CRITICS PRAISE THE NATIONAL BESTSELLER FROM
THE EDITORS OF THE ONLINE MAGAZINE
SALON.COM

MOTHERS WHO THINK
Tales of Real-Life Parenthood

"A must-read for anyone contemplating motherhood and a bible for all of us whose lives have been warped, splendored, and expanded by our dear little ones."

—Austin Chronicle (TX)

"Most popular press articles on the joys and tribulations of mothering are mildly insulting. Good friends may share true feelings with you, but not the press. [The web site] 'Mothers Who Think' is where you go when you realize you've been duped. . . . Heartfelt, exuberant essays. . . . Funny, straight-talking. . . ."

—The Bellingham Herald (WA)

"Full of dames both besotted and fed up. . . . Essays by these mothers who think deal with the sweet, the sour, and the unthinkable."

—Mirabella

"Here, at last, is a parenting book for those of us who have made the desperate search for some literature (any literature!) that reflects our own intense, horrific, hilarious, joyful, maddening, bewildering, sublime experiences as mothers."

—Minnesota Parent

MOTHERS
WHO
think

TALES OF
REAL-LIFE
PARENTHOOD

EDITED BY **CAMILLE PERI** AND **KATE MOSES**
OF Salon.com

FOREWORD BY ANNE LAMOTT

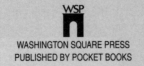

WASHINGTON SQUARE PRESS
PUBLISHED BY POCKET BOOKS

New York   London   Toronto   Sydney   Singapore

For David, Joey, and Nat;
For Gary, Zachary, and Celeste

A Washington Square Press Publication of
POCKET BOOKS, a division of Simon & Schuster Inc.
1230 Avenue of the Americas, New York, NY 10020

Copyright © 1999 by *Salon* Magazine

Most of the essays that are published in this work originally appeared in the online magazine *Salon*. Pages 280–282 constitute an extension of this copyright page.

Published by arrangement with Random House, Inc.

ISBN: 0-671-77468-9

First Washington Square Press trade paperback printing April 2000

10 9 8

WASHINGTON SQUARE PRESS and colophon are registered trademarks of Simon & Schuster Inc.

Cover art by Jose Ortega

Printed in the U.S.A.

ACKNOWLEDGMENTS

IT IS NO exaggeration to say that this book would not have come about but for our husbands—David Talbot, founding editor of *Salon* magazine, and Gary Kamiya, *Salon*'s executive editor. For their roles as our colleagues, editors, advisors, dinner makers, and partners in raising our children, no amount of thanks is enough.

We also wish to extend our gratitude to the following:

Ellen Levine, for her immediate enthusiasm and wise counsel.

Mollie Doyle, Brian De Fiore, and Elizabeth Rapoport, for their votes of confidence and their stewardship.

Salon editors Joyce Millman, Lori Leibovich, and Dawn MacKeen, for helping to shape *Salon*'s "Mothers Who Think" and for their daily support; art directors Elizabeth Kairys and Mignon Khargie, for translating our words into elegant images; Suzette Lalime and Fiona Morgan, for filling in whenever needed; and the rest of the *Salon* staff, for their continuing camaraderie, good humor, and faith in us.

Our parents, whom we never justly appreciated until we too became parents, especially our mothers, Alice Peri and Kathleen Wagner.

Our astute and thoughtful and patient female friends, whom we have not seen or spoken to since starting this book. Special thanks to Connie Matthiessen, for her early advice and encouragement, and Ruth Henrich, for her contributions as a friend, colleague, and godmother.

Our staunch babysitters, Season Jensen and Rachida Orr, whose flexibility and dedicated care of our children were essential to this project.

Salon magazine, which gave us the opportunity to make "Mothers Who Think" both virtual and tangible.

Finally, we would like to thank our children—Zachary, Joseph, Nathaniel, and Celeste—who filled us with the passion that inspired this book and who are happier than anyone else to see that it is finished.

—C.P. and K.M.

FOREWORD

ANNE LAMOTT

HOW CAN YOU even try to capture what it means to be a mother, both in the most daily and ordinary ways, and in the deepest parts of yourself? How can you present some sort of truth about bearing and caring for children, when that takes place wordlessly inside the center of your soul? I think the answer is that you can't; but maybe we can. So a kettle of water was put on the stove, and a bunch of women were invited to bring the best ingredients they had to offer, both the freshest and the sorriest, produce picked just today from the garden and produce on its last legs in the vegetable bin, to add to the pot. And it simmered and became something bigger, something both specific and limitless, became in fact this salty stone soup of a book about mothers who think.

I love the stories in this book for the same reason I love soup: They're delicious, life-giving, sometimes both. Sometimes they're plain, sometimes highly spiced. Both have sprung from the stuff of our lives. Sometimes they're made out of next to nothing except broth and love and sheer survival. And both are like the whole world in solution, the essence of everything boiled down until it surrenders itself entirely to the heat and the broth and the flavors, the quirks and surprises; and both are about the wonders of surrendering to something bigger without ceasing to exist.

In this book, we write about joy, we write a lot about love, and we write about rage. We write about figuring it all out as we go along, or certainly meaning to, as soon as we get a little free time; and we write about, in the meantime, just doing it. We write about the moments that changed us forever. We write about the changes in our bodies, especially in our hearts. We write about the changes in our vision, about the new pair of glasses motherhood wrestles onto you; about the ways in which children teach us to pay attention. We write about how hard we work, how tired we get, how bored, how exposed—about the terrible close-ups of our most glaring character defects that parenthood provides. We write about softness, we write about strength, we write about the places where those rings intersect. We write about how much harder it is than one could have ever expected, and how much richer. We write about discovering that we are perhaps a bit more volatile than we were before we encountered our children. We write about their sexuality and about our own. We write about just barely getting by, with a little help from our friends, and about transcendence and amazement; we write about blowups and breakdowns. We write about grief and hopelessness and resurrection.

There is cool water in being a mother, there is steam; there is salt, there is sweetness, there is bitter, there is utterly delicious. There are stories here that will make you laugh and so give you a new lease on life. Some may make you gasp with recognition or relief that, thank God, you've never gotten quite that bad—yet. Many are about confusion, some are about solutions. Many are, in some way, about learning to let go, about learning the terrible truth that when we are doing a good job, we are raising our kids to leave us. (And about how accepting that goes better on some days than others.) Some are stories where mothers just tell their truth; and this, in the end, is all that any of us has to offer.

Some of these pieces are about poor mothers, some about wealthy. They are by and about the mothers of babies, so the rest of us can remember the fleshy joy of holding infants, those warm bodies melting into ours, the tickle of that soft hair under our chins. They are by and about the mothers of sick kids who get well, and of sick kids who don't. They are by mothers who sometimes don't feel like taking care of their kids, and about kids who need their care—and boy, oh boy, do you discover what strength you had inside you then. They are by mothers of kids big enough to notice how strange the world is, and how unfair. They are about really big kids, with their lusts and smells and problems. They are by and about the mothers of only children and the mothers of children with brothers and sisters. They are by and about single mothers, divorced mothers, happily married mothers, working mothers, famous mothers, sick mothers, losing-their-minds mothers, back-in-the-saddle mothers.

But they are not by or about normal mothers, because we've finally stopped falling for the great palace lie that such a person exists. Somewhere along the way, we figured out that normal is a setting on the dryer. That there is only us—mothers who think and feel and love, who do the best we can, struggling and laughing more than we thought we would, and yelling and learning and regressing and pleading, sometimes crying in frustration and then, a little later, in gratitude for the blessing of being mothers, as all the while, one day at a time, we watch our children grow.

CONTENTS

INTRODUCTION: THE MAMAFESTO

CAMILLE PERI AND KATE MOSES

TWO MONTHS BEFORE her first child was born, Jane Smiley was struck by the seeming contradiction of teaching a course on Kafka and being pregnant. Would the baby somehow be marred for life, she wondered, by its in utero exposure to literature's master of anxiety? Would Smiley be forced to repudiate great novels with murky parent-child relationships, such as *Native Son* and *To the Lighthouse,* in favor of family romps like *Please Don't Eat the Daisies?* But Smiley found that in giving birth to a child, she also had given birth to her subject, the interplay of love and power that was the seed of her novel *A Thousand Acres.* "Far from depriving me of thought, motherhood gave me new and startling things to think about and the motivation to do the hard work of thinking," she wrote in her slyly titled essay "Can Mothers Think?"

Can mothers think? Of course—the question doesn't merit a response. But it's no easy task to find written accounts of real-life motherhood that haven't had their sharp, thought-provoking edges sanded off. The general media continues to treat the raising of the next generation as a lifestyle issue, while the magazines, Web sites, and books for parents (but aimed almost exclusively at mothers) seem on a desperate mission to wrestle child-rearing into chirpy Twelve-Step guides and ten-best lists, as if the complicated range of dramas and emotions that really defines motherhood were a wound best not probed too deeply.

This book is intended to be an antidote to the saccharine, oversimplified literature of motherhood. Motherhood is the most essential relationship to the continuity of life—and the wiping of snotty noses. It possesses the tenderness of a Mary Cassatt painting one minute, the surreality of a Diane Arbus photo the next. Some mothers abandon their children, others cripple them by holding them too close; nearly all mothers discover an unnerving helplessness in the face of the passions that motherhood arouses. Far from a soft-focus celebration, the essays gathered here are an uncensored exploration of the subject—an articulate, heartfelt, and sometimes mystified acknowledgment that being a mother is a lifelong lesson in embracing contradiction.

Both as readers and as writers, we had longed to see motherhood addressed as the intellectual and emotional challenge we had found it to be. We felt stifled by the popular labels our culture reduces mothers to: soccer mom, sneaker mom, stay-at-home mom, working mom, supermom—we knew we were all and none of those things. Becoming mothers had given us more to think about, not less, but only rarely could we find the outlets to express the complexity of those thoughts except among friends. And we believed that other mothers, like us, had learned to take their intellectual nourishment by any means necessary. We wanted to widen access to the dialogue already long in progress in sandboxes and on sidewalk stoops—unlikely settings for intellectual life but often the only places where mothers can talk about the world and our place in it. We began "Mothers Who Think" as a daily department in the on-line magazine *Salon* in June 1997 to provide an ongoing conversation that mothers could pick up whenever they could snatch the time—in the middle of the night, during naptime, while pumping milk at their desk at work.

The very creation of our Web site was itself a testament to the blurred boundaries that characterize mothers' lives. For some misguided reason, we decided that we could sketch out the concept during an outing to the zoo with our children. As our older sons spied on us through the bushes, the toddler with his pants on backward refused to budge from his perch on a rock, and the baby felt blindly around in her stroller until someone noticed that her hat had slipped down over her eyes, we simultaneously discussed whether "Mothers Who Think" could reach its intended audience of like-minded mothers, whether women with small children and cobbled-together childcare could put out a daily magazine section working part-time, and whether the zoo had an espresso machine. To our amazement, the answer to all our questions turned out to be a resounding yes.

Salon's "Mothers Who Think" was launched by three part-time working mothers—Camille was a freelance journalist, Kate a literary critic and editor, and Joyce Millman was stealing time from her already packed schedule as *Salon*'s television critic; assistant editor Dawn MacKeen and associate editor Lori Leibovich rounded out our team. It immediately became one of the most popular sections of the magazine, and the outpouring of letters from readers confirmed to us that mothers are searching for new ways to connect and new models for defining contemporary motherhood. "Thanks for reminding me that I'm a woman who is also a mother," wrote one reader, "not a mother who is also a woman."

In less than two years, "Mothers Who Think" has evolved into a truly global mothers' group, a place for intellectual companionship across the gulf of national, racial, and cultural differences, where we can talk about our shared and vastly different experiences of raising children. It also provides a place for mothers to let off steam: Our "Drama Queen for a Day" contest, which invites readers to share their stories of motherhood at its lowest, is an ongoing hit—mothers flock to the opportunity to send in their dispatches from the front and readers love to be reminded that it could be worse.

This book is a collection of thirty-seven essays from prominent and new writers, including the most memorable stories from the first year of "Mothers Who Think." Thoughtful, probing, hilarious, fierce, lyrical, wrenching—these stories tell of the experiences we had been hungry to hear about, the ones we knew we shared with other women but that somehow remained strangely obscured in the culture at large. They also made us aware once more of something easy to lose in the harried dailiness of taking care of a family—the vividness of our complex feelings for our children.

The stories spread over a broad canvas—from childbirth to child death, from the sensual fleshiness of babyhood to the havoc children wreak on our sex lives and self-image, from microscopic examinations of our own mothers' defects to the ambivalence with which motherhood is viewed by our culture. Idiosyncratic as the essays are, what they offer in common is that flicker of recognition that motherhood imparts. Our own experience of putting this collection together while working in the same office with our husbands—both doting and devoted fathers—reflects the incomparable makeup of motherhood. While our rising work pressures barely created a ripple in our spouses' routines, we had to become a streamlined machine—coordinating schedules, consolidating errands, sharing babysitters and washing machines, allotting time at the frantic height of deadline week to search out candy sprinkles for the cookie-decorating booth at the school fair. At times, we felt like we were sharing the same brain: We developed that odd intimacy, the intuitive shorthand that happens between mothers simply because it has to.

If there is any one theme that runs through this book, it is that, in the end, no one raises a child alone. The stories here testify over and over again to the vital importance of connectedness—to other people, to the world, to the debits and credits incurred when mothering a child. Rather than causing us to shy away from the bleakness of Kafka or the atrocities in the nightly news, we believe that raising children requires us to look squarely at both the dark and the bright.

For this reason, it seems fitting to us that this book is being published on Mother's Day. Although it has come to be derided as the ultimate Hallmark holiday, Mother's Day had nobler beginnings. In the aftermath of the bloody Franco-Prussian and American Civil wars, abolitionist Julia Ward Howe— author of "The Battle Hymn of the Republic" and a mother of six—wrote a stirring appeal to mothers worldwide to protest having their sons taken from them "to unlearn all that we have been able to teach them of charity, mercy and patience." Her Mother's Day Proclamation gave birth to annual mothers' meetings in Boston, where women strategized how to make the world a better place for their children. Howe's "mothers' days" were not designed to congratulate mothers, but to recognize the true power of their role.

In the spirit of all the other mothers with big ideas and half-formed thoughts and voices waiting to be heard, we offer this book. We hope it injects new perspective into a discussion that began long ago, and that it does equal justice to what Howe called "the august dignity of motherhood and its terrible responsibilities" and to the annual treasure of grubby construction paper lettered with alphabet macaroni and festooned with glitter.

MOTHERS
WHO
think

Reparations

JANE LAZARRE

I AM A SMALL CHILD, somewhere between the time language opened up the world of meaning to me and six years later when my mother died and key words lost their meaning. Words in the dictionary. Words I could no longer comprehend. *Forever. Dead.* Like *elephant*, which had suddenly turned from solid sign into a mysterious drifting sound in an extraordinary moment when my mother, perhaps unknowingly, enabled me to see the precariousness of meaning, its constructed fragility.

"Knock, knock," she said, having taught me the routine.

"Who's there?" (I might have clapped in excitement. I was only four or five.)

"Ella." (I think I recall her dark eyes twinkling, or she may have shook her head, displacing her carefully shaped, short dark hair.)

"Ella who?" I whispered, obedient and aroused.

"Ella-Fant," she said.

It took a few moments for me to grasp it. *Ella-Fant.* What was that? For what seemed a very long time I repeated the words over and over, searching for the double meaning I knew must be there, and finally the strange name slipped back into the image of the familiar animal I saw nearly every Sunday in the Central Park Zoo. I would hold my father's hand as we watched the huge creatures lift their trunks with dark holes at the end that seemed to stretch and constrict rhythmically around peanuts, leaves, the world.

When it was *elephant* again, I stared at my mother in silent amazement, but she may have had no idea what was happening inside me as I stood there repeating, "Elephant, Ella-Fant . . ." The long gray trunks, hard and erect and opened at the end. My father's hand in mine. My mother's voice, her laugh—as I stood there falling in love with the indefinite plasticity of words.

After she was dead (but I never said "dead," not until much later, when I was in my twenties; I said *died*, "she died"; the action suggesting a possible reaction, a lack of definite ending), I kept saying "elephant" to myself—meaning, I think, that the word *dead*, which I wouldn't say, might have within its mysterious sound the same magical ambiguity.

I AM ABOUT four years old, dressed in some ruffled, stiff thing my mother likes. I cannot see its pattern because it is under my coat, which is wool, navy blue, with a pretty indented waist. My defective feet (weak ankles, turned-in toes) are pushed into smart patent leather shoes, Mary Janes. Under a thick, red plaid woolen blanket that reeks of animal hair, I cuddle next to my mother in an old-fashioned open carriage that is being pulled by a tired-looking black horse around Central Park. This is a special date—"excursion" is the word my mother uses and I have come to love. We are on an excursion together, only the two of us. My father is someplace else. My sister is only a baby, left at home with our grandmother. I notice the weariness of the horse's movements, his mangy mane threaded with what looks like gray dust, a great sadness in his eyes. As with the twin worlds of elephant (in one world, the word meaning something perfectly comprehensible; in the other, nonsense), I imagine twin worlds of a different sort for the horse. I can see he is an exhausted animal in ordinary life. But held in my mother's arms, my aching feet warmed by the stiff wool and my cheeks icy from the cold, I can feel the saliva of excitement gather in my mouth and I am certain the horse is really majestic, powerful, his coat glistening. I see him lift his hooves high off the ground, prancing. His mane grows long and shines like I imagine midnight might if you were alone on a dark sea reflecting a sky full of stars. And that is how I come to remember the horse that pulled our carriage around the park. Years later, when my father takes my younger sister and me for a ride one afternoon, trying to replicate my mother's excursion and, perhaps, preserve a bit of her dramatic nature for her daughters, I will be shocked by the sickly appearance of the black horse and, despite my previous insistence, refuse to go for the ride.

MANY YEARS LATER, I dug out my old books about black horses for my son. He loved *The Black Stallion* series so much he read all the novels one summer, and I felt a strange thrill. But when I gave him *Black Beauty*—the story of a powerful colt who is orphaned, sold here and there until he becomes a carriage horse and is then overworked, whipped, underfed, and generally so mistreated he is eventually retired to a farm—my son disliked it, finding it too sad, and his dislike filled me with an annoyance I did not understand at the time. I gazed at the illustrations of the ill-used, exhausted horse and tried to push behind my idealized memory to a vague, uneasy familiarity, where I recognized that worn-out animal from someplace in my past.

I started the knock-knock jokes as soon as my sons began

speaking words. We moved from Ella-Fant on to more complex ambiguities—"Ida" becoming "I da know," "Willie" becoming "Will e win the race?" Both boys became fascinated with the magic of the game, which ignited other passions, so each time the double meaning became clear, they would throw themselves into my arms, kiss my neck, and declare their love for me.

THINKING ABOUT PASSION and words, after my children are grown, I begin a novel with the memory of the knock-knock joke. I want to write about a woman writer—a subject that demands, or seeks, a self-confident mood—so I feel hopeful when I realize I am drawn to mirrors. I do not pass them by with a quick glance as has been my habit for years. Nor do I sit and stare into them as I did as a child, searching for evidence of my dead mother's features shadowed in my own. I look at myself—my face, my body, clothed and naked. I gaze closely at my shoulders, my neck, my thighs. And then I hear my father's voice admonishing me long ago: "Stop admiring yourself in the mirror!"

My father was a storyteller, and when I was a child, about to go to sleep and full of anxieties that had taken hold since my mother's death, he would try to calm me with tales about his long trip by train and foot from the Old Country—even the Atlantic Ocean months away, let alone the eventual goal of America. But when he finally arrived, there were unimagined riches to behold, and he'd begin the story of seeing an orange for the first time in his life. He would hold up an orange for me to admire, looking at it as he must have years before, and I would imagine the taste of real orange juice emerging from succulent, dripping crescents outlined in delicate, edible white thread, all meeting in his mouth for the very first time. The orange came to represent all the possibilities one might hope for even at the most hopeless times. The story about the orange became a tonic for our grief.

He elaborated on his stories as the years went by. Stories of Ordinary Life, he called them: the day my younger sister learned to pump herself on the swing in the park; our ride in a Central Park carriage drawn by a powerful, beautiful black horse; our Sunday trip to the zoo, where I stood holding his hand at the fenced border of the elephant's cage and watched in wonder as those long, powerful trunks threatened to ingest the whole world.

If my mother's laughter and her death introduced me to mystery, it was my father's voice that taught me how stories might be a railing when the chasm seemed to fall too far and steep below. Of course, he would no more approve of these mirroring sequences of my life I am calling a novel than he liked me looking in mirrors. Nevertheless, he bequeathed the obsession. When *Ella-Fant* becomes "elephant," it is my father's hand I feel pressing around mine, the hardness of his thigh against my cheek.

During those years of childhood and adolescence when a beautiful young girl looked back at me from the mirror, I was incapable of what he was accusing me of. More than forty years later, I am admiring myself. In a beautiful old Cape Cod house where I stay for a few weeks of uninterrupted writing, I shower outside under a large tree and admire my aging thighs. In my quiet room at night, one small light near my bed casting a soft glow, I stand before the large, mahogany framed mirror and admire my face. Then I return to my bed and open the notebook where I am recording memories of my childhood and my children's childhood; drafting scenes, passages, sentences; making lists of magical words.

What My Mother Never Told Me, or How I Was Blindsided by Childbirth and Survived

RAHNA REIKO RIZZUTO

THERE ARE six billion birth stories in the world. Good luck finding a woman who will tell you what hers was really like.

Perhaps you have a wise friend who understands that you need to hear more than "it isn't easy, but it's all so worth it." Perhaps you have stopped accepting dinner invitations from new parents because you know that the moment your hostess has finished serving the poached pears and sorbet she will say, "Hey, do you guys want to *see?*" and you will trudge into the living room for yet another endless videotape of some red, mewling infant's entrance into the world. I, however, don't know these people. In New York City, where we refuse to look bums in the eye as we step over them, no one wants to be responsible for breaking the bad news.

Of course I tried to get the "truth" about childbirth. The answers were just a little bit vague. My mother-in-law: "It doesn't hurt. You are too fascinated by what's happening to think about pain." One of my only friends with children: "All I remember is the sun rising over the Charles River at the same moment Sarah's head appeared." Then there were the friends of my friends: one who entertained visitors in her private hospital room with the brownies she had baked during labor, and the other who proclaimed, "I've had period pain worse than that!" But when my mother—whose mantra while I was growing up was "I was in labor with you for forty-eight hours. The doctor said if you weren't dead you were going to be brain damaged"—suddenly changed her story to "Honey, I can't remember. It was so long ago," I knew I was in trouble.

Was I the victim of my mother's well-deserved revenge? Of misplaced sympathy for the pregnant woman who can no longer call the whole thing off? Could the responses of these experienced mothers have been corrupted by that celebrated fuse in your brain that short-circuits, wiping out all memory of pain and trauma? Was it as simple as shame? The details, after all, tend to be smelly and wet.

No matter, I thought before my first birth. There are classes. Books. I could pay for this information and I did. How to toughen my nipples, turn my abdominal muscles into bungee cords that would spring back the minute my son was born, how to find and flex those crucial sphincters, and, of course, how to breathe. I even rented a video: The pregnant woman looked like Jabba the Hutt with a Farrah Fawcett hairdo and her supporters included a midwife, a sister, two friends, three children (one of whom was under age two), and a bearded, hand-holding husband who kept reminding his wife to breathe. It was difficult to relate. In fact, it occurred to me that if my husband dared to tell me how to breathe, I would beat the crap out of him.

None of the information I actually needed to know was forthcoming: how to keep my sense of humor when I was two weeks overdue in an un-air-conditioned house in July; that

Pitocin-induced contractions feel like, oh, having your teeth smashed in with a hammer; whether I should bring my own airbag to protect myself as my hospital cot ricocheted toward the operating room, where my emergency cesarean section would be performed. No need to alarm the paying customers, I guess. Instead, the teacher in my childbirth class directed all the partners in our class to pinch our arms (hard) so we pregnant women could "practice breathing through the pain of labor." Let's just say I was unprepared for my first birth.

About my second birth, though: I have never been so unprepared for anything in my life.

MY SECOND BIRTH was going to be different. I was going to go into labor spontaneously, on time, and at home; I was going to give birth vaginally. It wasn't until I was eight months pregnant that I realized that my first experience hadn't actually given me the insider's information I felt I had earned. I had forgotten how to breathe, how to time my contractions, even when to go to the hospital. Clearly I needed a refresher course, so I found a midwife who offered private counseling sessions on "vaginal birth after cesarean." My husband and I sat on her living room couch; she straddled a large rubber ball. We learned that my labor would be easier (since natural labor pains are gentler and build more gradually than induced ones) and shorter (my first labor lasted thirty hours and, for some reason, I decided this one would last only six). Maybe it was the way her head swayed gently as she rolled, but I didn't even question her when she told me that an epidural—or any pain relief—would increase my risk of another cesarean section significantly. She demonstrated the very uninhibited painkilling sound she used to get her through both her births without drugs and advised me to spend some time finding my own. My husband and I topped that evening off with a single glass of wine, and I remember thinking, Maybe I really can do this.

It was the equivalent of discovering religion in an airport. But I didn't know.

I didn't know.

So when I woke in mid-contraction at 5:00 A.M. on the day before I was due, I was cautiously happy. I had been having similar pains on and off for weeks and always, just as I was about to proclaim myself in labor, they went away. By six o'clock, though, I had achieved the milestone the books set for you: an hour of contractions five minutes apart and one minute long. I was in labor. This is the point at which you are told to ignore the mild discomfort and make cookies.

I jumped into the shower, which I had been advised to "save" for pain relief, because I knew that if I didn't I would be immortalized on film unwashed, uncombed, and unaware. Before I could rinse the shampoo from my hair, though, my forehead was pressed against the tile wall and I couldn't see through my tears. I woke my husband, Craig, and told him he better get some coffee, which he may have done but I don't remember because I was trying to get my doctor on the phone. Her partner, whom I barely knew, told me I wasn't ready to come to the hospital yet; apparently, since the cervix dilates at an average rate of one centimeter per hour, she felt I needed several more hours at home. So I swore (quietly, so as not to wake my visiting parents) and followed orders.

I knelt over the side of the bed while Craig applied counter-pressure on my tailbone—a blessed lesson from the rolling midwife. After an hour of watching my hands twist while searching for my own painkilling sound, my water broke and I discovered just how slowly I could form the thought, *What in the hell was that?* Let me illustrate: First, something shuddered inside me and I heard the far-off sound of, say, a potato exploding in a microwave oven, and I thought, *What in—.* Then I felt my underwear bulge and I got as far as the *hell—.* Then the baby's no-longer-pillowed head came crashing down on the bundle of nerve endings in my tailbone and I thought, *was that?* just as the amniotic fluid turned into a small lake around Craig's feet and he said, "What in the hell was that?"

That was the moment when I decided that there was no way I was going to let any doctor tell me where I should be. Craig called her back and told her we were leaving for the hospital and I wanted my epidural. In rush-hour traffic across the Brooklyn Bridge, we were an hour away.

FIRST WE HAD to wake my mother and ask her to pack our bag. "The books" had warned me to do this three weeks before my due date, but I figured, How hard is it to throw a T-shirt and some film into a bike-messenger bag, and what if I need that clean pair of underwear in the interim? I sent my groggy father outside to push the front passenger seat in the car all the way forward so I could ride behind it on the floor and Craig could maintain the pressure on my back—a configuration I devised when my contractions were two minutes apart and at least one minute long, and I realized that my husband and I were not going to be able to drive to the hospital in private or in good humor. As I patiently explained to Craig that no, he could not go to the bathroom, and no, I did not want to change out of my sopping shorts or put on a pair of shoes, my mother reappeared at the bedroom door with the news that "they" (I never found out exactly who) were trying to close off the street so they could dig it up. Dad was downstairs warning them that if they didn't let us take our car and leave, they were going to be delivering a baby. Soon, he said.

My parents had raised three children. Yet I have never seen them in such a state of shock.

Once it was agreed that we would be allowed to leave, our mad dash to the car went something like this: Feel my contraction subsiding, run to the hall; have another contraction, stumble down the first flight of stairs (we live in a brownstone, and, of course, I was on the top floor); lean over our unstable banister to have another contraction while telling my mother, rather loudly, to take my two-year-old son into the living room instead of letting him stand at the front door waving good morning to the backhoe in the street, run down a second flight of stairs; have another contraction on the stoop for the benefit of the construction workers (just in case the sweat pouring down my father's face had failed to convince them of his honesty), run to the car; throw myself against the side of the car cop-show style for yet another contraction, crawl into the backseat. Then the pinball-machine ride to the hospital: me crouched behind the passenger's seat on my knees leaning forward, Craig behind me pushing on my tailbone, my father—whose driving experience, for the past thirty years, has been limited to glorified sugarcane trails in Hawaii—weaving in and out of traffic like he had to hit all the bumpers to get the highest score. I couldn't decide which was worse, moving or sitting in the traffic, and I had just about decided that we should say the hell with my doctor and go to the nearest emergency room—which was only seven blocks away, and where I was sure I could faint on the sidewalk and get immediate attention—when my father made the mistake of patting my back during a contraction. My response effectively opened a path through the cars around us, and the opportunity was gone.

. . .

IN A COURT of law, I could not tell you how we got there, but we finally pulled up to the correct hospital. By that time, my legs were numb and I had gashed one of my bare feet trying to wake them, so I was bleeding as I staggered to the elevator, supported by my husband's arm. We didn't raise a single eyebrow and certainly didn't impress the staff in the labor and delivery ward, even when I threw myself dramatically across the admitting counter, gave my name, and proclaimed my need for an epidural. I was given a set of papers to fill out (as if!) and was told a nurse would find me a room as the two women behind the counter continued to talk about lunch.

Remember this: You are not allowed to have an epidural in the hall.

After two contractions, I decided not to wait for the nurse and started down the hall myself, to the great relief of several other mothers-about-to-be who were seated behind me, trying to have their own "fascinating" experiences. I refused a wheelchair on the grounds that Craig must be able to reach my back at all times, but someone came up behind me, ran it into the back of my knees, and began rolling me to a room. I must still have been whining for my epidural because I was told I needed to be in a hospital gown before I could have one. That was one too many conditions; I stood up, stripped off my shirt and bra, and threw them to one side in a smooth, arcing motion. (I think we were in the room at that point.) Then I hooked my thumbs under the elasticized waist of my bike shorts, bent forward, and dropped my pants, mooning everyone behind me.

I never saw the guy who had been pushing the wheelchair again. Craig, however, came toward me as I began relieving myself of my clothing, so when my pants dropped, the mucus plug that had released when my water broke fell out of my underwear and onto his shoe. It looked like a large tiger slug that someone had sprinkled with salt: tan with rust streaks, and definitely melting, but with enough body and tenacity to cling to the top of his loafer. His foot slipped on the floor the next time he tried to apply his entire weight to my tailbone in response to my screams. He tried to shake the mucus plug off, gently at first, and then with more and more vigor, until at last his shoe and the plug flew off and went sailing somewhere in the direction of my clothing.

I have a mental picture of this and may actually have seen it, but I was busy insisting that someone give me a goddamn IV so I could get my goddamn epidural—in fact, as Craig told me later, I said, "They told me it would be waiting for me!" which I truly believed at the time. The nurse explained that she had to wait for my doctor, and then for the anesthesiologist, both of whom came into the room at the same time and began extracting needles and tubes from the air. Craig was sent into the hall to listen to the chorus of more distant screaming during my three-needle, fifteen-minute procedure, where he impressed the other exiled family members and hospital staff with the fact that he was wearing only one shoe. When he was allowed back into my room, the nurse frowned at him and demonstrated extreme disinterest in his story of the mucus plug and in the mucus plug itself, which he began cleaning off his shoe once she told him he didn't need to keep it.

THE PAIN was gone. I apologized to the nurses, who, strangely enough, said they had seen such behavior before—and worse! I gave Audrey, my doctor, who had just come back on duty, a proper greeting. Then I spent the next nine hours in the tiniest and last available labor room listening to Hawaiian slack key guitar music, sneaking bits of chocolate graham cracker, and itching. A side effect of the epidural: I felt like someone had staked me to an anthill. My hands responded by chasing the imaginary creatures across my skin, often lifting my gown and exposing various thigh, groin, and belly areas to whoever happened to be in the room.

When I woke, I found that I had temporarily regained a few shards of modesty when it occurred to me that, although the midwife had assured me that my bowels would empty naturally during early labor to clear any "obstructions," they hadn't done so. Who knew what lay in my child's path? I mentioned this to Audrey, but she merely shrugged and warned me that, since she was five months pregnant herself, her heightened reactions to smell might force her to leave the room from time to time. It was too late for an enema since the epidural had effectively quashed both my pain and my ability to move at all. I had a brief, violent fantasy about what my reaction would have been if, before my epidural, any hapless doctor had tried to insert flexible tubing and a quart of warm water into my rectum, and decided whatever will be, will be.

My attention span was short, to say the least. My father mentioned that he was hungry and presto! I saw a sandwich in his hand. My mother wondered if they were overstaying their welcome and wham! the lights had been dimmed and Craig and I were alone. I stared at the wall, I listened to the heart-rate monitor, but I spent no time fantasizing about the joyful moment when I would welcome my second child into the world. Instead, I thought about a friend of mine who, just a few days before, had delivered her daughter in less than twenty minutes. Talk about a fantasy. I had been there before—on the brink of pushing a baby out—and failed after four hours of trying. Yet, I actually dared imagine that the worst might be over. Again, I thought, I can do this.

Clearly, I had lost my mind.

Maybe I was praying. Toward the end of that nine-hour interlude, about the same time that the lights dimmed, the baby's heart rate began dipping with each contraction. He was in distress. No one had to tell me what we were dealing with: Craig, Audrey, and I had faced this situation together once before. The baby would be fine if we could get him out quickly. Unfortunately, it turned out that time—as well as luck, fate, the odds, and the stars—was against us. This child, like his big brother, wanted to come into the world face up: the very long way.

It was time to push. Big fanfare, right? Complete with ready, set, go. I lay on my side as Craig held one bent leg in the air, the nurse braced my lower knee, and Audrey stuck her fingers inside me to spread my vagina a little wider for the baby's head. We all turned our eyes to the television screen mounted above my head that was broadcasting my contractions and the baby's heart rate to everyone in the ward and waited for the next contraction to begin. It did and—I discovered I had forgotten how to push.

It sounds impossible.

All I had to do was to bear down three times during each contraction, for a slow count of ten each time, taking a breath in between. Which I did, with no success. Audrey suggested I hold my breath while I pushed, but I had been warned that this could cause the blood vessels in my eyes to pop, so instead I released my breath slowly, an alternate method that was supposed to help relax those nether sphincters and let the baby's head pass through. The problem was, there were muscles down there I didn't want to relax.

Audrey asked, a little hopefully, if I felt the "urge to push." I answered, equally hopefully, "Maybe." Then I threw up.

Luckily, Craig had told the midwife about the three hours he spent holding a vomit tray for me when our first son was born. Her response was cheery, something along the lines of "Oh, yeah, the pain, the drugs . . ." She had recommended peppermint oil, a vial of which Craig had bought and was inserting into one of my nostrils. I spent the next hour in that room sniffing, breathing, and trying to coordinate my pushes. Then I decided that, since no one else seemed to care if I pooped, I wasn't going to let it bother me either, and began pushing so effectively that a parade of doctors stopped by to see what was wrong with the baby's heart rate. I used them, rather than the monitor, to gauge the severity of the dips; I also used the nurse's tone when she snapped, "Not now, we're busy!" every time the door opened. I could feel the baby moving down, but too slowly to suit Audrey. He wasn't getting enough oxygen. My temperature was high and climbing. If it went much higher, the baby would have a mandatory forty-eight-hour stay in the intensive care unit. We were approaching emergency cesarean number two.

Meanwhile, I had discovered the urge to push, and it was no "maybe" impulse—it was more like the urge to breathe when your head is being held under water. If Craig and the nurse didn't move fast enough when the contractions began, I pulled my own leg into the air and started counting without them. I clenched the side rails of the bed for extra leverage so tightly that my forearms came away with bruises. The epidural was wearing off, but each push was so overwhelming that the pain was bearable in comparison—just.

And still the surgery loomed, forestalled only by the possibility of vacuum extraction (exactly what it sounds like—they put a suction cup on the baby's head to help him along while you push). I had the presence of mind to gasp out some question about the risks, and Audrey was quite candid. We knew the baby was big, but we didn't know how big. If she tried to pull him out and he got stuck, we would be really screwed.

For some reason, I couldn't process this response. I had taken the first step toward control—gathering information—only to discover I couldn't use it. I wasn't scared; I had used up that energy worrying that the baby would strangle himself on his umbilical cord during the pregnancy. The baby was so close. I just wanted him out. Audrey took a blood sample from the baby's scalp to check his pH level, which was somehow related to how much oxygen he was getting, and decided that we had enough time to try the vacuum but only for one contraction. I trusted her. I waited, pushing on my own while she assembled the equipment and the team required by the hospital: a pediatrician, a nurse, and a backup physician (a young man who will hereafter be known as "the golf guy" for reasons that will become clear). Craig held my hand. Then Audrey was ready. She stuck the suction cup on the baby's head.

Here's where I make my pitch for women doctors.

Everyone in the room knew I had about one minute to get the baby out. They all, presumably, wanted to be encouraging. So Audrey, who is a woman, gave me a progress report: "He's almost there, you're so close, he's almost there." And the nurse, who is also a woman, chanted: "Great job, you're really doing great." What did the golf guy say? "Drive it, Mommy! Come on, drive it!"

At that moment, perhaps not coincidentally, Audrey lost the seal on the vacuum and fell backward, splattering everyone with blood and amniotic fluid. Everyone, that is, except the golf guy, who was wearing a windshield to protect his precious face and had had the presence of mind to take several steps backward when the pushing began.

Audrey hesitated, then decided we could try it again for one more contraction. She put the suction cup back on the baby's head. I heard, "Come on, Mommy, drive it!" and pushed, reminding myself that, if I was going to have a cesarean section, I should have done it three weeks ago and skipped the whole labor thing.

And again. "Drive it, Mommy, drive it!" I pushed and thought that if this kid wasn't born right that minute, my nightmarish ride to the hospital would be completely meaningless.

One more time. "Drive it, Mommy, drive it, drive it!" And at last, I found my own painkilling sound, but instead of screaming—"Shut up! Shut up! Shut up, you bastard!"—I used all my anger and my energy to push. Audrey pulled. We were three pushes past my last chance and—pop! Out came the head.

Breaking my tailbone in the process, although that wouldn't become obvious for a couple of hours.

There was a pause in the delivery, then, as Audrey held the baby where he was and told me not to push. The pediatrician came over and inserted a tube into the baby's nose to suction out his airways so he wouldn't breathe meconium (that's baby poop) into his lungs. I could feel my son wriggling inside me, only partially born, but couldn't see him, having opted against a mirror. (I could have used the windshield the golf guy was wearing, but I couldn't bring myself to look at his face.) When the next contraction came, I didn't push—and let me tell you how easy that is when you have the urge and there is a head sticking out of you. Then the next urge came and I could push again. As I did, Audrey grabbed the child, turned him in the direction he was supposed to be facing all along, and his body fell into her hands. She tossed him like a fish into the incuba-tor, and it was over. As simply as that.

And what, you may ask, of the "but it's all so worth it" moment? That came days, even months later—about the same time I stopped reminding my husband each night that "Yes, he's very cute, but I am never going through that again!" At that moment, I felt only relief. When the baby's head came out, the sound was palpable; I could feel it in my heart. As I watched the pediatrician pull on my son's limbs and massage his small body from tan to pink, I thought, *This is the part I missed last time.* The curtain of surgery had obscured my first child; I could only hear him cry. But even this time, my son was out of reach, so I was left to try to recognize him from afar. Audrey was showing me something—a knot in the umbilical cord—something rare, dangerous, something I really should have taken a picture of, but at the moment, I didn't care.

It was finished. Over. I had done it, and I was still trying to believe it was true. Could I actually have done this thing? Could any woman, anywhere? Six billion births notwithstand-ing, my own two-year-old child aside, somehow it just didn't seem possible.

At least, no one had ever told me that it was.

Boy Crazy

SALLIE TISDALE

I SING A SONG of teenage boys! I defend them (no one else will), these giant, awkward creatures with their smelly feet, faint beards, and inconvenient erections. Teenage boys, mostly too big or too small and sometimes so damned perfect they bring tears to the eyes of watching, wistful adults, who are afraid to say out loud how beautiful, how desirable, how strange these creatures are. Teenage boys: graceful, gauche, wafting musk through the room, vigorous, lit from inside by a barely restrained power, an untouched and misunderstood virility—most of them so scared of their own shadows and what the world holds in store that they can't leave the house unless they're wearing clothes big enough to hide in.

Teenage boys come to my door, knock politely, call me "ma'am." They try to sell me magazine subscriptions so they can win valuable prizes and college scholarships, shucking and looking at their feet. They want work, lawn mowing and weed pulling. They want friends—not me. I visit my own friends and talk to their teenage sons, who must be courteous to me, and I grill them about new movies and changing mores and how they feel about the president's personal life. Young men unfold their long limbs and climb out of their roughly idling old cars patched with rust and lift the seat forward so my just-grown sons can say their hearty hail-fellows and leap up the steps, two at a time.

Teenage boys with pimples and careful haircuts sell me slices of pizza, reams of paper, cups of tea, lightbulbs, a line of goods. The whole world, and certainly the coffee bar counter, feels too big and looks too small for them. They crowd doorways and sidewalks and school desks. Even football fields shrink when a half-dozen teenage boys are running across them, shouting.

I have a girl just entering her own teenage years. "Cute" has always been a word she reserved for puppies and newborns. Suddenly, it's popping out all over—alternating with complaints. She was supposed to write a story last week about a "pest" in her life.

"How about the boys at school?" I asked. "They pester you."

"Boys aren't pests," she said. "They're *enemies.*"

A few days ago, I was at the mall with said teenage girl, who needed an invisible haircut right away. She never used to need these things. I left her in the $10 walk-in salon to wait her turn, and ran up to the ATM on the third floor, the one near the food court and the fly-by-night jewelry booths. This is something like the watering hole for the herds of teenagers who prowl these stores; they mill around in groups, alert, dipping their heads now and then while they watch for predators, and prey.

There was a big crowd around the Piercing Pagoda, which was selling a lot of gold chains on discount—even then, at $119, $139 each, far more than I can afford for jewelry. A dozen young men lined the glass cases in hunger. All wore low-slung fat pants and roomy shirts, all had their left ears pierced with gold hoops. Several wore red or black scarves tightly wound around their heads, and when they moved, they moved with a sullen, bouncy step, arms flung wide. They were a mob designed to clear a path through any mall, to throw the other shoppers into a faint. Steer clear, these big clothes and bobbing heads cried. Pay attention, shouted the giant athletic shoes and gold rings. ("Wish fulfillment," one teenage friend of mine called those clothes—wishes of getting bigger someday, filling out.)

And people steered clear, making wide arcs around the Piercing Pagoda. An armed security guard leaned on the rail nearby. The boys were perfectly well behaved, waiting their turn, not even raising their voices to get the salesclerk's attention. But that wasn't the point. They had that look, expensive and carefully cultivated—that prowling, dangerous look.

We treat this kind of teenage boy with kid gloves and confused anger, reacting without thought—crossing streets, ducking nervously into our cars. We can't decide if teenage boys are our children, our peers, our hope, or just a menace. They are, of course, all these things: strong but often stupid, naïve and powerful, evolved for hard labor and reproduction and defense of the cave in times of siege. Here they live in a world of boring jobs and shopping malls. Something has to give—them or us. They are victims, and killers, but teenage boys are victims and killers mainly of each other.

Even in fat pants and black scarves, they look like babies to me still. I gave birth to one more than twenty years ago, when I was only twenty myself, and didn't like men much and hoped desperately I was giving birth to a girl. "It's a boy!" someone said in that dim, dreamy, everlasting moment when he came free of me for the first time, and I thought: I knew it. A day later, he and I dozed together on the same bed where I'd given birth and he became Baby. It was an immense discovery for me, to find I didn't care that he was also Boy. Later I discovered that Boy was something wonderful, too.

For years he had to wear studded black leather and Doc Martens to compensate for virginity and confusion. His brother chose the fat pants, a bad dye job, the slouching, insouciant walk to compensate for being short and bewildered. I lived so long with Gothic and Gangland that it's hard for me to remember that a lot of teenage boys are babies—but big scary ones, with teeth. We keep some of our babies in jail, some for the rest of their lives. We have babies with guns, worried about pimples—babies wondering how to buy the next gold chain.

I wondered vaguely where their money comes from.

I went back to the walk-in salon. It was late afternoon, and one, two, three teenage boys wandered in, signed up on the waiting list, and tried to cool their heels. Teenage boys do a fair amount of hanging around, but they aren't very good at cooling their heels. The tallest of the trio wandered around for a few minutes, picking up big black cylinders full of magically expensive shampoo, and then slumped down in one of the revolving salon chairs. A few minutes later he was unceremoniously chased out by a hairdresser and went back to his shelf wandering—picking up, putting down, glancing around, picking up again. The other two crouched, overly large, on two of the small, fragile-looking chairs near the magazines.

I sat on the floor behind them, reading *Newsweek*. They picked up *Mademoiselle* and *Vogue*, chortling to each other.

"There's no *Cosmo*," said one. "*Cosmo* has breasts."

"No, it doesn't," said the other, quite firm.

"Yes, it does," said the first one. "I've seen them."

He looked over his shoulder at me, below him—forty-one years old, in a sweater and faded jeans. "I bet you read *Cosmo*," he said.

I demurred. "I don't."

"But you've seen it, right? It's got breasts, doesn't it?"

And I told him yes, it does, wondering if he was just showing off for his friend or wanted to see if he could startle me. I am often surprised to discover that teenage boys consider me old. Old enough to be their mother, old enough to be worth shocking, old enough to ignore without a thought. I am also occasionally surprised at the intense heat of my own sexual desire. Without warning my entire middle-aged body seems to recognize the mandate of the human race: Something in me still thinks it should couple with the most powerful, healthy, young, and fertile animal around. Conversation isn't on the agenda. Only pheromones, hormones, genetics, and now. Younger than my sons, I remind myself, but the body knows that's exactly the point.

The boy in the salon accepted my information, a bit smug, and went back to *Vogue*.

I *have* been shocked by boys—shocked each time by the suddenness with which childhood ended and teenage began in their young, childish bodies. Shocked twice again at how persistent childhood proved to be in their minds. The outward turning of childhood became the dishevelment and annoyance of puberty overnight; their bedrooms filled with a miasmic funk, odor streaming from every pore—from feet, skin, hair, like swamps in spring. They sweated continuously into T-shirts and socks and sheets and the bath towels they conveniently left crumpled on the sopping bathroom floor. Shoes were too small, bicycles too small, dinner portions too small, backpacks too small, dreams too small—and the world too big. Scary.

Cuteness disappears. The big drawback of cuteness is that kittens turn into cats and puppies into dogs—and babies into boys, into teenagers, into men. The one, short and cocky, still dresses in fat pants, giant shirts, and the big athletic shoes he somehow believes make him look fast and tough as he stumbles down the steps. The other is tall and lean, with sculpted biceps he likes to show me. He's a Teamster, a conspiracy theorist, still afraid to take his driving test, truly in love—timid one moment, then suddenly on fire. They are works in progress; old enough to vote, to drink, to buy guns. I make a joke out of it, because it's so hard to believe. Just so they don't do all three at the same time, I say, crossing my fingers that they do one and not the rest—because my opinions are no longer relevant. I am a small, steady, dependable, and clearly ordinary spot in their vast world.

I am the mother of men and still getting used to it.

Teenage boys, their lives, are different here in the United States than anywhere else in the world. Here, they sell lattes and deliver newspapers and save up for invisible haircuts before the weekend. Here they play soccer and football, dodge drugs and crime with more and less success, blow off their history homework and loiter in the park, smoking. Here, they usually grow up.

Elsewhere, that peculiar combination of power and naïveté is their undoing, their raison d'être. They have a traditional role in the human tribe—genetic material and sacrificial lamb. In other countries and throughout time, teenage boys are acolytes and castrati, slaves and soldiers. They carry automatic weapons instead of backpacks; they dig all day in the fields and underground for diamonds and coal; they kill large animals and get killed in turn; they are sent out alone into the forest and the desert to survive and find a name and learn their purpose in life. They get married and have children. They don't go to school. Many don't grow up. A lot of them spend their youth making soccer balls and athletic shoes and giant pants for luckier teenage boys in other places.

The boys I watch in the mall, the ones who ask me with seeming innocence about breasts and magazines, the ones who sell me a slice of pizza, dreaming about Saturday night—these boys are the world's soldiers, its rapists, its raw meat, its Brown Shirts and cannon fodder. Elsewhere (and sometimes here, when no one offers anything else) they learn that pain builds character, war is manly, armies are family, glory is more important than love.

I am the mother of men, venturing forth, blossoming, doomed as are we all. So I sing for teenage boys; I think we all should sing. Sing for Huck Finn, for Pinocchio, for Peter Pan and the Lost Boys, sing along: "I won't grow up." Sing about the Greek athletes running endlessly on the broken urns, made beautiful by capricious gods. Sing about the eternity of youth, which doesn't last forever.

I Love You Both Unequally

KATE MOSES

EVERY PREGNANT WOMAN awaiting the birth of a second child steels herself for the onslaught to come. Two kids are more than twice as much work, the common wisdom goes, and alongside the hopeful mental images we allow ourselves of enchanted, careful older siblings cuddling "their" babies are the scary pictures of wailing arguments over disputed toys, dinnertimes disrupted by imagined slights, and the logistical nightmare of schlepping six bags of groceries, a stroller (with sleeping child), and a car seat (with hungry infant) from the garage a block and a half away to your apartment three flights up—in the rain.

"It's hard," warn friends with more than one child, and you can see the evidence of how hard it is in the dark circles under their eyes. But why is it that nobody tells you that the hardest part of having a second child is kicking your first beloved child out of the nest of your heart to make room for a baby?

For reasons obscured by time (probably prompted by the familiar question, "Who do you love more—me, the older kid, or the baby?"), my mother once told me that, as the pregnant mother of a toddler, she couldn't imagine how she could love another baby as much as she loved her firstborn. "But then you were born, and I loved you just as wildly as I loved Billy. And later, when I was pregnant with John, I worried again—how could I have enough love for three? But John arrived, and it seemed that my heart just expanded to make room for him."

I suppose it's true that we have an infinite capacity for love, certainly where our children are concerned. But I question whether we have an infinite capacity for the type of passionate, consuming, distilled essence of love that one feels for a baby. The love I felt for my newborn son—that deep, visceral bond, as vivid and tender as heartbreak—was a feeling I retained for nearly eight years. Then his sister arrived and broke the bank of my heretofore ever-expandable heart.

In the months prior to my new baby's birth, I spent a lot of time thinking about my old baby. Not only was I wistful for the seven years I'd spent in undivided loyalty to my one and only child, I was also worried about how a new baby would affect Zachary's life and his place in our family. Zachary was the fruit of my failed first marriage; my new baby would be his half-sister, technically. Since he was two, Zachary has shuttled every few days between my home and his father's. He doesn't remember his life before his stepfather was in it, and he calls both of the fathers in his life Daddy. As enthusiastically as Zachary had campaigned for a little brother or sister, once he had one, I wondered, would he really be happy? When that baby got to stay home all the time, and he was still shuttling back and forth between houses? Would he feel jealous when his stepfather doted on the baby?

In the weeks just prior to baby Celeste's arrival, all three of Zachary's parents quietly plotted to make his transition into brotherhood as secure and untroubled as we could. As summer's meter ran low and the annual parade of day camps ended, before the start of second grade and my due date, Zachary and I even went away for a week together at the family retreat in the Sierra foothills. It was the week of the Perseid meteor shower, and we planned to sleep on the back porch of the big log cabin and watch the stars fall over our heads. We would walk the creekside trail with our lunches and spend afternoons at the lake, swimming and reading *The Chronicles of Narnia* and trying, dogged despite years of failure, to catch a frog.

Perhaps in part because of the unexpected and painful end of my relationship with his dad, Zachary and I have always been very close. Even too close—or so I sometimes worried, especially during the black year when Zachary was a moody, tyrannical, unappealing three-year-old. But that phase passed, and I was left with a whimsical, cuddly dreamer whose company I relished.

In fact, shortly after Zachary was born, I realized that, through some mysterious alchemy, he had taken over my memories. Zelig-like, he appeared throughout my past. Though he wasn't born until I was in my late twenties, I seemed to remember carrying him to the podium as I collected my high school diploma. I could almost remember holding him by one hand while holding a plastic cup of beer in the other at a college fraternity party. And wasn't that Zachary in his stroller on the family vacation to a Florida alligator farm when I was twelve? No doubt my memory confusion was due to the exhaustion of sudden single motherhood, but his ever-presence in the movie of my life made its point obvious—I could not imagine myself before him or beyond him. Neither could I imagine, truly, how it might be possible for me to love another child as hopelessly and effortlessly. As desired as this second baby was, I felt a little sorry for her.

So Celeste was born, but only after a difficult seven-week preamble set into motion by premature labor. Though drugs and bed rest stopped the early labor, my instincts moved inexorably forward, and I could focus on nothing but the Force of Motherhood. I reminded myself of a friend's pet rabbit, who inexplicably plucked out all of the fur on her chest one morning and then—surprise!—gave birth. Ten minutes before Celeste's arrival, I looked up at the clock between pushes and realized that Zachary's school was about to let out for the day. To everyone's amazement, including my own, I barked at my husband to call his parents and the school, so that Zachary could be ushered in as soon as the baby was born. Gary hesitated, so I handed him the receiver. Not for a minute—not even on Pitocin—could I forget my sweet boy. Celeste was born at 3:27 P.M., school got out at 3:30, and Zachary walked into the room to meet his sister a few minutes later.

A fierce, uncontrollable, feral instinct to protect the infant crept noiselessly upon me over the first few days of Celeste's life. Two days of wonderment and bliss gave way as a heat wave burned off my postnatal euphoria. My breasts grew hard as melons, and Zachary's hovering over his focusless, moonfaced sister grew increasingly irritating and oppressive. Everything Zachary did infuriated me. To my horror, I realized that the "thing" I was protecting my newborn from was the huge, dirty, graceless creature my older child had become overnight. He receded in my heart, becoming a cipher for my older child instead of Zachary, my first baby, my little love, and he spun away from me like a figure waving just beyond my focus in the reflection of a mirror. Meanwhile, Celeste (beautiful, delicate, peaceful Celeste) took up more and more space in my psyche, quietly demanding to be reckoned with, inflating exponentially, like the balloon of Bart Simpson in the Macy's Thanksgiving Day Parade.

No one who has been through the experience can deny that the first weeks after childbirth are emotionally charged and hormonally merciless. Even as it was happening, as I gravitated helplessly toward my newborn and felt a gap widening between me and my eager, confused little boy, I knew we were part of an organic transformation not controllable by emotion or intellect. It was the will of the body—my body—that I focus my attention on the survival of my baby. And yet, sitting across the dinner table from my son, listening to his chatter while I nursed his infant sister, I often felt the urge to gather him up and beg, "Don't go!" though I knew that I was the one who was going.

"I love you both equally"—the age-old answer sputtered by querulous, stammering parents to their querulous, suspicious children—is a myth we would like to believe. But it's simply not possible to love any two humans equally—to do so would defy the nature of humanness in all its individuality. I wouldn't even want to love my children equally if that meant without regard for their uniqueness, without discretion, a sort of blanket love policy that didn't itemize their gifts and quirks and weak spots. And yet, until my second child was born, I would have been furious had anyone suggested that I might love my first child less.

As much as it saddens me, the truth is that my heart did not simply "expand" to accommodate my second child. Though I do, unequivocally, love both of my children deeply, it is also true that I have been more connected to my baby than to my son since the baby's birth. The baby needs that connection, I tell myself; babies require the most passionate, most thorough love we are capable of. I also tell myself that, for eight years, I've been in the honeymoon phase—the baby phase—of my emotional relationship with my son. With Celeste's birth, we entered the realistic phase.

Which isn't to say that my love for my son is now finite. Like anything vital, it changes. And grows. And perhaps this change, which feels like such a loss, is also necessary and healthy. Perhaps we are now forging the relationship that will carry us, connected and yet separate, not just loving each other but with enough distance to like each other, into Zachary's adulthood. That's a comforting thought, but one with a cool breeze blowing through it, since the payoff seems so very far away.

On the final night of my week alone with Zachary last summer, the tattered shreds of cloud that had started to appear in the sky over the last couple of days finally bunched up, obscuring the stars in their flight. It was just as well: Zachary was so tired that I couldn't rouse him from his nest of blankets on the couch, where he was "resting" until, as promised, I woke him for the midnight show overhead. But earlier that day, late in the hot, still afternoon, as the sun dropped below the tree line and cast us and the lake into shadow, in a quiet broken only by the occasional liquid trilling of a grosbeak, we caught a frog. Or rather, we found a tiny frog in the tall grasses at the water's edge.

The length of my thumb and two shades of green, he had glimmering golden eyes and tiger-striped legs. Sprinkled over his cool back were black speckles, as if someone had just ground pepper over him. For the longest time he patiently let us examine him, and we touched our fingertips to his creamy belly and watched him breathe. He was new, we decided, too young and confused to be afraid.

But finally he hopped away from our open hands and back to the edge of the lake, where he floated in a pool made by the matted grass. I know I will always remember that day—not just because, as Zachary whispered triumphantly, we finally captured a frog! or because the next day, back in the city, I went into labor seven weeks early. I'll remember because I carry in my head a picture of Zachary, my firstborn, on his wet belly in the grass, his nose sprinkled with new freckles, his arms impossibly scrawny and pink with sunburn. For one last fleeting moment, he was my baby, my one and only. And then it was time to go.

On Not Having
a Daughter

JAYNE ANNE PHILLIPS

A son will leave and take a wife;
a daughter's a daughter all her life.

I'M A KID, drying dishes for my mother. On summer evenings
a slow caramel light plays across the yard and dapples the narrow two-lane out front. Cows stand in the north corner of the
hilly field across the macadam, leaning up against one another
in a velvet shamble and scratching themselves on the barbed-
wire fence. All day the shade of a giant somnolent oak casts
shadows across their broad, dumb faces. Evenings they stand
as though sensually stunned, in light so thick and sepia gold
they can't move.

In winter it's pitch dark by five and the cattle huddle in shelter on the other side of the hill. My brothers are wrestling
across the twin beds in their room at the end of the darkened
hallway; I hear their metal bed frames lurch on groaning
wheels. We have a Maytag dishwasher but my mother prefers
to wash dishes by hand; she says she gets them cleaner than
any machine. And besides, this is our time to talk. It's when I
hear all the stories about high school, her boyfriends and suit-

ors, our town and everyone in it. I hear all she knows about my father's people and his other life, the one he led before he met her in 1948. I hear about her rather outlandish father, wealthy before the Depression ruined him, her much older sister and brother and the three siblings born after them, all dead before she drew breath: stillborn twins and a toddler who died of diphtheria. I hear about the woman who lost those babies and feared in the beginning that she would lose my mother as well. She was nearly forty when her last child was born, as the Depression came on and the money was gone; the infant was scrawny and sickly, and her much older husband increasingly eccentric. *I used to worry so,* my grandmother told my mother, *and the neighbor woman would tell me, "Don't you fret, she'll be the joy of your life." And it's true, you were.*

My mother refers always to my grandmother as Mother but the term seems neither formal nor distanced. The word is her comfort. I learn early that a woman who loses her mother aches. Much happens in life and miracles unfold, but that central absence of voice and image persists. It's as though a room of the spirit remains just as it was the day my grandmother died, the day her long illness was over and my mother had nursed her through it into the mouth of time. In that room possessions are undisturbed and the August air smells of roses. The town stands still; the hour, closed like a bud, pulls softly shut. *You only have one mother . . . As Mother used to say . . . I don't know how many times Mother told me . . .*

I know her through words. She died when my mother was three months married, but her story is my mother's story. Together they chose my name when my mother was twelve, and referred to me as someone who would exist. Their story is so complex and layered and shot through with luminous sorrow that I will exist, and become a writer to make sure the stories don't vanish. I grow up believing that I too will have a daughter. After all, a woman with no mother or daughter is a woman alone on earth.

I'M TWENTY, FINISHING college in a world my grandmother wouldn't recognize, but the sprawling house I live in with assorted others is circa her era. The generous, sagging porch and bay windows have seen better days; next year the house will be razed for a parking lot, and the landlord gives us free rein. We fill the place with antique odds and ends in various states of repair, plant a big garden, cover the torn floor with remnant linoleum. My lover, a recent Harvard grad school dropout, has come home to work construction and play music; he's one of those men who is so charming and vital that he's slept with every woman he knows. In fact, when my roommate and I moved into this house, he was sleeping with the woman who sublet to us, in the big first-floor bedroom. Now he lives on the second floor, with me. When he isn't living with a woman, he lives in his van. He keeps his belongings in milk crates, which are quite portable; he stacks them in our room on their sides, like an open shelving system. I'm crazy about him, though I've had numerous liaisons since leaving home, two or three a year, not counting spellbound one-night encounters, and I know enough to recognize we're completely dissimilar; he's a politicized extrovert musician, I'm a reader and scantly published poet. When we're together three months or so, I find that I'm pregnant, despite my IUD.

I remember locking myself in the bathroom, bathing in the big tub, sitting in hot water with the tap on full and loud, and sobbing. I make the appointment right away though, glad I'm only six weeks along. Abortion is illegal here; we drive out of state to the nearest big city, walk into an anonymous brick building. At first we get the wrong office—a roomful of women in various states of pregnancy look up from their magazines. We exit quickly, as though someone's played a bad joke on us. It's the third time my lover has impregnated a girlfriend, but I'm the first he's actually accompanied for the consequent abortion. He feels it's a simple thing. Still, he leaves the building as soon as I'm checked in; he'll wait in the car or take a walk while I go through the obligatory counseling process and have the procedure. I'd like to go with him, but I sit in the waiting room and calculate my approximate due date on a conveniently provided paper dial: January 28th, his birthday.

I'm an articulate, composed client during the interview. Yes, I'm certain; no, I don't wish to consider other alternatives. Then I'm in the gown and on the table. My counselor is holding my hand. The nice young doctor comes in with his female assistant. I realize they're volunteers; we're all volunteers here, acting on our convictions. My mother has told me not to have sex before marriage. I've rejected her dictum; I'm a responsible sexual being whom technology has failed, and my mother would be horrified at any option available to me now. Here at the beginning of my life, my option is escape. A twinge, and the IUD is gone. The doctor explains what will happen next, adjusts the machinery, and begins. An appliancelike sound swallows the room. The counselor takes my hand and says to squeeze as hard as I like, then locks gazes with me and keeps talking. I'm wondering how many times a day she does this, then thought abruptly stops. I go completely blank, as though I'm floating through my own astonishment. I've heard the phrase *knowledge beyond words* but I've never been inside it, or known it was real. Independent of my motionless, abandoned self and the sharp, manageable discomfort, there opens some field of time in which sentience begins or floats or waits, both death and life; into it something separate from cells and blood withdraws, some ineffable breath, deeply whispered, withdraws.

It's done. Across a vast divide I've heard phrases, *almost over, just another moment.* Then the women help me sit up, into the doctor's open gaze at the end of the table. He's so startled and alarmed by the look on my face that he steps toward me and says quickly, What's wrong? I burst into tears, my face in my hands, and he leaves immediately.

In the recovery room the others read paperbacks and I continue weeping, a strange gasping distant from myself, lacking even tears. Nurses come by and take my temp, my pulse, inquire about my "support system"; they're surprised I've taken this turn. My lover has been here three times to retrieve me. "She's resting," they've told him. When I finally stand up I'm dry-eyed and increasingly relieved, a body freed from a trap. I'm hungry, ravenous: I realize the thought of food has not occurred to me for days. On the way home we stop at an inn along a country road, under a bower of dark trees, and have a wonderful meal, holding hands across the table like two glad, weightless voyagers. I don't tell him about the due date, or about anything; all of it disappears into the space between us, bridged in our fingertips. Together, we hold on.

The abortion doesn't separate us. That happens weeks later, when he sleeps with another girl and I won't adapt to a more open relationship—not with him. In love, I revert to my mother's passionate need for contact and protection. *I won't be tortured,* I hear her say, dispensing with some irritation or weighty annoyance. It's the phrase that occurs to me as I turn away. I'm not a modern woman. I sleep with men only in love, or convinced of its possibility. When possibility ends, there's nowhere to go and I step out: a single soul. It's almost a religious stance.

I take up the solitary life. On a lark, my friends talk me into coming along to see a psychic. She's a working-class, middle-aged woman who comes to town, stays with friends, does readings for fifty dollars. I'm told she asks to hold a bracelet or a ring, then describes pictures—things that have happened or may happen occur to her in disconnected images. She sits alone in a room and we enter one by one. I go in first, but she doesn't ask to hold anything. She looks at me before I even sit down and says, "I see you've lost a child, a girl." In response to my silence, she adds, "They stay near you for a while. There's a shadow in your aura, an essence that's female." Still I don't speak. She admits she doesn't know how it works, she mentions incarnation and karma. "Maybe it's like a knock at a door," she tells me. "You can answer the door, or not. Perhaps the visitor will return, and perhaps not." She opens her hands. I put mine inside them. Then she tells me other things.

THE DREAMS START in a month or so. I graduate and leave, travel cross-country, live in New Mexico and California. The dreams, little guilt dreams, regret dreams, keep pace with me, repeating in a cycle of their own. Something's misplaced or missing. Alone, like any pilgrim, I'm looking through long, disconnected hallways of houses and apartments I've lived in. The houses are all mixed up, or have wings of rooms not obvious in life.

By January I'm living in Colorado in a gorgeous cowboy town, waitressing in a Greek-owned greasy spoon that serves mostly eggs and fried potatoes, food familiar from home. Late one night I fall asleep with a candle burning, and dream I'm walking into the yard of my childhood home, through the pines, onto the wide lawn in front of the house. The house has been turned into a home for mothers and babies, and my lover and his father greet me as though I'm expected. I understand that I live here, and my lover's father embraces me, lifting me up into the air as though I'm a child. Buoyant, I float above him, then I'm in the house, walking down the long hallway. This is the room my brothers shared, but it's small now, just wide enough for a narrow bed with a cardboard box full of puppies at the foot. I look away and the box is full of kittens. I look away again and the box is fluffed with sheets and pillows; inside stands a baby a year or so old. I see her clearly, her face, her dark curls. She reaches for me and I lift her into bed. It's as though we've been separated a long time. She kisses me on the mouth. They are strange kisses, sensual, unhurried, but not sexual or probing. I awaken, instantly alert, as though the dream has broken some spell, and open my eyes to see the flame of the candle opposite my bed lick the air in a high thin column. There's a faint burning smell, and I see that a book sticking out from a high shelf is smoldering. It is my grandmother's old cloth-bound copy of Gibran's *The Prophet,* the one she requested my mother read from at her funeral. The book is so old and dry that the heat of the candle has burned a hole through the cover. I know, without looking, the last words of the text: *A little while, a moment upon the wind, and another woman shall bear me.* Beneath these words, my grandmother, who died five years before my birth, has written my mother's name, a girl cousin's name, and my name, each with a question mark.

I open the windows. The faint acrid scent of seared paper mixes with the drifted cold of a heavy, blowing snow. Somewhere far from here, snow blankets the rumpled cattle, the graves in deserted, separate glades, all that was offered and refused. A moment of undisputed presence holds steady in the blinding fall, like evidence, a live promise in a cloud that moves.

DRAMA QUEEN *for a Day*

How I Beat a Bull with
My Three-Speed Blender

CATHY WILKINSON

THERE ARE MANY charming advantages to living out here in the Wild West. Beautiful sunsets, eccentric characters named Chester, closeness to all things wild and beautiful. But I must draw the line at large bovine creatures that wander freely wherever they please. I occasionally shoo away the stray steer nosing around in my petunias. It is part and parcel of living in ranch land. But my sanity was tested (I believe I failed) when an enormous bull came calling in my backyard.

"Mom, there's a *reallllly* big bull in the yard and you should see his nuts," my shy and retiring twelve-year-old son yelled one day.

By golly, they were very big. I went out with my broom and assumed my usual pioneer woman stance and said, "Shoo, there, shoo!" He responded by charging very quickly in my direction. I lost the broom in my eagerness to enter the house. The bull blew snot all over the kitchen windows. This was bad.

I called my husband, who promptly assigned the bull-chasing task to my boys, ages twelve and eleven. The boys charged up the stairs to "get stuff" while I pounded on the windows and yelled very bad words. Soon, my angels were scrambling downstairs, BB guns cocked, plastic swords waving, handcuffs stuffed in their pockets. "Don't worry, Mom, we'll take care of this!" I felt like the mom in *Old Yeller*.

They dashed out the back door and I stood by the window, distracting Mr. Big Balls. Soon, I could see the boys cautiously moving up behind the beast. My heart was in my throat. This was really stupid, they are so little, my babies! Suddenly, with a strangled war whoop, they let fly a barrage of BBs into the offending bovine's butt. The bull bellowed, jumped straight up three feet, whirled around, and charged my boys!

That is when that blind, motherly instinct hooked me under the armpits and moved me. I grabbed the nearest item, a blender, and dashed out to protect my young. I ran up and conked the bull right on the noggin with my grandmother's 1946 Oster three-speed blender. He stopped, turned around, and faced me. Unflinching (do you think Demi Moore could play me in the movie?), I hit him again. He took off like a shot. Through my flowers, through the fence ($259 repair), and away. I never saw his big balls again.

Best of all, my boys have a high regard for my bravery and they know not to mess with me, especially when I am whipping up some milk shakes in my Bovine Blaster.

One Drip at a Time

SUSAN STRAIGHT

IN THE GROCERY STORE parking lot, across from my daughters' elementary school, I leaned into the open back of my dust-covered van, wielding the can of frosting I'd just bought. Twirling the knife I'd remembered to bring, I covered the top of each cupcake I'd made that morning before work. The chocolate cupcakes had been sitting on their metal baking sheet in the van while I was at work, so they felt warm as if they'd just come from the oven, I thought.

Yeah, right. Other women passed behind me, and I thought I felt their glances, like a cold breeze, like pity or disdain, through the cotton of my shirt.

I glanced back surreptitiously. A couple of moms wearing Keds and shorts, hair styled, nails done, moms I knew stayed home with their kids, pushing judiciously filled carts of groceries to pack carefully into their clean vans before picking up their children from school.

They looked so good.

A few older women walked by, wearing comfortable knit pants or dresses and heeled shoes, gray hair also styled, their eyebrows drawn into slight frowns when they saw what I was doing. Yes, I know, I wanted to say, I know this looks foolish and last-minute and not at all the way you probably did it. I know. I know how the frayed edges of my life are showing right now, like hems taped instead of sewn, like glasses missing a temple, like safety pins holding up a strap.

I WAS MARRIED for thirteen years, to the boy I met in eighth grade who became the teenager I dated throughout high school who became the man I married when I was twenty-two. He became the father of our three daughters, but by then, he'd also become so progressively unhappy that he decided he needed to become independent. At this point in my internal recitation of what happened to my life, I always envision the elf in the animated version of *Rudolph the Red-Nosed Reindeer* spelling out that all-important word for the others heading off into the snowy wilderness. *In-de-pen-dent.* That helped, the pronunciation, when I had to explain it over and over to the girls.

Our third daughter was four months old when he repeated that phrase to me. "I need to learn to live on my own, be responsible for myself," he added.

So I did, too.

But he got a one-bedroom apartment across town, and a new car. I had a two-bedroom, eighty-seven-year-old farm-house in a crumbling neighborhood, suddenly and increasingly full of single women. I had three kids, a job, a big yard, seven rabbits, and two hands.

That first year he was gone, I confess I felt a sense of exhilaration at times. I was proud of myself, handling everything. (Even though I worked, I'd been one of those women who did 80 percent of household chores anyway, like the studies show; that was part of the inequity of my marriage.) I boldly set out to trim the big fruitless mulberry tree we'd planted a few years before. I took the clippers to get sharpened, I stood on the ladder and then on the tree trunk, kamikaze mom, impressing the children and my neighbors with my prowess. I'm short, I weigh 105, and they didn't think I could hang. Oh, baby, I thought, you just don't know how tough I am. Between the tree trimming, cutting up the branches, pruning the fruit trees and roses, washing the windows, hammering in loose fence boards, and hanging up laundry, my biceps were better than if I'd been going to the gym. Which I sure as heck wasn't.

At night, though, the emotional adventures were different, much more draining. The kids cried, which hurt me more than any cuts or scrapes or sore muscles. We had a nightly ritual of lighting saints' candles, *veladoras* from the Mexican grocery nearby, and saying prayers. Of course, they prayed for their daddy to come back. I prayed for strength and peace, which made them stare at me.

This all took an extra hour or so, after homework and baths, and then they insisted on sleeping with me, tossing and turning all night. I'd wake up with toes in my nose and elbows grazing my eyebrows. Hands patting me to make sure I was there.

After a few months, I was down low, too, so sad and scared and mad that I had to call my friend Holly, a former single mother, at midnight her time to hear, "I know. I cried until my eyes felt like fists. It takes a long time." I had to call my friend Elizabeth at 10:00 P.M. just to make sure I wasn't going to have a heart attack. She'd been divorced when her four children were only slightly older than mine, and her calming words were like cough syrup that made me stop hacking at night and let me sleep. The emotional rough stuff of the first year was her specialty, and she told me one evening, "It's like you're in a room with a hundred dripping faucets, and you have to turn them off, one at a time."

That was the greatest metaphor I'd heard for dealing with

the boundaries and memories and twist ties of a long marriage and life together. The first year, that's how it felt, with each wrangle over the kids or money or responsibility—the past weighted everything with anger and sadness. Each trickling faucet took a lot of wrenching to stop.

Now, after three years alone, some of that emotional Chinese water torture is over. However, I laugh with Elizabeth about the phrase now, in the throes of solitary responsibility for everything, still.

"Great," I say. "Just something else to fix."

THE BATHROOM FAUCETS, tub and sink, have been dripping for months now. Outside, the hose connection drips unless I turn it exactly the right way. Roof shingles are missing from the ferocious winds of winter, and the house is dusty from the smoky winds of summer. The van I bought has sweeping dents and paint smears from where a jerk, being chased by a cop, raced down my street and sideswiped my parked vehicle. My only vehicle. Which is why the dents are over a year old, and I can't motivate myself to take the van in, find another way to get us all to work and school, and care about how the bumper looks. It looks slightly run-down, like the rest of my life.

My street is looking pretty ragged, too. The guy who hit us was living in his station wagon. The windows had been shattered with a baseball bat by his brother down the block, who'd just been put out of the speed lab business. My next-door neighbor's husband had left her with her three kids. My across-the-street neighbor's husband had died at forty-four after spending half his life addicted to heroin. She was living on eternal yard sales (which I have to admit made my lawn seem less cluttered, since mine only displayed children's toys and garden implements rather than motor parts, old clothes, and furniture).

My best friend on the street, Jeannine, whose four kids had baby-sat mine and played with them, lost her husband, too. He was killed in a car accident. Jeannine and I were both thirty-five that year. We couldn't believe we had to do this alone. Seven kids. Old houses with flickering electrical wires and flooding basements and overgrown hedges and missing shingles. Jeannine was in her last year of nursing school. I was working. We were stunned.

That's how we got through the year. We called each other at ten or so, because we couldn't leave the sleeping kids alone, and said, "How are you?" "Stunned." This was our answer, our mantra, our comfort. I couldn't have made it without her wry laughter.

Some nights we were both mad. She'd met her husband at fourteen, like me. After we talked, I would lie in bed, my body aching, my hands raw from dishes and floors and branches and baby shampoo, thinking that when I got married, I always assumed I'd work hard, have kids and a house and some fun. We all think that when we sign up for this particular existence rather than high-powered career or endless party.

And when my husband first left, I thought, So I work a little harder. But now, the realization has set in, piled high and crackling as the mulberry leaves falling from those spear-straight branches one more year: I have to do all of this forever. Fix the vacuum cleaner, kill the spiders, correct the spelling and make the math flash cards and pay for preschool and trim the tree. Trim the tree.

Now, sometimes, I feel like a burro. A small frame, feet hard as hooves, back sagging a little. Now the edges of my life are a bit ragged, and things don't always get done as they should.

The void yawns beneath me. And I understand now how life slips when you're on your own. I don't always remember that the three-year-old is supposed to dress in green for a nature walk, or that the seven-year-old owes money for the field trip, or that the nine-year-old needs new shoelaces. So we all look slightly askew. And instead of crying about it, when it seems overwhelming and spirit-crushing and *dull*, I make myself go out in the yard and touch the teepee we made out of last year's mulberry branches, covered with an old white sheet spray-painted with leftover Christmas copper, the designs of deer and snakes held together with an old bungee cord.

I know how it looks, but we like to sit in there and eat, pretend we're not here. We're not here, where the grass is too long and some fence posts are missing and we are up too late, keeping one another company.

THIS IS WHAT always gets done, because it means a lot to me: The kids wear clean, unwrinkled clothes, and their hair is always clean and styled. We eat really good breakfasts and dinners, and we are never out of Swiss chocolate, English Breakfast tea, or Vermont maple syrup. The sink is never full of dishes, and all trash is taken out of the van when children exit.

This is what doesn't get done, because I can't do it: If they lose a button or need a strap sewn back on, they'd better pray they grow slowly, because it could be months before I get to sit down and mend or sew. We are sometimes out of juice boxes or bread, and they have to take water bottles and peanut-butter-smeared crackers in their lunches. The outside of the van is so dirty we could grow corn in the soil collected on the windshield wipers and potatoes on the roof.

The kids always go to the doctor, for checkups and shots

and immediately, incessantly, it seems, when they are ill. They take their medicine when they should.

But I haven't been to the doctor since I had Rosette, who just turned three. Before that, I had seen my primary-care physician once in five years, for severe bronchitis. She had no idea who I was. Usually I drink herb tea, light a saint's candle and pray that I won't get sick, and go to bed.

When a branch-loaded trash can fell on my right thumb last fall, as I was trimming that damn mulberry tree for the second year, feeling much less exhilarated, I couldn't bear to go to the doctor. The kids had just had strep throat, and I felt like I'd lived at the clinic. The swelling in my thumb would recede, I told myself. I would be able to move it next week. I took Advil. I typed without that hand and couldn't write at all. But a week or two later, during another strep throat episode, the kids' pediatrician saw the bruised mess and carefully examined the thumb. He knew how my life went; he knew that for two years, I'd seen him more frequently than any other male adult except my stepfather. The pediatrician sent me for an X ray, with his authorization, and then gave me a child's splint.

As for medicine, the only prescription I have is for birth control pills. And it's so hard to drive all the way to the pharmacy when none of the kids are sick that I don't do it. So I'm lucky I don't even date, much less fool around, since I often take the pills late. The only reason I still take them is because they make my skin look so good. And what does that matter, since the rest of me looks like the stereotypical single working mother who hasn't glanced in the mirror for months, because after combing the kids' hair in the morning I don't have time for anything but a clip, and besides, the mirror is, of course, eighty years old and hazy with grimy little fingerprints?

So my clothes are hand-me-downs. My glasses are nearly

three years old, and the baby girl has bumped them so many times that they hang askew. One eyebrow shows and one doesn't.

Okay, it's not that bad. But my hairstyle—long hair in a bun and bangs I cut myself when I can't see anymore—has worked for three years now. That's when I made my last annual salon trip. Two hours sitting in a chair? With no kids? And it costs money? Please.

REMEMBER THAT MOVIE we saw in school, the one about your body? The brain was represented by a roomful of drawers, like an office full of file cabinets. When you slept well, your brain got rested and the room stayed orderly. When you didn't sleep, the room got trashed—Daffy Duck appeared and ran around trying to stuff papers back into drawers, dust and spiderwebs collected in the rapidly filling corners, and Daffy finally gave up, exhausted and looking disheveled, since his brain couldn't function without rest.

That's how it feels, I think: the house and my body and my brain. I don't sleep very much, because I finish chores and work until about midnight, and then at two or three, I'll hear a noise in the yard. A raccoon, or possum, or wild dog trying to get the rabbits. I prowl around to make sure it's not a human. I have pepper spray and an unloaded shotgun, left behind by my independent former husband for my protection.

When I finally fall asleep again, one of the girls comes to me with bad dreams.

After black tea at dawn, we begin again. Breakfasts, lunch boxes, scrunchies and hair ribbons and last-minute spelling tests and permission slips and gas and work and the preschooler and groceries and rabbit food.

It's the sacks I mind most, after all this time. For three years, no one has ever helped me carry in the ten bags of groceries or the fifty-pound bags of rabbit food. Why does that bother me?

Because at this point, lots of still-married working moms are saying, "Yeah, I do all that. My guy channel-surfs while I do all that."

I know. I know most of us women do most of the child care and housework. What, then? What can't I do that men do?

I don't know. Men change the oil or take the car in for service, ostensibly. Buy the tires, fix the roof shingles and gutters, repair the fence. Trim the trees. They go up in the attic to kill the rat rolling pecans that sound like huge bowling balls thundering down the boards over our heads. Which makes the rat seem, at night, the size of a Tasmanian devil to the girls and me.

Husbands are just there, on those nights when you have to go to a school meeting or science fair and the baby's tired or the older girl's class play, *The Wizard of Oz,* is in ten minutes and the middle girl has strep throat.

Most marriages divide themselves—naturally or not—into roles. One does inside work, the other outside. One pays bills, the other washes the car. One cooks, the other does dishes.

But what marriage is really about is backup. Physical, moral, emotional, simple. I think what I'm saying is I don't have backup. Ever.

When we were teenagers, in our rough neighborhood, the most important thing to say to a friend was "I got your back." I will watch out for you, protect you and help you, be your backup. I felt that loss keenly when I fainted during a bout of winter flu and the girls had to rouse me from unconsciousness, had to kneel on the floor shaking me and crying, asking who to call.

When I feel it now—like tonight (really, I'm not lying, three hours ago), when the girls had all bathed and gotten nightied and then we remembered the videos—we have to cruise as a team through each big or little crisis. Videos due today. No money for overdue fees.

"It's still hot anyway," I say, and it's true. Near a hundred degrees today, and our house has no air-conditioning (that should be evident by now!) and it was nine. Bedtime, for some-one with backup. "Jump in," I said, and we cruised through the streets with the windows open and the radio blasting Aretha.

When you see us, don't shake your head and think, How irresponsible. Responsible is all I'm good at anymore.

THERE ARE so many of us out here. My friend Kari, who lives a few streets over, lost her husband to a brain tumor the same year I lost mine to independence. She is eight days younger than me. She has three kids, too, and a job. We eat pizza with our kids in the yard or the park, and while they spin and run and whisper, we look at each other. "Stunned" is one of her favorite words, too. We compare whose van is dirtier. No one wins. Kari says her sprinkler system is broken, her faucets are leaking, and so, like me, she saves the water in buckets and soaks her plants with it.

When we see each other on the sidewalk at the elementary school, waiting to pick up our kids, we look at the well-tended mothers—the calm, prepared, accessorized mothers who carry elaborate science projects or room-mother lists. Do the other single mothers think what we do sometimes? We think: Why them? Why not us? Some days we all have this look I can only imagine as gaunt and haunted, like the Dust Bowl mother with her fingers to her mouth, her eyes fixed far away.

We have jobs, though. We are not starving. We are lucky. My mother reminds me of this. My mother did this, too. My father left when I was three and my mother was eight months pregnant. Shortly after that, she gave birth to my brother and called her stepmother, who told her she had made her bed and had to lie in it. My mother brought us home to a tiny house in a rural area not far from where I live now. A windstorm had covered the few rooms with layers of dust. My baby brother threw up all over the yellow bassinet cover my mother had sewn. She was alone in the house with us and a few cans of beans. But she had a job, she always told me. She went back to work three days later, sitting gingerly, leaving us with a neighbor who she hoped wouldn't drop my brother on his head the way a drunk baby-sitter had once done to me.

MY MOTHER, my stepfather, my friends never tell me I made my bed and must lie in it. Instead, they bring me food, or run by a carton of milk, or just talk to me on the phone. They are the shoulders and hands making my improvised backup, holding my tired back up.

My mother watches my girls on her day off, which is a workday for me. She helps them with their homework and then they make cookies or fudge for our dessert. I couldn't survive without her or my stepfather, who changes the filter in the central heating duct and fixes the dripping faucet once again and gets me a used printer so I can write. That first year, he watched the girls for an hour on Monday nights so I could go jogging, pretending to need the exercise but in reality just floating, breathing, alone.

"Your stepfather?" some women said. "He's always helping you. You're not a kid now. You need a man."

My friend Terri, a landscaper and former single mother, told me, "So hook up with a contractor for a year. You got this old house. Give him something in trade, you know what I mean? Get things in shape."

I laughed. I couldn't even envision it.

Instead, I asked my stepfather to hold the ladder, because I had to learn to crawl in the attic and put out the rat poison and nail a board over the chewed hole in the shingles. I trapped the skunk that was digging under the foundation to nest in the basement. And in the evenings, the baby just had to come to the class play, which was okay, because she had to learn the songs to *The Wizard of Oz* anyway, with the rest of us.

And at night, when I didn't feel like a writer but only a burro, I called Holly, who talked to me not about kids and divorce but about books and words. When I knew I couldn't make the parent orientation meeting, I called Kari, confessing to "stunned," and I felt better when she said she wasn't going either. And when one daughter refused to touch or talk to me for a week, simmering about our abandonment, blaming the nearest warm burro body, I called Elizabeth, who counseled hugs, even if that required persistence and possibly full-contact tackles, her time-honored and successful technique for misplaced anger. It worked.

We wouldn't work, my household, alone.

When I wrecked my thumb trimming the tree, Elizabeth brought over clippers and her husband, Dave, and we finished the branches in a morning, but more important, I wasn't alone.

I was laughing, telling them why we had to leave the one awkward branch jutting out to the sky: Delphine, my seven-year-old, likes to straddle that one and touch the moon at certain times of the year. They understood. When feral dogs from the riverbed kept crashing into the yard trying to kill the rabbits, and I had to chase them off with a rake and my shouts, my neighbor Juli, daughter of a single mother, came over with gloves and a measuring tape. She said I could build a fence. We did, pounding in a six-foot board fence protecting that corner of the yard.

My daughters are older now. They watch all this. Am I teaching them that men aren't necessary? I don't think so, because I don't believe that. I believe what my mother taught me: You get left, you get busy. You get tired, you get frustrated, you get crazy, and then you get up again and make the lunches, braid the hair, and go to work.

I JUST WISH I didn't look so bad doing it. Closing up the van that day, the cupcakes cheerful with their handful of sprinkles, a dark fudge smear on my good khaki pants (of course), I headed over to the school to be a good mom. And I was. My oldest daughter said, "Everybody loves the cupcakes. Especially the sprinkles. You're the best mom in the world." Her eyes darted nervously. "But you have chocolate on your pants."

That wouldn't be true if I'd frosted the cupcakes the night before, leisurely, efficiently. But the real reason I didn't have time for homemade frosting, the kind my mother taught me to make, the kind my children always have, is that the girls wanted to help, and they'd had tons of homework the previous night. So that morning, we got up early, and the youngest wanted to separate the muffin cups by color and put them in the tin. The two older girls wanted to drop the batter from soup ladles, and we only have one. They're my backup now, whether that's always good or not. And we're a team. In everything. No matter how much longer it takes.

By the time the cupcakes were in the oven, everyone had eaten and gotten dressed and braided hair and found papers and backpacks, and I handed them lunches, there was no time to make frosting. "I'll buy some on my way to work," I told Gaila, and she didn't mind.

"Most people get frosting in the can anyway," she said. "And lots of moms just buy cupcakes at the store." Then she said hesitantly, "Can you put sprinkles on them, though? Please?"

So I pressed sprinkles onto each cupcake, in the parking lot. Thirty-two cupcakes, and I'm thinking, That's way too many kids for third grade. Why are California schools so over-crowded? They're cutting class sizes for first and second grade, but they learn all that math in third grade, and they need smaller classes too. . . .

Of course, I'm spilling multicolored sprinkles on the van carpet, near the alluvial soil deposits that are probably sprouting foxtails, and other women are staring, and then I'm thinking, Yeah, so I wish I could write to the governor, or to the newspaper about smaller class sizes, but I can't even see, because my bangs are falling in my eyes again because I didn't have time to trim them. And if I don't finish these cupcakes, pick up the baby in the parking lot where the sitter's meeting me, then help with the birthday party, take the kids home, feed them and the rabbits, help finish a book report and a diorama of a scene from *The Velveteen Rabbit,* return phone calls I'm probably getting from work right now, pay the bills and change the sheets and vacuum, load the dishwasher, look over insurance papers, and sleep . . .

Yes, I should sleep so I can start again in the morning. Whether or not I sleep, I will not be able to make the right celery–cream cheese ghosts-on-a-log for Delphine's Halloween party. I lost the recipe.

I will make brownies. A batch big enough for my mother, Elizabeth, and Kari and Jeannine. All of them single mothers of the past or present, their hands reaching out over the void, their rueful, funny words and mesh of linked fingers reaching for the faucets still dripping in my life, their thumbs over the end of the hose, keeping the pressure back, making life slightly more livable.

I will lie there in the dark, trying to sleep. Still scared, until one of the girls comes in and pats me on the face. "Mommy's right here," I'll whisper.

Mother Roux

ERIN AUBRY

GROWING UP I always considered myself to be my mother's child. I liked what that meant: My mother was kind but entirely unsentimental, self-possessed but unassuming, practical above all things. She got married in a plain tea-length dress and short gloves and then gave the whole outfit away because she said she didn't need it anymore; she and my father never took a honeymoon, even when they could afford one years after their wedding, because she didn't attach great importance to such events. I admired my mother's efficiency, her equipoise and lack of wasted motion—these were the models I used to streamline my own imagination, to build my own aspirations of becoming a writer.

I turned out to be like my mother, but also a departure from her. I wanted reasonableness but also excess, flourishes, inconsistencies, stories; as I got older I wanted to dredge up and let fly what she had unceremoniously put away long ago. I was most curious about New Orleans, her and my father's hometown, a place that defined me to myself even though I was born and raised in Los Angeles. When she left there in 1956 to marry my father and settle here, she didn't go back home for a long, long time, which I hardly understood. New Orleans was magic to me, a place I'd never been to but had heard endlessly regaled in stories told over my head as a child, an acutely

Southern but wholly singular city that I had come to revere as
the molten spiritual core of our family—shouldn't somebody go
back now and then to tend to the heritage, pull up the weeds
growing around it? My mother didn't think so. The city lived for
her in a diminished capacity, perhaps packed up and given
away with the dress and gloves. "Ah, New Orleans," she'd say
brusquely. "I don't want to go back there. It's a big ghetto."

New Orleans might well have been a ghetto—like other
black children, I knew the rudiments of Southern history practically from birth—but evidence of my mother's greater New
Orleans faith filled our dinner table every week and teased my
curiosity: hot sausage and red beans, panne meat, jambalaya,
stuffed *mirlitons,* French bread and butter to go with everything. When my grandmother was visiting, she made apple pie
and biscuits from scratch, or pitched in with my mother to
make the pièce de résistance of New Orleans cooking, filé
gumbo. At a time when L.A. was institutionalizing the popular-
ity of brave new foods such as wheat germ and soy meat, New
Orleans was implacably fed to us; it described much of our
workaday world and all of our special occasions and it lingered
in our psyche as indelibly as the acrid smoke from the frying
sausage lingered in the blackened stove hood—letting anyone
who stood beneath it and caught the faint but unmistakable
pungence of spice and char and nascent roux know what our
origins were.

Here was the excess, the story I sought, yet my mother did
not teach me how to cook. At dinnertime I always pulled Kool-
Aid and place-setting duty; the closest I ever came to food
preparation was sitting out on the back porch peeling shrimp
for the gumbo or shucking corn with a paper sack between my
knees. At first I thought my mother regarded me as incompe-
tent or herself as too competent to be bothered with training

novices—too much possibility of wasted motion. But there was more to it than that. As proprietary as she was about cooking, she was also laissez-faire about it, an attitude that spoke to her own L.A. yearnings to divest the old and investigate the new. She would set the dishes before us but let us make of them what we wanted, and if we chose to murk up the gumbo by adding too much filé powder, or if we chose not to eat gumbo at all and make a peanut butter sandwich instead, well, that was our business. She wanted us to have space enough for our own lives, for our own dishes—what else was this city for? Why else had she come?

Cultivating choices was something my mother revered, in her quiet way. I remember her telling me when I was young that I had better not think about marriage until after thirty "because after you're married," she said with a kind of finality, "there are certain things you just can't *do*." When I was six, shortly after the birth of my little sister, I followed her into the bathroom one day to inquire whether or not it hurt to have babies; she hesitated only a second before answering evenly that yes, it did, and I sensed even then that she meant more than physical pain. Despite her loyalty to family, I felt early on that she probably would have loved being a professional woman or a business owner just as much. The part of me that was like my mother empathized deeply with her unrealized wishes, the part that was outgoing but self-protective, brooding and often emotionally oblique—what they call in New Orleans *comme il faut,* holding the feelings close to the chest like trump cards. I loved her for taking me to the library each week, reading to me out loud, encouraging my writing merely by letting me be. I wanted her to follow where I was going, but I came to realize that she was content by then to stand where she was and see me off. She had made her choices; now she was going to watch me make mine. As far as cooking was concerned, I understood that my mother wanted her own space, to be given as wide a berth as she gave me. It was not hostility but a great need for privacy that drove her, a need to have full run of the world she had constructed for herself; I could look and admire, ask questions and one day be invited in, but I couldn't intrude—exactly the rules I tacitly established for my life as a writer. So it was with all the best intentions and with the desire for mutual respect, I believe, that my mother never taught me to cook.

I accepted that, though the funny thing is I still considered Creole cooking mine in the way that New Orleans, that place I never saw until I was twenty-two, was mine. When people asked me where I was from, I answered, "Los Angeles," and briefly reveled in my native city's hip quotient—denim bikinis, *Soul Train*—but I always hastily added, "but my family's from New Orleans." People's faces relaxed into understanding; that explained my fair skin and straight hair, the hybrid lilt that sometimes edged my voice, and rapid speech that often jammed into a stutter and put me in speech therapy by second grade. Too wound up to be Californian, not quite urban-tough enough for Spanish Harlem, I fancied myself to be exactly the mélange that was New Orleans: wide open and dankly mysterious and, even if you couldn't figure out which it was, always delightful to the taste.

People assume, because of my New Orleans bloodline, that I have inborn culinary talent. Not much is further from the truth; not only do I not make red beans and gumbo, I can barely make pancake mix, the kind that only needs water, come out right. But I don't mind the lack because it has, ironically enough, provided my mother and me with a reliable source of closeness—while she didn't teach me how to cook, she's always been a willing source of information, should I choose to ask. When I have the smallest food question, I call my mother to plumb her expertise. She enjoys this kind of deference and in these moments overcomes her emotional reticence and is most confident in her affections of me. There are even a few rare instances when I am able to air a little accumulated knowledge of my own; I say, "Well, I just used lemon peel instead of the juice, it's the same, you know," and my mother concurs or says, "Peel, sure, and you know it only takes about six lemons to make a glass of juice," as if I already knew that. And for a moment or two we are equals, confidants, two women exchanging timeworn shop talk that enables one of us to call the other in the morning for no particular reason.

More and more, I appreciate that kind of family intimacy. The Creole network that was firmly in place in postwar L.A.—that helped define the massive Southern migration here and give Creolism a uniquely local character—has slowly vanished over the years. In Crenshaw and South Central, there used to be my Uncle Leon's barber shop, Henry Marine's, Sid's Louisiana Cafe, Feast of Saint Joseph, and a thousand events based out of Catholic parish church halls like Transfiguration and Saint John of God. All of my relatives lived within a five-mile radius of one another, which is as tight a community as L.A. offers; I visited some aunt or uncle every Sunday and sat in the backyard or on the front porch drinking punch out of a paper cup and consuming whatever they had on the stove. Food and family were at every pit stop, impossible to escape, as warm and inextricable a part of my L.A. experience as sand and surf.

That experience has changed texturally over time, not for the better. My extended family exploded at its center and moved out to hot, far-flung suburbs like Diamond Bar and

Hacienda Heights. The only Creole must-stop from old times is Pete's Louisiana Hot Sausage, which is on Jefferson just west of Crenshaw. Jefferson used to be a Creole thoroughfare, the street where my Uncle Leon held such political and community sway from his barber shop that folks called him the Mayor. But people no longer use storefronts or porches or sidewalks as gathering sites. Visiting relatives, or anyone in central L.A., is a qualitatively different proposition—you don't hang out in the front yard and, well, there's really no one left for us to visit anymore. My mother spends Sunday afternoons now in the aisles of behemoth grocery stores and tells me I really should consider moving away from my midcity apartment, it's gotten too dangerous; she's been saying this ever since my landlady was unable to install an iron security screen on my glass-paned front door. The expansiveness I grew up with has been supplanted by fear, and the whole notion of cultural preservation seems not nearly as important as individual preservation. Now the closest I can get to those old family Sundays is in making seasonal pilgrimages to my crosstown homestead, positioning my face over the stockpot that steams gumbo mist up into the stove hood that holds a generation of L.A.-permuted Creole dreams—fissured dreams run through with cracks that could be either highways, which bind this city together and keep it apart, or simply cracks of age and disrepair.

I do consider—and record—stories. I ask old people questions when I see them, I ask my mother such questions every day (she is not yet old), but casually, offhandedly, as if an account of my great-uncle Lester's exploits in World War II is something that just occurred to me, like a measurement for sugar or baking powder. I must have my mother believe that I'm looking the other way when it comes to New Orleans; only then will she give it to me, and she even interrupts herself suddenly sometimes with a wary half question, half warning: "You aren't going to write about this, are you?" To that I answer, in my head, that these things are very much part of the space that she allowed me to architect. This is my choice.

I know my mother recognizes this choice more than she can admit. She is more relaxed now, less strict about keeping our functions apart. Yet she knows the power she still wields as keeper of the gas flame. When I fell into a crippling depression last year, from the depths of which I decided to stop answering the doorbell and returning phone calls, my mother sent my younger sister by with a Tupperware bowl full of gumbo she had made for Labor Day. This was a holiday, she had cooked— where the hell was I?

I didn't answer the door straightaway—all right, my sister had to force her way in with keys borrowed from my landlady. I didn't talk to her, couldn't talk to her; I had my mother's tight lips that day, and she left after a while, exasperated. But the bowl she brought for me worked its magic. In my slippery-slope misery, I went to the kitchen, poured the gumbo over the rice my mother had packed along with it, settled in front of the television, and watched something I can't remember at all. I had no more words in me, no more inclination to speak, but some weight rolled slightly off the center of my being as I spooned up the gumbo in silence, savoring the broth-tenderized chicken and sausage and shrimp on my tongue like an unutterable prayer, letting the oily roux coat the roof of my mouth like a salve. In these leanest of times, New Orleans was again being fed to me, in its own time. Whatever things I imagined were lacking, I had family enough. I had mother enough. *Laissez le bon temps rouler.*

How Many Working Fathers Does It Take to Screw in a Lightbulb?

ELIZABETH RAPOPORT

A SURVEY published in 1998 by the Families and Work Institute trumpeted the good news that working fathers are punching in for a bigger slice of the Second Shift: spending more time caring for, or at least hanging out with, their kids. During the workweek, they spend an average of 2.3 hours per day with their kids (up from 1.8 hours in a Department of Labor survey done in 1977), closing in on the average three hours that working mothers spend daily on child care. On days off, dads spend an average of 6.4 hours with the kids—up from five hours in 1977, but still lagging behind the 8.3 hours moms spend. Plus, men are spending more time on housework than they did twenty years ago, and women less.

Cigars all around? Not so fast. The authors of the study owned up to some suspect methodology—parents self-reported the results (allowing dads who watched the Bulls while Junior snoozed in the Swyngomatic to theoretically log 2.5 hours of "child care"), and they could "double-dip"—getting credit for both child care and chores if they, say, folded the laundry while prepping the kids for a spelling quiz.

Critics of the study noted that it didn't cover activities outside the home—school, sports, etc.—where the rubber really meets the road. They also cited competing surveys with more rigorous record keeping that indicated no major difference in working dads' participation on the home front.

Yeah, yeah. I must confess I'm a little jaded by these sociological pissing contests. Just wake me when the dads are doing 50 percent. Period. There's your headline news.

Or at least give us a survey that yields more useful data. A survey that reflects and quantifies the real psychic energy and time-suck of child rearing. Who really gets stuck with shouldering more of the immense data bank of information about caring for the kids, plus the intense, guilt-saturated drive to implement it? I reject any claim of gender equity that doesn't account for these factors, and no study I've seen has done that. To remedy the situation, I propose a new SAT: Superparent Achievement Test.

OK, moms and dads, grab a No. 2 pencil and let's begin.

PART I: VERBAL (or Preverbal if your child is under age two).

Score yourself one point apiece for each of the following correct answers.

HOME
—What are the names and numbers for the pediatrician, pharmacy, and fastest pizza delivery? (Partial credit for speed dial, but only if you programmed it yourself.)
—When's your child's next checkup? Dental appointment?
—What are your kids' clothing and shoe sizes?
—What's a good price for boneless chicken breasts?

—How much is a three-pack of Funtoons underpants on sale?

—Where is the extra toilet paper? (Subtract one point if you know and never replace the empty roll.)

SCHOOL

—What are the names of your kids' teachers? The principal? How much should you spend on a teacher's present at Christmas and at the end of the school year? (Subtract one point if you didn't know these gifts are mandatory.)

—When are your child's gym days, and why does that matter?

—To whom must you recycle egg cartons?

—When is bus pick-up and drop-off?

—How much does a school lunch cost? A carton of milk?

—How many PTA meetings have you attended in the last year? (Score one point per meeting; double if you had to bring cookies and pretend you baked them yourself.)

EXTRACURRICULAR

—What are the names and phone numbers of the kids' emergency backup play dates? (Double credit if you know the parents' and/or babysitters' names.)

—Who has custody of the Cookie Cupboard? How much is a box of Thin Mints? Which are lower in fat, Iced Ginger Daisies or Lemon Pastry Cremes?

—When are drop-off and pick-up for gymnastics, baseball, basketball, chess club, ballet, and Musical Mondays? Who could cover you at car pool if Save the Earth Day runs overtime?

—When is camp registration due?

—How many minutes a day must your child practice his or her musical instrument? What days do instruments go to school? If the instrument has a spit valve, do you know how to empty it?

—Are stud earrings allowed at soccer practice? Do socks go over or under the shin guards?

POP KIDDIE CULTURE

—Who are the three Hansons? Which is the youngest? The cutest?

—Who is "Leo"?

—If you had to choose between Spunky, Valentino, and Garcia, which Beanie Baby must you have? (Subtract one point if you didn't know that the answer is all of the above.)

—Who is Lisa Frank?

—What kind of animal is Arthur?

—Quick—kittens, puppies, or unicorns?

—Can you dance the Macarena, Electric Slide, Chicken Dance, and "YMCA"? (Score one point per dance; subtract one point if you still remember how to do the Hustle.)

—Who were the original Spice Girls? (Subtract one point if you forgot Scary.)

PART 2: MATH

WORD PROBLEMS

—You stayed home from work, waited two hours at the pediatrician's until they could "squeeze you in" with a feverish, whiny child plastered across your lap, and

bullied the receptionist into phoning in the
prescription so you wouldn't have to wait at the
pharmacy too. Given your current state of depletion
and the fact that you are developing both a fever and
an embarrassing diaper rash across your thighs,
calculate how long it will take you to scrub out the
bubble-gum-pink stains when your child spews every
drop of antibiotic on the new Persian rug. (Score one
point per minute.)

—You reserved the time at Discovery Zone for your
child's birthday party, mailed out the invitations,
shelled out a low three figures for themed paper
goods, and, on the appointed day, assembled and
doled out the goody bags despite your throbbing head.
How long after the designated parent pick-up time will
the last straggling adult come to claim the screaming
child whose idea of a gracious thank-you is "But I
wanted a *blue* balloon"? (Score one point per minute.)

BONUS ROUND: 5 POINTS APIECE
—You made up a grocery list and shopped for a week's
worth of meals. (Double credit if you took the kids
along; triple credit if you did all of the above without
once asking, "Honey, do we need . . . ?")

—You took the kids to buy new shoes. (Ten points if you
took them to Stride Rite to have their feet properly
sized, then doubled back to Marshall's and bought
Stride Rite shoes at half price. Subtract 10 points if
you bought the kids $90 Nikes or allowed them to
persuade you that jellies are acceptable "school
shoes.")

—You noticed that the rug had weird pink stains and arranged for the steam cleaners to come on your day at home.

—You called the nighttime sitter and reserved the restaurant. (Double credit if you know which baby-sitters tidy up and which snarf down the secret stash of Peak Freans like truffle pigs.)

BONUS ROUND: 3 POINTS APIECE

—You sequestered two-liter soda bottles for the class's terrarium project. (Double credit if you sent in a few extras to cover for the negligent parents; triple credit if the bottles were for caffeine-free soda.)

—You emptied the kids' backpacks every evening this week and separated the paper detritus into piles for "one parental signature required," "both signatures required," and "your child has been exposed to head lice/pinkeye/strep."

—You gathered up all the library books and returned them before the due dates. (Double credit if you took your kids with you for a refill.)

—You poured the milk, microwaved the chicken nuggets, peeled the carrot sticks, and mopped up the spilled milk before changing out of your work clothes.

—You bathed your four-year-old and gave her rapt, undivided tubside attention while she told you a five-minute story about a rock she'd seen—or maybe it was a bird, or a book; it's not completely clear—even though the new issue of *People* just arrived.

MULTIPLE CHOICE:
SCORE ONE POINT FOR EVERY RESPONSE

—What would it take for you to volunteer as field trip parent?

A) The prospect of spending more time with my child and his/her little friends

B) The chance to suck up to the little friends' parents so I can arrange more "away" play dates

C) A mid-six-figure bribe

D) The National Guard

—What do you love most about Brownies and Scouts?

A) They instill good values in my kids and help them learn caring and cooperation

B) The chance to spend two hours grocery shopping alone

C) Someone else shows my child the joys of camping while I get to stay home where the flush toilets live

D) They can take my Shrinky Dinks and shove them where the sun don't shine

TRUE/FALSE (CIRCLE ONE):
SCORE ONE POINT FOR EACH "TRUE" RESPONSE

You braved the dreaded Pink Aisle at Toys 'R' Us for the third birthday party this month and still didn't get stuck using gift wrap that said "It's a Boy" or "Happy Hanukkah."

T   F

You packed the lunch boxes every day this week and never forgot who needs the turkey not to touch the

mayonnaise and who cries if they get the grape juice box instead of the apple one.
T F

You never once considered feigning that you didn't notice the baby's dirty diaper.
T F

You guard your sippy cup lids like pieces of the True Cross.
T F

If Your Total Score Is:

65 points or higher: Congratulations! You are a Superparent. Please seek therapy.

50–64 points: You're not there yet, but you fake it well.

35–49 points: You're an average parent. You should feel guilty. Really guilty.

20–34 points: You're being lapped in the Superparent race. The rest of us have been talking about this behind your back.

19 points or lower: You are a male.

I've now administered the new SAT to dozens of working couples, analyzed the results, and discovered some fascinating findings. Unfortunately, I don't have time to write them down. I need to get to Caldor's right away. I hear the Funtoon underpants are on sale.

One Week Until College

SANDI KAHN SHELTON

MY DAUGHTER, Allie, is leaving for college in one week. What this means for today—when it's still not time to say good-bye—is that it's impossible to make a path through her room. The floor is cluttered with bags from Filene's and J. Crew: They're filled with extra-long sheets for her dormitory bed, fleece blankets still in their wrappers, thick dark blue towels, washcloths, new pairs of jeans and sweaters, baskets of shampoo and loofahs.

She won't talk about going.

I say, "I'm going to miss you," and she gives me one of her looks and finds a reason to leave the room.

Another time I say, in a voice so friendly it surprises even me: "Do you think you'll take down your posters and pictures and take them with you, or will you get new ones at college?"

She answers, in a voice filled with annoyance, "How should I know?"

I was also eighteen when I left home in 1970, but instead of moving to college, I was leaving to live with my boyfriend. I had been angry with my mother for months before I left. I flung my belongings in cardboard boxes, taking everything with me because I was never, never coming back home again. My mother stood in the doorway, her arms folded, and said I was making a huge mistake. "If what you're hoping for is marriage, this isn't the way to get it," she said. "He'll just live with you and then toss you away when something better comes along. I know that type." "I'm not looking for marriage," I responded. "I'm just looking for a chance to get out of here."

My daughter is off with friends most of the time. Yesterday was the last day she'd have until Christmas with her friend Katharine, whom she'd known since kindergarten. Soon, very soon, it will be her last day with Sarah, Claire, Heather, and Lauren.

And then it will be her last day with me. My friend Karen told me, "The August before I left for college, I screamed at my mother the whole month. Be prepared."

We in our forties have mostly learned to forgive our mothers for the crimes they committed in raising us. We have paid therapists thousands of dollars and spent endless hours talking with friends, going over and over the mistakes that were our legacy, and we have figured out how not to make the same errors with our daughters. We know just what kind of support girls need.

In the cooperative day-care center my daughter attended, the young mothers sat down with storybooks and patiently crossed out all sexist references. We told them they could be anything they wanted to be. We said, "Don't let the boys win. You're as big and strong and capable as they are!"

So they simply can't be as angry with us as we were with our own mothers.

Yet I stand here in the kitchen, watching my daughter make a glass of iced tea. Her face, once so open and trusting, is closed to me. I struggle to think of something to say to her, something friendly and warm. I would like her to know that I admire her, that I am excited about the college she has chosen, that I know the adventure of her life is just about to get started, and that I am so proud of how she's handling everything.

But here's the thing: The look on her face is so mad that I think she might slug me if I open my mouth.

I can't think what I have done. One night not long ago—after a particularly long period of silence between us—I asked what I might have done or said to make her angry with me. I felt foolish saying it. My own mother, who ruled the house with such authoritative majesty, would never have deigned to find out what I thought or felt about anything she did. But there I was, obviously having offended my daughter, and I wanted to know. I felt vulnerable asking the question, but it was important.

She sighed, as though this question were more evidence of a problem so vast and fundamental that it could never be explained, and she said, "Mom, you haven't done anything. It's fine."

It *is* fine. It's just distant, that's all. May I tell you how close we once were? When she was two years old, my husband and I divorced—one of those modern, amiable divorces that was just great for all parties involved, except that I had to quit my part-time job and take a full-time position. When I would come to the day-care center to pick Allie up after work, she and I would sit on the reading mattress together, and she would nurse. For a whole year after that divorce, we would sit every day at five o'clock, our eyes locked together, concentrating on and reconnecting with each other at the end of our public day. In middle school, when other mothers were already lamenting the estrangement they felt with their adolescent daughters, I hit upon what seemed the perfect solution: rescue raids. I would simply show up occasionally at the school, sign her out of class, and take her somewhere—out to lunch, off to the movies, once on a long walk on the beach. It may sound irresponsible, unsupportive of education, but it worked. It kept us close when around us other mothers and daughters were floundering. We talked about everything on those outings, outings we kept secret from the rest of the family and even from friends.

Sometimes, blow-drying her hair in the bathroom while I brushed my teeth, she'd say, "Mom, I really could use a rescue raid soon." And so I would arrange my work schedule to make one possible.

Anyone will tell you that high school is hard on the mother-daughter bond, and so it was for us, too. I'd get up with her in the early mornings to make her sandwich for school, and we'd silently drink a cup of tea together before the six-forty school bus came. But then she decided she'd rather buy her lunch at school, and she came right out and said she'd prefer to be alone in the mornings while she got ready. It was hard to concentrate on everything she needed to do with someone else standing there, she said.

We didn't have the typical fights that the media lead us to expect with teenagers: She didn't go in for tattoos and body piercings; she was mostly good about curfews; she didn't drink or do drugs. Her friends seemed nice, and the boys she occasionally brought home were polite and acceptable.

But what happened? More and more often, I'd feel her eyes boring into me when I was living my regular life, doing my usual things: talking on the phone with friends, disciplining her younger sister, cleaning the bathroom. And the look on her face was a look of frozen disapproval, disappointment . . . even rage.

A couple of times during her senior year I went into her room at night, when the light was off but before she went to sleep. I sat on the edge of her bed and managed to find things to say that didn't enrage or disappoint her. She told me, sometimes, about problems she was having at school: a teacher who lowered her grade because she was too shy to talk in class, a boy who teased her between classes, a friend who had started smoking. Her disembodied voice, coming out of the darkness, sounded young and questioning. She listened when I said things. A few days later, I'd hear her on the phone, repeating some of the things I had said, things she had adopted for her own, and I felt glad to have been there with her that night.

I said to myself, "Somehow I can be the right kind of mother. Somehow we will find our way back to closeness again."

We haven't found our way back. And now we are having two different kinds of Augusts. I want a romantic August, where we stock up together on things she will need in her dormitory. I want to go to lunch and lean across the table toward each other, the way we've all seen mothers and daughters do, and say how much we will miss each other. I want smiles through tears, bittersweet moments of reminiscence, and the chance to offer the last little bits of wisdom I might be able to summon for her.

But she is having an August where her feelings have gone underground, where to reach over and touch her arm seems an act of war. She pulls away, eyes hard. She turns down every invitation I extend, no matter how lightly I offer them; instead of coming out with me, she lies on her bed reading Emily Dickinson until I say I have always loved Emily Dickinson, and then—but is this just a coincidence?—she closes the book.

Books I have read about surviving adolescence say that the closer your bond with your child, the more violent is the child's need to break away from you, to establish her own identity in the world. The more it will hurt, they say.

My husband says, "She's missing you so much already that she can't bear it."

A friend of mine, an editor in New York who went through a difficult adolescence with her daughter but now has become close to her again, tells me, "You're a wonderful mother. Your daughter will be back to you."

"I don't know," I say to them. I sometimes feel so angry around her that I want to go over and shake her. I want to say, "Talk to me! Either you talk to me—or you're grounded!" I can actually feel myself wanting to say that most horrible of all mother phrases: "Think of everything I've done for you. Don't you appreciate how I've suffered and struggled to give you what you need?"

I can see how the mother-daughter relationship could turn primitive and ugly. One night I go into the den and watch *Fiddler on the Roof* with my younger daughter. She's nine, and she cuddles up next to me on the couch. We weep over the daughters saying good-bye. "It's a little like Allie leaving," she says. I hug her to me ferociously, as though I could hug all daughters trying to break away. I am not unaware that I am hugging my long-ago self, standing there so furiously, glaring at my mother, unable to forgive her.

Late at night, when I'm exhausted with the effort of trying not to mind the loneliness I've felt all day around her, I am getting ready for bed. She shows up at the door of the bathroom, watches me brush my teeth. For a moment, I think wildly that I must be brushing my teeth in a way she doesn't approve of, and I'll be upbraided for it.

But then she says, "I want to read you something." She's holding a handbook sent by her college. "These are tips for parents," she says.

I watch her face as she reads the advice aloud. " 'Don't ask your student if she is homesick,' it says. 'She might feel bad the first few weeks, but don't let it worry you. This is a natural time of transition. Write her letters and call her a lot. Send a package of goodies. . . .' "

Her voice breaks, and she comes over to me and buries her head in my shoulder. I stroke her hair, lightly, afraid she'll bolt if I say a word. We stand there together for long moments, swaying.

I know it will be hard again. We probably won't have sentimental lunches in restaurants before she leaves, and most likely there will be a fight about something. But I am grateful to be standing in the bathroom at midnight, both of us tired and sad, toothpaste smeared on my chin, holding tight—while at the same time letting go of—this daughter who is trying to say good-bye.

2-4-6-8, I'm the One They Appreciate

JOYCE MILLMAN

LIKE YOU, I had my suspicions about the rah-rah moms, the ones who made a hobby (or a career) out of their kids' school years, who were always available to chaperone field trips and cut construction paper for art projects and make jigglers and dirt cake for classroom parties (who didn't even have to *ask* what jigglers and dirt cake were), who called the teacher by her first name and went gung-ho over every fund-raising drive. I looked askance at these moms (and the occasional dad), thinking that no normal, well-adjusted person could possibly care *that* much. My old high-school contempt for the popular kids, the joiners, was deeply ingrained—school spirit was for nerds. So I dismissed these so-happy-to-help moms as control freaks who couldn't let their kids out of their sight, or as goody-goodies who were reliving their student council glory days.

And then I became one of them.

I'd like to say it happened insidiously, imperceptibly, creepily—first the denim shirt, then the leggings, then the insatiable desire to handle school paste. But it didn't. I made the decision to become a classroom volunteer with my eyes wide open and my knees shaking. We live in a nice suburb with a perfectly fine neighborhood elementary school. My husband and I went to public schools ourselves and, good liberals that we are, we always felt a little guilty about the homogenous, high-end private preschool we'd sent our son to. We were disturbed by the barely veiled racism and classism of so many parents we'd met there, who spoke of public school as something their kids needed to be shielded from. We would send our son to public school and we would make it work. It was the right thing to do.

When, after a suitable period of procrastination, I finally put my name down to help out for a couple of hours a week in my son's kindergarten class, I thought, OK, no big deal: I'll pass out the snacks, I'll feed the goldfish, I'll get to see how smart my kid is, then I'll go to work and forget about it. I didn't imagine—couldn't—how much help a kindergarten teacher with a class of twenty-seven kids and no such luxuries as a regular paid art teacher or library aide would need.

On my first day of school, I sat at a little table in the back of the room while the teacher, a woman so young and enthusiastic it almost made me cry, went through the lengthy and complicated ritual of Circle Time. While she was doing that, I was to go down the class roster and take four kids at a time to my table and have them cut out pictures of pumpkins, paste the pictures in sequence from vine to jack-o'-lantern, color the pictures, and try to write their names on their papers. After my first group of four, I was in a panic.

In my fantasies of being Snack Mom or Fish Mom, I left out one little possibility—that I would actually have to interact with strange children. Oh, I'm great with my own kid, but I still get tongue-tied around other people's kids. I don't want to overstep my boundaries; I don't want to be *responsible*. But that's exactly what this volunteering gig required. Some kids couldn't get the pumpkin sequence right; I was instructed to give them a few hints. But how many hints were too many? Some kids couldn't spell their names. Should I show them how to make the letters? Some kids wanted to color their pumpkins purple or red. I was supposed to gently prod them into thinking about the color of real pumpkins. But, often, I didn't have the words—I frantically tried to call up bits of my high school Spanish. *Naranja? Verde? Por favor?* This wasn't trivial stuff I was doing with these kids; these were projects that the teacher would have done herself, but it would have meant she'd have to abandon other projects. What right did I have to be playing school?

When the teacher thanked me profusely—too profusely—as I walked out the door in a daze, I knew that there was no graceful or decent way I could get out of this. She truly needed the help. And if not me and the other volunteers—always the same half-dozen parents, I soon found out—then who? So I went back, because I was needed and because my son was proud to have me there and because I wanted this school to be *great*, like my elementary school had been in a far less affluent town.

I went back and got to know my son's classmates: Cody, who loved horses and who would rub his head against my shoulder, horselike, by way of greeting; Angela, who was an aspiring writer and a bit of a know-it-all and who reminded me of myself at age five; Zelda, who had beautiful, sparkling black eyes; Alan, who was a chatterbox; meticulous Ann, who was always the last to finish her work and it was always perfect; Felipe, who would shyly tell me about his big brother, whom he adored. There were some things that troubled me: Julio's pants were always too small and kept unsnapping, but it didn't appear that he was going to get any new ones. And George's cold was hanging on for such a long time. I developed a great respect for teachers, not just for the workload they carry, but for the emotional load.

I drove kids on field trips to the pumpkin patch and the post office. I walked kids to the school library and helped them choose books. I mixed finger paint and filled glue pots. I traced penguin shapes onto black construction paper and measured heads for pilgrim hats and Native American feather bonnets. (My husband's most tedious assignment: helping twenty-seven kids sort handfuls of nuts for a graphing project—walnut, filbert, almond, walnut, filbert, almond.) And this is what I got in return: a little time each week where I was too busy to stress out over work, a flowerpot decorated with each kid's name scrawled in gold pen, and the persistent goodwill of two dozen of my son's peers. A year later, I hear, "Hi, Mark's mom!" on the playground and at the mall and on the soccer field. I'm tempted to tell them, Don't remember me, remember your teachers— I'm just a helper mom. But I don't. Because, at long last, I have school spirit. And I like being popular.

DRAMA QUEEN *for a* Day

Is That a Tongue
or an Umbilical Cord?

BETH MYLER

MY FIRST CHILD came into our lives on an epidural/Demerol cloud. My three best girlfriends watched, supplying my husband with bourbon from a flask while I pushed for less than ten minutes and brought forth a beautiful little girl with two-inch eyelashes. In the hospital she slept. I ate pancakes and bragged that postpartum was less painful than post–horseback ride. All was well. Until we got home.

She screamed, my nipples bled, my husband committed innumerable crimes only detectable by me. But I had carefully planned for postpartum misery. I had foreseen the possibility that I might need an escape. Exactly one week after my daughter's birth, when I was able to shower and dress, I drove off to meet my shrink, who could once again prescribe for me the drugs that were forbidden during the little screaming darling's gestation. Oh, I was so happy pulling out of the driveway. It was December 23.

When I arrived at the doctor's office, I was already awash with the strange panic that I now know accompanies every mother in some degree each time she leaves her infant. The nurse took my name and said, "Your husband has phoned and wants you to call home immediately." The room spun, my knees were weak, and my stomach had that sick feeling. My baby was dead. Tears rolled down my fat postpartum cheeks as I dialed home.

The baby was alive, but the dog had been hit by a car and limped off into the woods. My husband had given chase, collapsing in the street with an asthma attack. True, my husband sounded very weak on the phone after having injected himself with his emergency epinephrine, and he paused once to vomit while asking me to come home and look for the dog, but I was on top of the world—it was only the dog!

I canvassed three square miles, telling each neighbor to be on the lookout for our limping mutt. At dusk I went home to a nauseous husband and a still-screaming infant. The next morning, the dog was found in our neighbor's yard. She was operated on that day—not for injury sustained in the car accident, but to remove a nail that she ingested sometime earlier. If she hadn't been hit by the car, we never would have found the nail that would have killed the dog. Unfortunately, the dog was also hurt in the car accident: She almost bit off a quarter of her tongue. On Christmas Eve, I nursed the baby and my husband nursed the dog's stitches and sore tongue. Late that evening I found a piece of pink flesh on the sofa and had to ask my husband, "Is that the dog's tongue or the baby's umbilical cord?" It was the tongue. The cord came off later that night.

Mother Anger:
Theory and Practice

ANNE LAMOTT

I NEED TO PUT in a quick disclaimer so when I say what I'm about to, you will know that the truest thing in the world is that I love my son literally more than life itself. I would rather be with him, talk to him, and watch him grow than anything else on earth. Okay?

So: I woke up one recent morning and lay in bed trying to remember if the night before I had actually threatened to have my son's pets put to sleep, or whether I had only insinuated that I would no longer intercede to keep them alive when, due to his neglect, they began starving to death.

I'm pretty sure I only threatened to not intercede. But there have been other nights when I've made worse threats, thrown toys off the deck into the street and slammed the door to his room so hard things fell off his bookshelf. I have screamed at him with such rage for ignoring me that you would have thought he'd tried to set my bed on fire. And the list goes on.

He is an unusually good boy at other people's houses. He is the one the other mothers want to come play with their children. At other people's homes, my child does not suck the energy and air out of the room. He does not do the same annoying thing over and over and over until his friends' parents need to ask him through clenched teeth to stop doing this.

But at our house, he—*comment se dit?*—fucks with me. He can provoke me into a state of something similar to road rage.

I have felt many times over the years that I was capable of hurting him. I have not done this yet. Or at any rate, I have hurt him only a little—I have spanked him a few times, yanked him and grabbed him too hard. I have managed to stay on this side of the line. If you've gone over the line and hurt your child, obviously you need to get help—and soon—but in the meantime, we want you to know we've all been there. (If you don't have the money or anywhere else to turn, please write to me care of this publisher and I'll do whatever I can to help you.)

When Sam was a colicky baby, it was one thing. I felt free to discuss my terrible Caliban feelings because I was so exhausted and hormonal and without a clue as to how to be a real mother that I believed anyone would understand my feelings. I felt confused, though, that no one tells you when you're pregnant how insane you're going to feel after the baby comes, how pathological, how inept and out of control. Or how, when they get older, you'll still sometimes feel exhausted, hormonal, without a clue. You'll still find your child infuriating. Also—I am just going to go ahead and blurt this out—*dull.*

A few mothers seem happy with their children all the time, as if they're sailing through motherhood, entranced. However, up close and personal, you find that these moms tend to have tiny little unresolved issues: They exercise three hours a day or check their husband's pockets every night looking for motel receipts. Because not only do moms get very mad; they also get bored. This is a closely guarded secret, as if the myth of maternal bliss is so sacrosanct that we can't even admit these feelings to ourselves. But when you mention these feelings to other mothers, they all say, "Yes, yes!" You ask, "Are you ever mean to your children?" "Yes!" "Do you ever yell so that it scares you?" "Yes, yes!" "Do you ever want to throw yourself down the back stairs because you're so bored with your child that you can hardly see straight?" "Yes, Lord, yes, thank you, thank you . . ."

So, let's talk about this.

One reason I think we get so angry at our children is because we can. Who else can you talk to like this? Can you imagine hissing at your partner, "You get off the phone *now!* No, *not* in five minutes . . ."? Or saying to a friend, "You get over here right this second! And the longer you make me wait, the worse it's going to be for you." Or, while talking to a salesman at Sears who happens to pick up the ringing phone, grabbing his arm too hard and shouting, "Don't you *dare* answer the phone when I'm talking to you!"

No, you can't. If regular people saw your secret angry inside self, they'd draw back when they saw you coming. They would see you for what you are—human, flawed, more nuts than had been hoped—and they would probably not want to hire or date you. Of course, most people have such bit parts in your life that they're not around to see the whole, erratic panoply that is you. Or they actually pay for the privilege of torturing you. But children—God, attending to all their needs is so exhausting that our blowups may be like working out cramps in our legs. You feel sometimes like male emperor penguins after the eggs are laid, standing there in the cold holding the eggs on their fuzzy, feather-warm feet. They have to stand there, because to lay the eggs down on the snow would mean death. And maybe in the deep freeze, emotions don't run so hot, because otherwise, I tell you, I would last about twenty minutes as a penguin.

The tyranny of waking up a sleepy child at 7:00 A.M. and hassling him to get him clothed and fed in preparation for school means you're chronically tired, resentful, and resented. Then, in this condition, while begging him to put on socks, you are inevitably treated to an endless and intricate précis of *Rugrats*. It's like having Pauly Shore administer the Chinese water torture.

This is how Sam told me about his school day while I was trying to watch the news last night: "So David says she didn't draw it and then she goes like, she did draw the picture herself, and then he goes like, 'Oh yeah,' and then she goes like, 'Yeah, I asked her to but she said I had to,' and then he goes like, 'Oh, yeah, riiiight,' then I go . . ."

I am not an ageist. If Jesus wanted to tell me in great detail how he runs the fifty-yard dash while I was watching the news, I'd be annoyed with Him too: "See, most kids start out like this—the first step is a big one, like this—no, watch—and then the second is smaller, like this, and the next—*no, watch*, I'm almost done—so see, what I do is, I start like everyone else— *watch*—but then my third step is like small, and the next one is bigger, so like, this PE teacher who sees me do it goes, 'Whoa, Lord, cool,' and then she goes . . ."

Before we go on, I want to say that people who didn't want children just roll their eyes when you complain, because they think you brought this on yourself. Comedian Rita Rudner once said that she and her husband were trying to decide whether to buy a dog or have a child—whether to ruin their carpets or their lives. So people without children tend not to feel very sympathetic. But some of us wanted children—and what they give is so rich, you can hardly bear it.

At the same time, if you need to yell, children are going to give you something to yell about. There's no reasoning with them. If you get into a disagreement with a regular person, you slog through it; listen to the other person's position, needs, problems; and somehow you arrive at something that is maybe not perfect, but you don't actually feel like smacking them. But because we are so tired sometimes, when a disagreement starts with our child, we can only flail miserably through time and space and the holes in between; and then we blow our top. Say, for instance, that your child is four and going through the stage when he will only wear the T-shirt with the tiger on it. With a colleague who was hoping you'd come through with the professional equivalent of washing his tiger T-shirt every night, you might be able to explain to him that you were up until dawn on deadline, or you've got a fever, and so did not get to the laundry. And the colleague might cut you some slack and try to understand that you simply hadn't had time to wash the tiger shirt, and besides, he's worn it now four days in a row. But your child is apt to—well, let's say, apt to not.

They can be like rats. I mean this in the nicest possible way. They may still be drooling, covered with effluvia, trying to wrestle underpants on over their heads because they think they're shirts, but in the miniature war room of their heads, they still know where your nuclear button is. They may ignore you, or seem troubled by hearing loss, or erupt in fury at you, or weep, but in any case, they're so unreasonable and capable of such meanness that you're stunned and grief-stricken about how much harder it is than you could have imagined. All you're aware of is the big, windy gap between you and your lack of anything left to give, any solution whatsoever.

Friends without children point out the good news: that kids haven't, thank God, taken all their impulses and learned to disguise them subtly. Maybe what kids want and when they want it is in your face, they'll say, but still, it's wonderful for people to be who they really are. And you can only say, "Thank you so much for sharing." Because it's not wonderful when kids ignore you, or are being sassy and oppositional. It's not wonderful when you're coping well enough, feeding them, helping them get ready, trying to get them to do something in their best interests—like "Zip up the pants, honey, that's not a great look for you"—and then, under the rubric of What Fresh Hell Is This? the play date for the afternoon calls and cancels, and then there's total despair and hysteria because your child is going to have to hang out here alone with *you*, horrible you, and he's sobbing like the dog has died, and you're thinking, What about all those times this week when I *did* arrange play dates? Do I get any *fucking* credit for that? And it happens. *Kaboooom.*

It's so ugly and scary for everyone concerned that—well. One of my best friends, the gentlest person I know, once tore the head off his daughter's doll. And then threw it to her, like a baseball pitch. And I love that in a guy, or at least I love that he told me about it when I was in despair about a recent rage at Sam. Because, while I'm not sure what the solution is, I know that what doesn't help is the terrible feeling of isolation, the fear that everyone else is doing better.

Of course, it helps if you can catch yourself before you blow up, if you give one of you a time-out. I'm sure it helps to have a spouse, and it also helps when people tell you their own terrible stories of blowing up, so you can laugh about it: At one of my lowest points, a friend—a teacher—told me that she looks at her child and thinks: I gave you life. So if I kill you, it's a wash.

What has helped recently was figuring out that when we blow up at our kids, we only *think* we're going from zero to sixty in one second. Our surface and persona is so calm that when the problem first begins, we sound in control when we say, "Now, honey, stop that," or "That's enough." But it's only an illusion. Because actually, all day we've been nursing anger toward the boss or boyfriend or mother, but because we can't get mad at nonkid people, we stuff it down; we keep going without blowing up because we don't want to lose our jobs or partners or reputations. So when the problem with your kid starts up, you're actually starting at fifty-nine, only you're not moving. You're at high idle already, but you are not even aware of how vulnerable and disrespected you already feel. It's your child's bedtime and all you want from Jesus or Baruch Hashem is for He/She/It to help your child go to sleep so you can lie down and stare at the TV—and it starts up. "Mama, I need to talk to you. It's important." So you go in and you muster patience, and you help him with his fears or his thirst, and you go back to the living room and sink down into your couch, and then you hear, "Mama? Please come here one more time." You lumber in like you're dragging a big dinosaur tail behind you and you rub his back for a minute, his sharp angel shoulder blades. But the third time he calls for you, you try to talk him out of needing you, only he seems to have this tiny problem with self-absorption, and he can't hear that you can't be there for him. And you become wordless with rage. You try to breathe, you try everything, and then you blow. You scream, "God fucking damnit! What! *What?* Can't you leave me alone for *four seconds?*"

Now your child feels much safer, more likely to drift off to sleep.

Good therapy helps. Good friends help. Pretending that we are doing better than we are doesn't. Shame doesn't. Being heard does.

When I talk about it, I don't feel so afraid. The fear is the worst part, the fear about who you secretly think you are, the fear you see in your child's eyes. But underneath the fear I keep finding resiliency, forgiveness, even grace. The third time Sam called for me the other night, and I finally blew up in the living room, there was a great silence in the house, silence like suspended animation: Here I'd been praying for silence, and then it turns out to be so charged and toxic. I lay on the couch with my hands over my face, just shocked by how hard it is to be a parent. And after a minute Sam sidled out into the living room because he still needed to see me, he needed to snuggle with me, with mean me, he needed to find me—like the baby spider pushing in through the furry black legs of the mother tarantula, knowing she's in there somewhere.

Bringing Up Bébé

DEBRA S. OLLIVIER

THE LAST DOG DAYS of summer in Paris: ninety-degree heat, second-stage smog alerts, petri dish air so thick you could cut it with a knife. For those of us living in the city's densest district, the only relief is a tiny square of blue called the Georges-Hermant Bassin d'Enfants. As the waning inferno burns holes in the tarmac, hundreds of people in various states of sweaty exhaustion make their way to this dilapidated kiddie pool. One recent scorching Sunday, I walked like a pack mule with thirteen kilos of baby—my Franco-American one-year-old, Max—in one arm and thirteen kilos of swimming gear in the other, methodically picking my way across a field of slippery tile and half-naked bodies.

The only official rule here is prominently posted in the front vestibule: No Swimming Trunks. This fashion dictate, which comes not from the pool management but all the way from the city council itself, is in effect in public pools all over France, presumably to prevent people from swimming in pants and dress shoes and for obscure reasons of hygiene. Only Speedo-type bikinis are permitted for men, which means that your average American guy has to shed a lot more than his baggies to chill out in this town.

Beyond this one rule, it's *liberté, égalité,* and *fraternité* at Georges-Hermant. The locker and shower rooms are coed.

(The display of public promiscuity here would make any faint-hearted Puritan run for the hills.) There are also no wall plaques listing the Ten Pool Commandments and no lane dividers for lap swimming, which makes the pool look like the Arc de Triomphe during a rush-hour pileup. When I asked the lone lifeguard on duty about the latter point, he probably didn't realize that his reply could pretty well sum up the national French ethos. "But, madame," he said, looking rather shocked, "lane dividers would be an infringement on the individual rights of people to swim as they like."

As I stood at the edge of this pool party, it dawned on me that France is a sort of inverse daguerreotype of America: In France, the rules that are respected are not the ones posted in public spaces to enforce law and orderly social conduct. Rather, they're the unspoken ones that are learned by living in a culture where conventions are upheld by history and tradition. The relative lack of tradition gives Americans the freedom to reinvent themselves in ways that are inconceivable to the French (the simple idea of, say, a midlife career change is almost unthinkable here), but in American public spaces, rules and regulations abound. And we obey them. We stand in lines. We signal when we change lanes. We play by the book. When we don't, we draw a Colt .45 to your head or sue you for everything you're worth. Americans are black or white, while the French are inscrutably gray.

Getting into the kiddie pool itself is a little like walking into a Hieronymus Bosch painting in your underwear. Hundreds of flailing children are packed into a pool the size of a carport, with no supervision in sight. I can see the lifeguard surveying the traffic in the adult pool below—he's on a seat hoisted above a concrete wall that separates the two pools. But unless he has a mysterious third eye in the back of his head, it's unlikely he'll be much help to any children. There are toy fights in the water, food fights on the pool rim, and children upside down in half-deflated capsized rubber duckies floating against the pool wall like unmanned vehicles in an airport tow-away zone. So where are all the parents?

From the look of things, many of them seem to be having a good time of their own in poolside smoking salons. The rest of them have overrun the small patch of drought-baked lawn, ostensibly a place for kids to run, now apparently an annex for sun worshipers who can't find space in the crammed adult pool area. They cover the grass in a tapestry of partially nude formations; total nudity is reserved for skinny-dipping toddlers—delectably delicious when you're potty trained but somewhat problematic when you're not.

Oddly, in this refuge of unregulated public intercourse, I'm surprised to note that there *is*, in fact, one authority figure, and when he arrives on the scene a sudden silence overcomes the crowd and brings activity to a halt. To the transfixed and slightly culpable stares of a hundred poolside toddlers, the man takes a long-necked aquatic pooper-scooper, casts an implicating glance at onlookers, then scoops out a small, wayward turd as if it were an expired goldfish. Then he goes away, engulfed in the throng, and the party resumes in all its bedlam.

I happened to be here with an American swim mate who was so concerned about her child having a "spill" she obliged her to wear a diaper under her swimsuit. After an hour, it got so waterlogged it finally ruptured along its seams, and a gelatinous porridge of saturated silicone beads flowed out of its sides onto the pool steps. The ultimate consumer test. Later, while we roasted like pork rinds—my son, Max, hollering incomprehensibly at birds and her daughter violently attached to her plastic Elmo—my swim mate made a list of the litigious opportunities that could bring in big bucks were we in the States.

"Well," she began, "for starters, there are a hundred safety risks and violations," and she went on to describe things I didn't see—jagged, broken tiles that had become small tide pools of debris, an unprotected ledge with a six-foot drop. "And oh my God, there's that kid over there peeing on the embankment where people sit." She shook her head in disgust. "Microbes. Another public health risk." Then she took another good, hard look around the pool. "And there's indecent exposure," she added quietly, referring to nearly one third of the women, who were topless.

The day burned on. Despite the medieval funfest and its study in multifarious forms of cultural life, we thanked God that this small oasis existed. Where else could our little love bunnies cool off in this hot town? It will continue for just a little while longer. But soon, the unyielding curtain of Continental weather will fall, and bring this unruly show to its most certain close.

The Line Is White,
and It Is Narrow

BETH KEPHART

THE LINE GETS DRAWN, and the line gets drawn again. There are, as they say, so many degrees of separation, so much growing up that must go on: The bottle replacing the breast. The book the child reads alone. Something whispered so that the mother cannot hear. Children retreat and return to us like the tide—tripping out beyond our reach, lapping back in, turning once more to greet the sea. They are discovering themselves, of course. But we are also discovering them.

JEREMY IS EIGHT when he decrees his love for all things soccer. He is at the kitchen table telling the sort of story that sends my stomach to my knees. It's a recess story, my least favorite kind. I'm not an optimist when it comes to recess.

"James and me were selling walnuts," Jeremy starts out earnestly, sparing me context, as he is wont to do, and peeling the cheap white paper from an ice cream sandwich. "Then we dug for China."

"Did you find it?" I ask.

"What?" Jeremy blinks. The ice cream sandwich has slouched.

"China?"

"Of course not," Jeremy says; he has learned to be so patient with me. "We were just digging for it." He finishes his treat, and there he sits, slathered with white and dark-brown sugars.

"So then what happened?" My question: quiet and cautious.

"Some of the other kids were playing tag, but most of them were playing soccer. Second, third, fourth, and fifth graders. They're good. They really are."

"Uh-huh," I tell Jeremy. "Hmm."

"I love soccer," Jeremy says, with operatic emphasis. "I love it. I really do."

"You do?" I say, fumbling for a comeback to this unexpected outburst of passion for a sport we've never once discussed, read about, or watched on TV. "You love it even though you've never played?"

"Yup."

"Why?" I ask, genuinely stumped. "Why soccer?"

"Because I love it," Jeremy says. "And I'm going to play. I'm going to get my foot on the ball and I'm going to kick it. I just want to kick it, see what it feels like to kick the ball in a game of recess soccer. I'm going to play soccer. I'm going to be good." He looks at me with his huge, lit-up eyes, and I'm won over. I believe him, because I am his mom.

THE NEXT DAY, at pick-up time, there are two salty stripes that streak from the lower ledge of Jeremy's eyes to the cliff of his well-defined chin. He is forcing his bottom lip to stop quivering by pursing his pliant upper lip shut. "How was school?" I ask him, deflated at once by the sight of his sadness.

"Fine," he answers, nobly. "Just fine."

"Are you feeling sad?" He sits behind me because of the purported dangers of the car's safety air bags, and I turn around at the first red light to get another good look at him. Those are the vestiges of tears, for sure.

"Nope."

"Did something happen?"

Nothing at all from the backseat.

"Did you get to play soccer today?"

"It's hard," Jeremy concedes after we've driven another several miles or so, after rural has become suburban, and we've left the country road and joined up with the highway. "Soccer's hard," he says again, and it's clear that that is all he can bear to tell me. I don't know what happened at recess. I don't know whether my son played and got pushed, or played and grew confused, or didn't get to play at all. But it's definite that something's happened and just as definite that it would hurt to explain, and I don't want to deepen his wound, so I do not force a confession.

"I know," I tell Jeremy. Inadequate words, and all that I have. "Soccer is hard. I do believe you."

But soccer's hardness, this much is true, will neither dissuade nor diminish my son. For at Jeremy's core is a rich web of fibers; it's pure persistence inside, the odds-smashing stuff of stars and star light. I respect and I celebrate the stubborn, awesome bone of him, the valor that knocks flat whatsoever inconveniently rises up, the strictures that throw themselves against his soul. When Jeremy was two, three, four, when he was five, obtuseness pressed in from every side. Words, for example, were bewildering to him, hard to assimilate, wring free of meaning, and mete out. Society itself was an underwater country—disturbing and irritating, offering few ports of entry. Spoons, tricycles, crayons, swings, balls—easy for other children, but infuriatingly difficult for Jeremy, diagnosed as he was with an autism spectrum disorder. Entanglements and set-backs and deep-seated frustrations were the stuff of Jeremy's childhood. The offices of therapists. The dismal predictions of so-called experts. Only one person, in the end, could expel the label, dispel the myth, repel the very notion that my only child was to live life at its margins. It was Jeremy, and only Jeremy, who masterminded his own survival.

So now Jeremy is eight, and he has friends, and he is academically sound, and he is my hero, make no mistake about that. But he's also my little boy, and I'd fight a den of lions on his behalf, defend his honor to the galaxy's end, hurl myself between him and any alien life force. Survival instincts, in mothers, always suggest themselves first, so that my first sorry inclination, when soccer starts troubling him so, is to tease him away from his newest passion. It seems the smartest, kindest thing to do, given the hurdles that remain. Impaired response time. Poor muscle tone. Limited spatial perception. No team experience. No experience with complex strategies. Besides, flowers full tilt with their blooms aren't as gentle as the child now inexplicably enamored with a sport that requires hustle, aggression, warrior tactics. "I really love soccer," Jeremy's saying, now that we're home. After a Popsicle and graham crackers, he says it again: "Soccer is the game that I love."

It's a good thing that we have a ball. It's a good thing that we have a backyard and two splintered, goal-like sawhorses and sneakers for the both of us. Out we go, and we start to practice, and since I'm deficient in soccer scholarship, our first home-front practice consists of tapping the ball meagerly to and fro. We stand close enough to each other to accommodate the modest momentum we drum up, and Jeremy squints when the ball comes his way, readies his feet, lifts his leg, aims, smacks the grass blades with the soles of his rubber shoes. The ball skips past him, over the crinkle of fallen maple leaves. Retrieving it, he taps it my way, and I lunge at his scattershots, nudge them right back to him, deploy my best coachlike repartee. The afternoon spills its shadows across our lawn. It's nippy out here in the near dark. We take a break and I ask Jeremy if he's happy now, if he realizes how many times he touched the ball.

"This doesn't count, Mom." He rolls his eyes. "You don't really count, even though I love you. Touching my foot to the ball only counts when I'm at school."

"Yeah?" I say.

"Yeah," he says. He retreats to his own fantasies.

WE NEED SOCCER books, and we get them. We need soccer videos; they're acquired, too. We need my husband, slight in frame and still graceful at forty, a Salvadoran by birth, a bit of an expert on soccer. Pretty soon, on the warm-enough nights and weekends, the two of them are out playing the game, and I'm cheering them on from the deck. We buy glowing red cones and string them like Christmas bulbs across the yard. We invite soccer-minded schoolmates to play. My husband teaches Jeremy the rules of the game on thick pieces of oversized paper. We are terribly indulgent parents. We do what we can to help our son fan his flame.

Still, school has become an unhappy trial; blanched trails of tears lengthen the verticals of Jeremy's face. Nearly every day now there's a quiver in his lip, a stoicism, an expressed desire to speak of anything but recess. It is only after weeks go by that Jeremy courageously drops his guard: "They make fun of me," he tells me. "Out on recess. When I play." We're in the midst of a dull, warm-weather winter, driving the familiar trek home. I'm aware, all of a sudden, that the sky is rammed against the earth. That the clouds are pressing close, like fog. My own imagination is a dangerous habitat as—rapidly, unstoppably— terrifying images grow crystal clear. Bestial children. Minor criminals.

"What do the kids say, Jeremy?" I ask, after I've already seen the whole awful mess in my mind's eye.

"That I shouldn't play." Jeremy starts to whimper. "That I don't know the rules. And why can't I stay in the sandbox with James and why don't I take some lessons or something, and soccer is for good players, soccer's not for me." Jeremy's words are hardly decipherable. He has started to wail in the back of the car.

"And what do you say, Jeremy?" I manage a civilized question in the quietest possible voice, hoping only, at this moment, to calm him down, make sure he breathes. *I'm going to kill them*, I'm meanwhile thinking. *I'm going to wring their little necks.*

"I say it isn't fair that I'm not any good and it isn't fair that I have to work so hard and it isn't fair that I'm not a hustler because I really love soccer, I really do, and I just want to play, just want to kick the ball once in a game, see what it feels like. I want to play." His words missile at me through a hailstorm of tears. Jeremy pounds his knotted-up fist against the plush taupe cushions of the car.

"Oh, Jeremy." I wish I could reach for him right now, bring an end to his sobbing. We're off the country roads, another five miles from home.

"And they say I'm stupid because I pick up the ball and you can't pick up the ball when you're playing soccer. That's the rules." Jeremy lets the whole story out now, it can't be stopped. His voice gets angrier and louder. His tears fall hard.

"You pick up the ball?" I manage to grab on to a piece of

what he's saying despite my desire, at this moment, to blame the whole damned world for his sorrow.

"I pick up the ball," he says, defiant. "I pick it up. I have to, Mom."

"But why, Jeremy, if it's against the rules? If it's going to get the kids mad, why do you do it?"

"Because how else am I going to get a chance at kicking if they won't let me close and I want to play soccer? I can't keep up. I can't hustle. I have to pick the ball up if I'm going to kick it, and I have to kick the ball, Mom. I have to practice."

MORE BOOKS, more afternoon practice sessions, more studied videos. More recess tears, more profane stories, a burst of truncated tales about show-and-tell soccer trophies. Too many drives home from school that leave us both with a bruise on our hearts, and I start to understand, as with all things Jeremy, that soccer is no longer a sport in our lives; it has become a metaphor. It's the key to another world, an access pass, and we realize, implicitly, that if Jeremy can learn this game, if he can master just one or two of its requisite skills, if someone will give him a chance—goddamn it—he will have pushed through yet another essential door. Closer he will have come to that fickle state "normal." No more will he be on the periphery at recess. No more standing on the sidelines cheering his classmates on, bestowing congratulatory smiles when they proudly showcase the latest in their long line of trophies. It is definitely winter now. I haven't been able to find Jeremy a private soccer coach. Recess is a disaster waiting to happen.

But Jeremy is not giving up. He practices every afternoon, studies his soccer books as if preparing for the bar. One day he announces that he's deriddled the problem. "How's that?" I ask.

His answer, straightforward: "I'm going to join the real soccer league. The one my friends play on. I'm going to get good that way. Going to get a trophy for me."

I get another of my furious famous mental pictures now—of tricky-footed kids, of crafty coaches, of upset over errors and defeats. I think about drafts, years of experience, uniforms, the not-so-irrelevant fact that we don't live anywhere near, aren't paying taxes to the township that sponsors Jeremy's chosen league.

"Are you sure, Jeremy?"

"Yes."

"Are you ready for that? I hear it's tough."

He rolls his eyes at his poor and unwise mother. "How am I going to get better, Mom, if I don't sign up and play?"

THERE ARE some things money can't buy and friendship delivers with aplomb. Let me say for the record that I'd be nowhere without my friends. Without the couple of ladies who have made my son part of their families, attended to his winding sentences, included him in every extracurricular gig. These ladies who, when I later report our predicament with the very league their sons have played on for years, promise at once to see what they can do. They lean on their husbands. They get me the paperwork. They let me know when secret draft meetings are conducted. After several weeks of holding our breath, it is outwardly and officially done. Jeremy has been given a berth on the league. He is a Shark, a purple-shirt and plastic-shin-guard guy, an up-and-coming Number 3. For different reasons we tremble, Jeremy and me, when we get the call from the league. This is the big time. This is the Big Jeremy Dream

Come True. Only one thing is left for him now, and that thing
is to get out there and play.

The first practice session is an out-and-out washout; thun-
derstorms have rivered the fields. The second practice is can-
celed, on account of the excess of absentees. We're coming up
on our first game now, and there's just one planned pre-season
practice to go. It's a Wednesday. The sky keeps its distance. The
practice field is prairie flat and dry. We're the first to arrive, by
a very long shot, and Jeremy rumbles out of the car, his long,
elk legs disguised with thick socks and padding, his feet
unsteady on the platform of their plastic cleats. He runs to the
field, then dribbles the ball up and down, all around, looking
up, frequently, to check for signs of his teammates.

Finally, the other Sharks materialize. We see them trundling
up toward the field, postures suggesting that nothing much is
doing. The parents, too, appear casual, informal, not particularly worried whether their kid will scoop up the soccer ball in
the midst of a frustrating moment. Impromptu drills get initi-
ated up and down the field; kids head the ball, knee the ball,
dribble it fiercely past their teammates.

Jeremy, meanwhile, skips up and down the sidelines, hopeful and solo as the tail on a kite. *God,* I think. *Oh God have
mercy.* And just then the practice coach arrives. Red-haired,
whistle-necklaced, impressively muscled and sound, she totes a
fisherman's net full of balls, cones, and nylon shirts, then lays
it down. She checks her clipboard and she blows her whistle.
On cue, the kids turn and race to where she's standing. Jeremy,
way out there, continues his skipping across the field. "Jeremy,"
I call to him. "Rascal! Get over here with your coach!" Overex-
cited, he fails to hear. I put down my purse, get myself ready to
fetch him. "You stay right here," a well-meaning, been-through-

this mother tells me. "He's on his own. The coach knows what she's doing." I nod. I agree. I give her credit for her infinite smarts. I pledge that I will not say another word, then promptly turn my back to the field so that I won't be tempted. If I cannot help, coax, urge, or pull, then right now I cannot watch.

THE FIRST REAL soccer game is just three days later. It's unseasonably cold, and I haven't slept a wink, but Jeremy is up before dawn, donning his purple. He's a handsome Number 3, proud as a colt that has mastered its own weak knees, and I have to admit, my heart is swelling with an arrogance all its own. I can't myself get over this. Never, in all these mixed-up, utterly fierce, and emotional years as a mother, did I imagine my boy suited up for a team. "You're the best," I tell him. "You really are." Because no matter what happens in this next hour or so, he's already beaten more miserable odds.

Now, I'm not going to nudge you through every shoelace detail of this first, bewildering game. I'm not going to say how unnerved I feel, how afraid of the opposing team, assailants in blue. I'm not going to say that the field seems vast and the netted goal cages loom large or that I have a bad case of chills by the time the whistle blows. I'm not going to say just how I feel when Jeremy, anointed left wing, trots gamely out to his position, or how I start trotting myself, acutely on edge, up and down, up and down, in the grassy sideline margins.

I'm not going to say much more, in short, than that it's hard, it is breath snatching, it is downright thrilling, this first game. It is Jeremy alive with challenge as I've never seen him before, Jeremy committing every inch of his devoted self to the rules, to the frenzy, to the wild, zagging play. Three times, right at the end, Jeremy taps his foot against the ball. Three times, in a real league game, he plays his part, while my husband screams and I scream and our voices get lost in the wind. Jeremy plays brave, and I hold my own—stay put, where I finally understand that I belong, on the parental side of the narrow white line.

I TELL JEREMY, many weeks later, that I am going to write his soccer story. I tell him this after the season of Wednesday practices and Saturday games has run its course, after I've widened our friendships with the other soccer moms and dads and with the coaches, who have given us every fair chance and more to earn our place on a team of purple shirts. I tell him this after the tears have stopped at recess because he's playing now by recess rules, because new friends and two coaches, at last, have taught him how. I tell him this after I have been given the delirious memory of watching Jeremy receive a trophy all his own. Jeremy of the Sharks, it says, a little gold plaque beneath a little gold man. A blazing glory, a shining tribute that now sits on our mantel among our most priceless things.

Jeremy says that it's all right to tell the tale, and then he tells me what plot points to inculcate. "Tell them, first, that I stayed away from the ball because I was afraid of the ball, even though I really love soccer," he instructs. "Tell them that I got better, I improved, that I'm still working on my hustle. Tell them about how we won the first game and tied another, and how we lost the rest, but once it wasn't our fault. That referee had no business calling that game. He was color-blind, couldn't tell the purple shirts from the blues."

"What else?" I ask, eager for more, and he says, "Tell them about the assist, tell them that. Tell them how, in the fifth game, I wasn't afraid anymore, how I took the ball from mid-field to the goal. I passed it to Garrett, because Garrett's the best, because I knew that if I got it to Garrett, he would score."

"Don't worry," I tell Jeremy. "That's going in there. That's really key."

"Yeah," Jeremy says. "Yeah. And you can tell them that you and Dad weren't the only ones screaming for me, Mom. Everybody else was too. All those other moms and dads. The coach. They were cheering for me, too. They were cheering like I was important. They were cheering like they cheer for real teams."

"Yeah," I say. "Don't worry. That's sacred. That's in."

"Yeah," Jeremy says. "Yeah. Scoring an assist is a whole lot bigger than getting your foot on the ball." He nods with thorough, disarming intelligence. I get the sense that he's trying to simplify the hard stuff for me.

"Either one," I say, "seems pretty special. And your team—all those Kevins and a Devin . . . I'm never going to forget them, will you?"

"Yeah. Well. That's pretty much it," Jeremy says, his forehead in a fit of lines as he tries to scrounge up any last relevant details. "I think that's it. Really. That's what you should say."

"Okay," I tell him. "That's plenty for the story I want to tell."

"Yeah. Except, maybe? If there's room? You can tell them about professional soccer."

"Professional soccer?" I ask, my pencil hung in midair.

"Yeah," he answers, so full of surprises, next steps, bigger dreams, star-blinding faith. "Professional soccer. Like how I'm going to play it, either when I'm a teen or a grown-up. Or I'll play in the Olympics. Or in the World Cup. I don't know which. But you can tell them, if there's room, that they'll definitely see me on TV."

"Yeah," I say softly, "I'll tell them that. I think I will." Because I'm flung back over that line and right smack in there with my little boy and his big ambitions. I'm on his side. I'm throwing caution to the wind. Because he can do it. He can do anything. Just give him the chance. Call him a Shark. Put him on your team.

You'll Get Used to It

NORA OKJA KELLER

I CRIED when my daughter was born. My husband cradled the capsule of her body, compact and pink as a new piglet, against his chest before he laid her on my still-rubbery stomach. Eyes closed, her tiny fists clenched, she mewled and rooted against my breast, already instinctively searching for reconnection. Exhausted, I was overwhelmed with the force of her perfection and individuality: a tiny being separate from and yet still so intimately tied to me.

My world shrunk to the size of her body. Immersed in her smell, her feedings, her needs, I couldn't imagine doing anything without her, that didn't involve her. I remembered my life before she was born as if it were a dream, as if it belonged to some other person I knew only vaguely.

That remotely familiar stranger that I used to define as myself could not have imagined the pleasure of being cocooned in the house, couldn't have imagined the desire, the passionate obsession, to enslave myself to another. Totally absorbed, I lost myself within the tiny coil, the perfect comma, of her body.

I spent hours watching her sleep, loving the way her body, seal-like, surfed the waves of my breathing. She grew heavier in sleep, somehow, more solid, as did the air around her. I sometimes placed my nose against the petals of her mouth so I could smell her sleep, her exhalations sweet and heavy, scented with dreams.

At night, she slept against my chest, my body a blanket for hers. In between dreams, we performed intricate dances, turning toward each other for feedings neither of us were fully awake for, limbs gingerly entwined, her body under my heart.

And then slowly, groggily, I became conscious of wanting to pull away. She started to feel too heavy. When I lay down with her at night, trapped in the nursery by a nipple, I listened not to her contented murmurs but to the noises outside the dim room: the clattering of dinner dishes, the static of television, the hum of conversation I could not quite hear. I began to wonder what I was missing.

I would count to 100. Though her eyes closed, her lips and tongue still sucked, demanding my presence. I then counted to 300, until her mouth became lax, almost releasing me with a sigh. Shifting slightly, I would try to pry the nub of my breast from between the teeth she seemed to have suddenly sprouted. When freedom became a matter of millimeters, she would clamp down and begin to suck furiously. I counted to 500. Then traced the numbers back to one.

I dreamt of freedom, for an unattached hour or two when I could go to an aerobics class, take a nap, or bathe without her banging on the steamy glass of the shower door. After eighteen months, I found a part-time baby-sitter, a nice woman with two children of her own at home. I paid for a full month's help: three hours, three times a week for four weeks. I became dizzy imagining myself weightless with unencumbered time.

During the second week, my daughter began to recognize the babysitter's neighborhood. When we turned onto the block of her abandonment, my daughter would grip the handles of her car seat and scream. Trying to soothe her, I sang, "I love you, you love me, we're a happy family," through clenched teeth. My baby cried louder and, by the time I parked the car, had turned purple. Even then, I tried to pull her out of the car seat. She held on. I pulled harder. We formed a tug-of-war, with her body sprawled horizontally half in and half out of the car door. Finally, the sitter ran out to refund my money, saying above the screams, "She's just not ready to be away from you yet."

A year and a half later, when my daughter turned three, I reasoned we were both over that first traumatic attempt at separation. I signed her up for preschool, where she was placed in the caterpillar class. "At the end of the year, she will be a butterfly!" the teacher happily promised.

"Isn't that great!" I crowed into my daughter's trembling face.

Wailing, she clutched my leg and wouldn't let go. I ended up spending the day with the caterpillars, pushing them on swings, eating sand pies in the sandbox. My daughter enjoyed playing with the other children as long as I was next to her to translate each of her desires. Every attempt I made to sneak away triggered some type of internal radar and she grabbed my arm. After several weeks, the baby caterpillars called me "Auntie." Instead of being unable to separate from one child, I now had fifteen guarding the gate.

The teacher told me, "You brought this on yourself. You should just say good-bye and leave. Don't look back. She'll stop crying once you are gone." Feeling like a bad mother, I listened to the teacher explain that I had been torturing my child with my inability to separate. She didn't say this with meanness, but with pity. I resolved from then on to say a cheerful but firm good-bye at the gate.

I had to pull her off of me, just as I once had to peel her out of the car seat. When we separated, my clothes were as battered and rumpled as the cheerful "Bye-bye, have a nice day" that stuck in my throat. As I stumbled away, she stuck her hands through the gate and called, "Mama, Mama! Don't leave me!" until I burst into sobs and the teacher ushered her into the room.

The teacher assured me she stopped crying ten minutes after I left. I felt better. But when I heard her tell another mother the same thing, I began to suspect the teacher of lying. I imagined a preschool conspiracy.

My daughter greeted the sunrise howling, "I don't wanna go to school!" The lament did not let up through the episode of *Barney*, through breakfast, through the ride to school, in the parking lot. After three months, she still mourned me at the gate every morning. Our school attendance trickled away, until I formally announced I was pulling her out of preschool. I felt joyous making that decision, like a burden had been lifted off my shoulders.

"She'll just have a harder time when she starts real school," the teacher predicted. Briefly convinced I was short-circuiting her emotional development and scarring her for life, I doubted my decision to let my daughter remain home with me for another year. Suddenly a year seemed a long time to be planning daily enriching, educational yet fun-filled activities. And I wondered how I would be able to last another twelve months without the uninterrupted time I need to write, to think enough to string a paragraph together.

Yet when the teacher added, "You're not doing her any favors," I remembered my daughter waking in the mornings, already hating the promise of a day at school, and realized: Yes, I am. And that was enough to remind me that a few more months of my undivided time was a gift—to her and to me. Knowing that the time was finite, perhaps, made it easier to give and to cherish.

We spent our mornings at the zoo or the beach, the museum or the library. In the afternoons, we sat in the backyard, waist-deep in the inflatable pool, and ate Popsicles that dripped off our elbows. Or we'd make chalk drawings on the sidewalk and play games of hopscotch in which it didn't matter if you jumped on a line; you could never be "out." Some days we spent mostly in bed, watching cartoons until we were numb enough to take a nap.

For countless hours we played "house" or—ironically— "school," where I would be the whiny baby. Once my daughter, playing working mother, pretended to drop me off at the sitter's. On cue, I cried: "Mamaaaaa! Don't leave meeee!" My heartless daughter grinned, waved airily, and said, "Don't worry; you'll get used to it." She walked out of the room and never looked back. I wondered if it would ever be that simple.

When the string of seemingly endless days of make-believe became a necklace of months, it was suddenly time for my daughter to start kindergarten. As we walked to her classroom, her small hand folded within mine, I was the one trying to find reasons for her not to go. "Are you sure you are ready for real school?" I kept asking. She didn't answer, to my relief; I would have been upset if she had said no, and just as upset if she had said yes.

"I'm nervous," I told her before we entered her classroom.

She frowned, puzzled, and said, "Why are you nervous? You're not the one going."

When the bell rang, she cried a little. She hugged me, and the preschool teacher's dire warning flashed through my head as I imagined my daughter hanging on to me as I dragged myself out the door. But then, with a little sniffle, she let go, releasing me.

I hesitated at the door before turning to walk blindly toward the parking lot. Stumbling, I offered a prayer into the air: "Don't let her feel so alone." The prayer was meant for my daughter, but looking back, I know it was also for me.

Without the ballast of my daughter, I felt off-kilter when I tried to do the things I had planned to do without her. At aerobics class, unable to follow the music and three steps behind the instructor, I left early. At the grocery store, I yelled at the clerk because he couldn't find the price of cheese. And at home, when I faced the computer and the "free" hours I had in which to write, I turned on the TV to watch *Jenny Jones* and *The Jerry Springer Show*. I couldn't even nap without my daughter's small weight pinning my arm; I jerked awake every ten minutes, afraid that I'd missed her pick-up time.

From this point on, I knew, our separation would continue to grow over the years, as she experienced things in her life that I wouldn't even know about. Imagining her in the world without needing the protection of a mother's body, I felt a small moment of panic, a sudden, clutching cramp not unlike the pain experienced at her birth. And it's not unlike the muted anguish I feel each time I have to travel for business, leaving her behind. Part of me wants to hang on to her and wail with sadness and fear. I have to force myself to smile and wave happily from the ramp of the plane.

Each good-bye, each separation, reminds me of our vulnerability—hers and mine. Because of our attachment, vital to life, I am afraid of death in a way I never was before; I cannot bear to think of that ultimate separation. I do not want her growing up alone, a daughter without a mother. Neither can I contemplate myself alone in this world without her. Life suddenly seems so tenuous, so brief. I wondered why I had tried to rush the separation that finally came so easily.

I drove to the school early and sat on a bench until the bell rang. I worried that my daughter might have been as off-balance as I was that day, but she came out skipping. When she jumped into my arms for a hug, her words tumbled over themselves in her excitement to tell me about the girls in her class, about a boy who had to have time out, about the play-dough they had mixed from scratch. I pressed my face into the cradle of her neck, inhaling her sweaty-sweet scent now barely reminiscent of infancy, before she squirmed away.

Thinking of You

ROSE STOLL

A FEW MONTHS AGO, I stopped opening my mother's letters. A small, dark event, unsettling in its simple promise, that if *I* wanted, I could step out of the frame of family. That I could hope to contain the choking accretion of thirty-seven years with such a disproportionately simple act—or could I? I remember coming upstairs and setting her letter down, turning to take off my coat, then pausing to pick it up again. Looking with some detachment at the familiar code of the immigrant's life: the overly glued flap catching parts of the contained pages, former defense against shifty third world postal employees carried over to her North American life; a continuous row of stamps patched together from what was found in purses and drawers, then supplemented at the post office window; a steeply cursive system of addressing that ignores all postal convention. I stand there unseeing, balancing the envelope on my open palm—then, I drop it into the basket on my dresser. *I do not have to open this.* That done, and slowly realized, I suddenly have to sit down. I *never* have to open her letters again.

"But she is your mother!" Years of hissing relatives come to bear on my sagging shoulders. She is my mother—as she has often reminded me herself, invoking God, my dead grandparents, and every Hallmarkism she can think of, and me passing from anger to weary amusement to indifference. Yet, now, I am not so sure it is indifference—it seems to be more of a closing, born of a frantic need to survive wasted, lost years. I don't want to open her letters anymore; I don't want to listen to pages of a life endured with imperfect sons, daughters, husband, daughters-in-law, sons-in-law, and other assorted relatives and people she knows. I don't want to sit through the numbing minutiae of her last fight with my sister-in-law or suffer the various ailments that now seem to afflict her every waking moment. I am no longer willing to be a part of the frozen landscape into which my mother has permanently carved herself a resting place, unwilling to break free even in response to the muffled screams of a daughter whose childhood was being ripped away from her.

But she is my mother. And every year at this time I stand in front of glistening row upon row of drippy sentiment: She is my mother and I have to send her a card for this holiest of all retail traditions, Mother's Day.

This farmer's daughter, this tall, large-boned woman with the wide, archless feet of a person born to the soil, this person who bore five children into a violent marriage, this frightened child who shuttled between the redemptive calm of her parents' home and the wrath of a vengeful husband, this uncertain adult—this woman is my mother. A mother I have held at arm's length for as long as I can remember, with whom I have never shared girlish confidences. We don't easily or at all display affection in our family. The last time I hugged my mother she was crying, because I had returned home for a surprise visit after a five-year absence. I recall how awkward I felt, how unfamiliar the physical closeness, and I remember an uncharitable thought: that the howling woman I was gingerly touching seemed to be crying less from release of emotion and more from the habit of coarse display. Because this is how she lived her life; by laying it bare to the nearest passerby. My mother kept no secrets and did not indulge in ruminative pastimes. Scandals were savored and quickly spread, illnesses were extended by detailing them to indulgent ears, decisions were by consensus of the community and weighed by the simple rubric of being able to hold her head up. And errant husbands earned one a place of honor in this society, allowing the sufferer many luxuriant hours of backyard chat with whispering neighbors.

And yet, there is the other woman, the mother who gives her insistent teenage daughter her last $20 to buy shoes she absolutely must have because all the kids in her upper-middle-class school wear them. My mother dishes up meals to a gaping family maw and retires to the kitchen ostensibly to finish some chore, but really so she can eat her own half-filled plate quickly. My mother is screaming from downstairs as she tries to fend off my drunken father and there we are, my brother and I, charging to her side, ready to kill in her defense.

It's Christmas Day and our family is sitting outside on the steps of our house. The landlord lives in the last house in the row, the second largest building. His is painted, with a fence and windows that have glass in them. He lives in the house with his wife, who has suffered a crippling stroke and can hardly walk, and his illegitimate daughter. His daughter is pregnant, and he is the father of the baby. The first house in this gray line of crumbling shacks is the largest and nicest of them all, home to the rest of his family, his son and daughter born of his marriage to his shrunken wife. His wife spends a lot of time in the first house, his son and daughter rarely visit the last house. I haven't seen them today, which is odd because it's Christmas and everybody visits at Christmastime. We're sitting outside because my father has returned home and in a drunken fit has thrown most of the dinner out the window, along with some glasses, a pot, and plates. He has long passed from frenzy into melancholia and is now sobbing into vomit-flecked sheets. Soon he will be asleep and we may even creep out to see our friends' new toys. We have to hurry back, though, because he sleeps fitfully and has been known to awaken and start hollering for us.

None of us want him alone and drunk with my mother, and I don't want it ever to get dark because my mother will be asleep in our bed and he will insist that I sleep in theirs. As much as I try to will blessed unconsciousness, there is no escaping the base perversion the night will disgorge. But it means that he will calm toward my mother, and in that pitiful cause-and-effect pairing of the young mind, I see that I can help her, I can alleviate our suffering. I can shield my mother by having my father visit his awful intentions instead on *my* body. How perverse that a child should bargain for her mother's welfare with her own self, that a mother should accept this heartbreaking gift—and that childhood should be dismissed in such a summary manner.

My father tells the same story time and again when he has had too much to drink, when reason mutates into mindless black rage. It begins with my mother leaving him just before I was born, retreating to the safety of her own parents and not returning until I was three years old; it ends the same way with each telling, with him sobbing and reaching for me, clumsily petting me and calling me his prize, his gold, his most treasured child, all the while spraying my mother in bespittled invective. He rails too against my mother's family, but I sense fear and something else beneath the bitter onslaught: My father is both afraid and grudgingly respectful of my grandfather.

. . .

I CLOSE MY EYES and search for those early years, but there is nothing in my memory of the time spent with my grandparents, and there is an odd absence of any baby pictures in my grandparents' photo albums. The earliest images I can find show a chubby, shy child holding hands with her brother in the front yard of my grandparents' home on the Pomeroon River. In the background is the house my grandfather built, and off to the far right you can barely see the muted gleam of the Pomeroon.

I love this river, the urgent, buzzing life of its banks and this creaky, dim old farmhouse wrapped in the dense, ripe promise of fruit-heavy trees. It takes us an entire day to travel to the farm: cousins, aunts, my mother, brothers and sisters, all one excitable, shrieking group, giddy with the realization that for a week or so, the long arm of my father will not reach us. My aunts arrive first, weighed down with bags of food and clothing, which they arrange around their feet underneath the steamer's slotted wooden benches. Once settled, they smile benignly at us, pass out sweets to clamoring hands, and we're free to run off. Which we do, up and down the narrow stairs, shoving and yelling from the bow to the lower sections, leaning out perilously over the iron rails. The day slides by in a dusty rumble of docking boats and bumpy land vehicles, until our bus rolls to a belching stop on the riverbank. And there is my grandfather waiting by the launch—familiar, comforting, faded craggy gray head crinkling in our direction. He gets up and lumbers over, a stooped, beloved giant of a man. We chug noisily down the river and arrive with the setting sun.

This is when I saw my mother at her happiest, with a father she loved and a life simple in its needs, generous in its return. We feasted hugely, childish appetites burst open by days of simple farm labor and excessive play, by climbing trees, swimming in murky river water, digging through piles of dusty old magazines, chasing after complacent chickens, and running screaming from imaginary tigers. Oddly, I discovered I missed my father on the journey back and was foolishly glad to see him. I came to realize this was but a vestige of hopeful childhood that faded and died in time. I couldn't make that journey to Pomeroon as often as I wanted, coming to rely instead on the embellished tales my siblings relayed back to me. My mother went many times, choosing not to see my terror at being left behind, seeking for herself the desperate relief of her childhood home.

That was the darkest time of my life, the years from my earliest memory until well after my eleventh birthday. I haven't seen my father in twelve years, and four years ago I spoke to him for the last time. There were no showdowns, no violent last scenes; I just never picked up the phone again and never responded to letters. I spent much of my life trying to figure out why I was the target of his terrible abuse, but at some point a shift must have occurred, because I stopped being angry with him—worse, I stopped thinking of him as my father. I grew weary of my own internal struggles and wanted very simply to move beyond them. And yet the anger didn't go away; instead, it shifted to my mother.

What is a parent's role? My West Indian ancestry stabs an accusing finger in my direction and swats the question away. It is the duty of the child to the parent that is more important. Your parents sacrifice their entire lives and this is how you turn out. *She is your mother!* But a mother, *my* mother, would have taken me away from the hell of my home, would have run away with me, would have protected me. Instead my mother needed protecting. She sought escape and she couldn't comfort, and in the end, the child could not continue being mother to her own mother.

But she is my mother. And it is easier for me to hide what I don't feel by buying her a brightly colored card. I will send it to her so she can display it and point to it proudly and say, "That's from my daughter in America." A small white sheet of paper, embellished with color and glitter, its safe anonymity tells nothing of the sender, but to an aging woman on the far side of the continent, it speaks of hope and reconciliation and family. And I'll compose a short note, replete with bright, soulless prose, heavily reliant on the plural "you." *Happy Mother's Day and hope you are all fine and in good health. Thinking of you. Rose.*

Stepmother

ALEX WITCHEL

EVERYONE SAID I was lucky they were boys.

Girls, they claimed, were notoriously difficult stepchildren. They identify with their mother, who, as a rule, never likes you. Also, they compete for their father's attention—and win. Boys, on the other hand, were simple creatures made of snips and snails and puppy dogs' tails. They required nothing more than a drawer full of video games, an endless supply of Oreos, and a minimum of questioning about the last time they brushed their teeth.

All of which was fine with me. The sum total of my stepmother fantasy came from *The Sound of Music*. While I certainly aspired to wear designer evening gowns and wield a cigarette holder like the Baroness and would have loved to play guitar and be handy enough to make puppets and play clothes like Maria the enterprising nun, I fell, with a thud, somewhere in between. Growing up the eldest of four children—the younger two being ten and thirteen years my junior—I was used to being a surrogate mom. I could only assume that my future stepsons, Nat, ten, and Simon, five, would resemble my two younger brothers—perpetually hungry bathroom hoggers who, once wrenched from either kitchen or shower, spent their time playing sports and reading comic books.

I was close. Everything but the bathroom hogging, because we had a spare. They were terrific boys, smart and funny. Yes, Nat was a little shy and Simon cheated at Monopoly, but mostly, they were good company. I had no desire to engage in any tug-of-war with their mother over emotional supremacy. It was enough for me to have a fulfilling marriage to Frank, their father, and hope that as we all got older, the kids would appreciate the benefit of having an extra adult handy who loved them no matter what. Even though as a child that's all you seem surrounded by, once you're grown up you realize that those people are a vanishing breed.

At our wedding, I fed Frank a forkful of cake and did the same with both boys. They opened their mouths wide and blushed. Everyone applauded.

Later that summer we went on our first trip together, to Chicago, where Frank had taken them before. Our itinerary was filled with their favorite places and everyone was happy. As soon as we unpacked, we got all dressed up to go out and indulge their premiere passion, steak. Their father supervised showers and jackets and ties while I primped in the next room, putting on a pretty dress, earrings, makeup. There I was, still fresh from my honeymoon, feeling bridal, that mixture of new and lucky and intrinsically *right*, having sailed into the happily-ever-after phase of life before anything else had a chance to prove otherwise.

We got into the elevator and headed toward the lobby. The doors opened. Nat cut in front of me, followed closely by his brother, whom I bumped into. "Sorry," I said, though he didn't seem to notice. What neither of them seemed to notice was that I was a *girl*, a woman, a lady, the person who walks out of the elevator first. There I was, all dressed up, wearing lipstick and my new husband. But to them, I wasn't a girl at all. I was a stepmother, whatever that meant. Mothers certainly weren't girls. Why should stepmothers be?

I felt shocked. Most women get a little more adjustment time. You marry and feel all gooey. You get pregnant and feel like a house until you have the baby and feel all gooey again. Then you have another one but this time you cut your hair because it's easier and who needs makeup, anyway? You learn to carry the extra ten pounds that have somehow appeared with humor and grace and elastic waistbands. And if your kids barely look up from the TV when you're all dolled up on a Saturday night, that's okay, too, as long as the sitter knows where to find you and there are snacks in the fridge.

But becoming a stepmother is instant. I never gave bottles or changed diapers. I joined the party late. Everyone else was right on schedule. It was mine that needed accelerating.

The first year was hard. Simon was used to sleeping in the same bed with his dad from the "bachelor apartment," as they called it, and Nat had only recently graduated to his own territory on the couch. They had always spent each weekend with Dad and they continued to in our new apartment, where they shared a room. For the first six weeks, when we tucked the boys in, Frank would say, "Knock if you need us," and every single time, there was a knock on the door and it would be Simon. Sometimes he had a stomachache, sometimes he had a headache, sometimes he had had a bad dream. All times, his dad brought him into bed and told him to lie down and rest awhile. Simon would then fall asleep, as he was used to doing with his daddy beside him, and Frank would carry him back to his bed, where he would wake up the next morning safe and sound.

There was a bad moment early on when the four of us were lying on our bed watching a video. I looked over at Nat and noticed he was fiddling with his braces, which were hurting him, using one of our pillowcases to get a better grip. "Don't do that!" I said and he jumped, looking at me with wide eyes. He hadn't realized he was doing it, of course. There he was in his father's bed, which had always been a safe haven, and all of a sudden there *I* was, the Hygiene Queen, coming between him and the bed linens. I felt awful.

That winter, I was in bed for two weeks with a debilitating flu, which, whenever I was awake, left me in the foulest of moods. When I dragged myself to the table for dinner one night (Dad cooked), the kids seemed to go out of their way to irritate me. Simon speared a whole chicken breast with his fork rather than cut it; Nat practically threw rice onto his plate from the serving bowl, leaving almost as much on the table. I lost it. I was sick as a dog and they were *purposefully* doing this to spite me, because they knew I didn't have the energy to say no. So I said whatever nasty thing came into my mouth, along the lines of them eating like pigs—and behaving like them. No sooner had I said it than I wanted to die. There went my record. Eight months and the only screw-up had been the braces. And, well, there was also that time I said some poisonous thing I've managed to block out to Simon, who was sitting next to me on the couch. He got up, moved to the other end, and proceeded to ignore me.

All right. So maybe I hadn't been perfect. In the awkward silence that followed my dinner table outburst (Dad was safely ensconced in the kitchen with the next batch of chicken breasts), I declared disgustedly, "I'm going back to bed." As I got up, I could have sworn I saw the same look pass between them that the von Trapp children shared when they put a frog on Maria's chair. So instead of diving under the covers, I pulled them back and double-checked first. Safe. Once inside, face-down on the pillow, I hoped I'd never have to get up again. Oreos and video games? Snips and snails and puppy dogs' tails? Someone had neglected to share with me the tiny fact that boys are people, too. Which means they're just as much work as girls, only with a cheaper clothing budget.

So how come, I reasoned, stepmothers couldn't just be people too? It seemed only fair, but it didn't work that way. This was the Grimm brothers' fault.

Maybe I would die, I thought as I lay there, and they would both be so guilt-stricken they'd have no choice but to chew with their mouths closed for the rest of their days.

No such luck. I recovered. When I did, I retreated to the kitchen, spending hours developing the perfect meat sauce while Frank and the kids watched baseball games, or Nat played his dad a "cool" CD, or Simon needed help sounding out words as he learned to read on his own.

It occurred to me, on the day I basted a chicken five times in ten minutes, that I was hiding. I was simply terrified of making more mistakes. Of saying the all-time dreadful thing that would leave the mark of the Wicked Stepmother upon them. I had worked with a woman once who called her stepmother Stepmonster. I didn't want that to happen to me.

It didn't. We got used to each other. We had good conversations ("An A in math? I'm so proud of you!"), boring conversations ("No, I don't know where your bus pass is"), and bad conversations ("You *knew* your curfew was one A.M.!"). Also, as they say, shit happened. All kinds. The four of us went to a Christmas cocktail party once at a fancy apartment on Manhattan's Upper East Side, where there were no other children.

While their dad worked the adult circuit, I slipped off my shoes, took my white wine and settled on a couch in a corner with Nat and Simon. We sat there talking, decorously enough, as they explained the allure of the singer Beck and what shows on MTV were good and why. My concentration was so great that in the process of leaning forward to ask more questions, I spilled the wine all over myself, including down into my shoes. They were so relieved that I was the one to screw up, they burst out laughing and I joined them. The three of us tried mopping me up with paper cocktail napkins while the grown-ups, all of whom seemed to have the same set of pursed lips, gave us dirty looks. We were in a roomful of Baronesses.

Then there was the Sunday afternoon when Simon was riding bikes with his mom, flew over the handlebars, and landed on his face. He had been wearing a helmet, thank God, but his braces went through his upper lip, requiring stitches, his nose blew up, his cheeks and forehead were scraped all over. While Frank joined them at the emergency room, I went to the kids' house—where I'd never been before—to wait with Nat. This was the place that had been my husband's home for eleven years and the place, at that moment, where I was needed, but I felt I was somehow trespassing. I concentrated on Nat, who was scared and alone—yet still hungry. Opening another woman's refrigerator seemed too intimate an act; I called out for Indian food from a place he liked. Even doing that, standing at the kitchen phone and glancing at *The New York Times Book Review* opened to a page where the boys' mother had left it, I felt like a spy.

The food came quickly and we seated ourselves on the couch in the living room, where we watched sitcom after sitcom and I laughed at every line. Nat started to relax. It was past ten when Simon came back, practically unrecognizable. We left quickly and when we got home, I cried. That beautiful little face, ruined forever.

When he showed up the following weekend, I couldn't believe it was the same kid. Except for the stitches still in his upper lip, he looked like he always had. Talk about the healing powers of the young. By the following week, with the stitches out, he had forgotten it even happened. I wish I could say the same. For months afterward, I would slide my eyes surreptitiously across his face, checking every possible angle. Was there something the doctor might have missed? Was he *really* okay?

He was.

As time went on, I came to realize that the situation was this: The Nat and Simon Corporation had a president and a chairman of the board—their mother and father. Though they were no longer married, this was a business arrangement that would never be dissolved. I was a consultant, albeit highly placed, whose two cents were considered in the mix, but who never made the final decision. Which was okay with me. The important thing was the way their father treated me, which taught the kids how to treat me. In the beginning, if I said no to something, they would immediately look to Dad. "Alex said no," he would respond, definitively, and that was that.

I also learned when to say no, how to say no, why to say no. I learned to say "I'm sorry" when I was wrong. I learned never to walk into their bedroom without knocking (they returned the favor), to say at the dinner table, "Why don't you try using your knife?" instead of "What are you, an animal?" and to be extra nice on the phone when girls called. I also learned how to look the other way at parent-teacher nights when first wives gave me dirty looks, when their husbands gave me interested looks, and when the teachers shook my hand, smiling pleasantly though clearly confused at who I was and what I was doing there.

Nat is in college now. He is so tall that when he puts his arm around me I fit under his armpit. Simon is in high school. Last summer we had our first vacation without Nat—he had his own busy schedule, so Frank and I took Simon to a resort hotel in Scottsdale, Arizona, where he gloried in the attention lavished solely upon him.

One day for lunch, we went to the local Ed Debevic's, a branch of the Chicago institution that is a parody of a fifties diner: waiters and waitresses in costumes straight out of *Grease* who jump up on the counter to sing and dance. Simon loves it because when they're not performing, the help is notoriously rude. They sit at your table and insult you—about your "square outfit" or "low IQ" if you have a question about the food.

We sat down and reviewed the menu. We had been back to Chicago since our first trip together and were eagerly making a list of all our favorite dishes as the waitress approached. Bleached blonde, a biker-chick type. I steeled myself for the onslaught. But as she came closer her face softened.

"Hello, little family," she said gently, almost wistfully. Simon looked up at her and smiled. Frank started to order. I glowed.

DRAMA QUEEN *for a* *Day*

No Diapers, No Coffee

CATHERINE A. SALTON

IT IS 5:15 A.M. on Good Friday when we hear the first thin wail of protest from fourteen-month-old Nicky's room. He has been expressing his displeasure with his earlier bedtime by waking up at the crack of dawn, despite our best attempts to fool him by lining his window with dark towels.

I was disgusted with myself for this petty trickery when we first did it. What an ignoble thing to do, duping your baby on such a small issue! Now, after four days of 5:00 A.M. wake-up calls, I am seriously thinking about boarding up the window. The wailing continues. My husband and I lie rigid in bed, feigning sleep, each trying to fool the other into getting up with the baby. The baby, however, is not fooled.

When I open the door, Nicky points dramatically to the window and says, "Boot dee," which I'm pretty sure means "*J'accuse!*" He is crabby and screechy as I take off his night diaper, which weighs as much as he does, and start fishing around on the shelf for a new one. Fishing around. Fishing around. No diaper. No diaper? No diaper!

"We forgot to get diapers!" I wail. I hear some flailing in the bedroom and shortly thereafter my husband appears, struggling into a tatty pair of shorts he's fetched from somewhere, cursing steadily under his breath as he heads for the garage. It's only after the garage door crashes shut again that I remember those shorts were in the trash because of a big hole in the seat.

I am left with the problem of what to do with a bare-bottomed kid until he returns from the diaper-fetching mission. Then Nicky suddenly stops wailing, looks at me intently, and his face turns bright red. "Oh, no," I say and witlessly pick him up, thinking, towel! I race to the linen closet, where there are no towels because I have been putting off doing the laundry. I put Nicky down on the floor while I race into the bedroom and dig frantically through the hampers. I triumphantly fish out an aged bath towel and return only to see Nicky beaming beautifully up at me from the floor, where it is obviously a little too late for the towel.

I clean up the mess and hose off the baby and mop the floor and feed my cats and we go off to have our breakfast. There is no coffee. I collapse on the sofa thinking that maybe I could watch the news, when I hear a very soft but utterly unmistakable barfing sound from behind the love seat.

The cat! Now, I know the routine because as far as I'm concerned I am the 1997 All-California Barfing-Cat-Toss Champion. I grab the heaving cat and whirl around to put it in the garage, where the damage will be minimized, when the garage door opens with its usual roar and my husband starts to pull the car in. Upon seeing this, the cat, who is already in some distress, throws up all over the love seat, the area rug, and the floor that I have just mopped at great personal effort.

My husband enters bearing an enormous pack of diapers and a poisonous expression. "There's a big hole in these shorts," he says slowly and clearly. "I only noticed it in the frozen food department because I felt this breeze." He places the diapers on the table and walks with rigid dignity into the bedroom.

Court of Last Resort

ARIEL GORE

I'VE WRITTEN two books. I put out a magazine four times a year. I write articles and columns every day. I am not usually at a loss for words. But right now I don't know where to begin. I want to tell you a story. When I think back on all that happened, I cannot pinpoint a beginning or a middle. I can't stand back, get the needed perspective. My story doesn't have the firm structure of usual court cases: accusations, counteraccusations, a trial, a verdict. It is not ordered or harmonious. Looking back it seems like pure chaos and storm. It went on for years, consumed whole seasons of my family's life, cost me forty thousand dollars and too many nights' sleep. It engendered strange dreams, and eventually caused in me a physical reaction that affected every muscle group in my body and made the whole world look dead.

"You're not crazy," a lawyer once assured me. "You're stuck in a crazy system." But over the years this fine distinction became blurred and gray.

I am talking about family court, that strange American institution designed solely, it seems to me now, to perpetuate family dysfunction and all of our culture's contradictory expectations of mothers. The system exists to uphold the status quo in society and in families—even when that status quo is unjust or dangerous.

But where to begin? Maybe in May of 1992, when, armed only with a pen and pushing my sleeping two-year-old in a stroller, I walked into a Sonoma County, California, courthouse and asked where I could get myself a restraining order. Or maybe I should begin when I left my daughter's father two years earlier. Or maybe on the day I told him I was pregnant and he punched me in the stomach. Maybe I should begin my story five thousand years ago, at the dawn of the patriarchy. Or maybe in the nineteenth century, when wives and children were considered a man's property. I don't think my story begins in the late 1800s, when the Industrial Revolution spurred a radical shift in family law, and old paternal ownership ideals were thrown out in favor of maternal preference. Maybe it begins around 1970, when those old-fashioned maternal-preference laws began to be seen as discriminatory, and the kids of divorce were suddenly up for grabs. Family courts around the country took the new "gender neutrality" guidelines and ran with them, creating the first generation of kids who would grow up under complicated "joint custody" plans, shuttled back and forth like transients between parents' homes. Those children would later describe their childhoods in terms of "morphology" and fragmentation. But I digress. Maybe I should begin my story on a morning that stands out in my mind for no particular reason I can think of.

"Remain seated, come to order, the Honorable Judge Blah Blah presiding, this court is now in session." I'm in court, but I'm not legally on trial; I'm here to be "heard." I've noticed the posted sign that reads YOU WILL HAVE ABSOLUTELY NO MORE THAN 10 MINUTES BEFORE THE JUDGE.

Already I know that nothing definitive, or lasting, will come of my hours of waiting and my ten minutes before the judge.

But I also know that if I leave now, if I do not stand when my name is called, I will lose everything.

There are no children in the courtroom—and no journalists, meaning no objective witnesses. Because every litigant knows that his or her parental fitness could be questioned, the room is filled with June and Ward Cleaver impersonators. My own navy-blue suit is plain, but so different from my usual wardrobe that it takes an old friend who happens to be in court this morning a full minute to recognize me. More than a million marriages are dissolved in American family courts like this every year, and countless decisions about money and children are made each day. Usually these decisions are explained away under the pretext of "the child's best interest," despite the fact that family-court judges rarely sport backgrounds in child psychology. The Supreme Court almost never hears family law cases, so even if a family member's civil rights are violated, parents have little recourse short of surrendering custody, and children have no recourse at all.

While I am waiting I also notice the pictures pinned on the wall that were, apparently, drawn by children who have been traumatized by divorce. They have captions like "Sometimes I feel ripped apart" or "I cried when Daddy moved away." As if I do not understand morphology and fragmentation. As if I need an illustration to remind me that I am here to let a judge decide the fate of my family.

ONCE, WHEN I WAS waiting to be "heard" in a courtroom in 1993, the judge saw fit to give us all a lecture on "broken" homes and told us our children would suffer irreparable harm because of our failure to keep it together. I wanted to stand and testify that my home was not "broken," that it was in much better repair than it was when my ex used to punch holes in the walls. But I was silent.

I was in court seeking protective orders for myself and for my daughter. Some of the facts before the court are more my daughter's story than mine to tell. But here are a few things I can tell you: My ex was convicted of domestic violence. Against me. He had a long criminal record. He was often homeless. He was once arrested after midnight, allegedly drunk in public, with our then four-year-old daughter during a visit. And he was an illegal alien from Europe.

I was eighteen when I got pregnant. He quoted his age alternately as thirty-four and thirty-seven. It took me less than a year to come to my senses and leave him. But by then it was too late. By then we were parents. By then he had started tracking my finances, controlling where I went and who I saw. By then the drinking and the violence had become a part of our lives. That's why I left.

For a couple of years, I tried to facilitate visits between my daughter and her father myself. I thought I could handle his erratic spells on my own. But things have a way of escalating, even long after a breakup. I started calling the police. They came. They were cordial. But pretty soon they told me they wouldn't be able to help me out unless and until I got a restraining order.

So off I went to that giant white courthouse on that bright spring morning, armed with a pen and pushing my sleeping two-year-old in her stroller, and I asked where I could get myself a restraining order. I was directed to the family-court clerk, who informed me that if I shared a child with my batterer I had to file a paternity suit to get my restraining order. And so, without the foggiest idea of what I was getting myself into, I filled out the paperwork and, in doing so, effectively appointed the state as my daughter's third parent.

We've all heard the horror stories that come out of family court: the Florida judge who decided that a convicted murderer was a more fit parent than a lesbian; the Michigan judge who awarded custody to a previously disinterested father when the mother decided to go back to school and put the child in day care; the New York judge who consistently awards custody to parents accused of child molestation to punish the accusing parents for "lying"; another Michigan judge who "sentenced" a man to marry the woman he hit. I could go on all day with the list of travesties that have made headlines, but I'll spare you the review. What I wished I'd known before walking into that courthouse was that these cases are exceptional only in that they made the news.

IN MY CASE, paternity was legally established very quickly, but my ex and I were soon drawn into a complicated joint-custody scheme engineered, primarily, by our family-court mediator. My ex was assigned more parenting responsibilities than he asked for and more than I offered. Instead of the restraining order I came for, I was advised to "bear with him." To "give him another chance." My ex didn't show our mediator the suitcase full of chances I'd already given him. Her decision was swift, and we left with a court order.

Now when I called the police they weren't even cordial. He had a court order. He was my daughter's legal father. And since I still had no restraining order, he had free rein in our lives.

IT WAS ANOTHER year before I finally got my restraining order, which turned out not to be worth the paper it was written on. Another year went by and my ex was finally convicted of violating that restraining order. I got a Criminal Stay-Away Order for my troubles, which was also useless. Now we had one court order that said he couldn't come near me, and another that said I had to deliver my daughter to him—in person—for biweekly visits.

When the police came they shrugged and sided with the friendly guy instead of the pissed-off woman. My ex no longer tracked my finances or told me where I could go or whom I could see. Family court did the job for him. Over the years, through suits and countersuits and endless continuations, the court had the jurisdiction to dictate even the most mundane aspects of my family's life, from whether or not I could have a glass of wine with dinner to when and if we could travel outside the town where we lived. As a lawyer once broke it down for me, "Family court is there to do one thing and one thing only— give Dad back the power he lost the day Mom walked out the door."

Clinging at once to "neutrality" and to the cultural idea that divorce is the great disrupter of lives, family court did in my case what it does in so many: It attempted to facilitate the breakup with as little disruption to our lives as possible. This theory might not sound totally illogical at first glance—if divorce is bad, then a good court should see that breakups take place with minimal disruption of the existing family life. But most people divorce because there is a *problem,* a big dysfunction that needs to be disrupted. I for one didn't go to family court to keep everything as it was. I needed maximum disruption. I didn't need someone to help me keep the peace. I needed someone to help me end the war. But the war had just begun.

Soon my restraining order expired and I knew better than to ask for a new one. I wanted out of the whole system. But it was too late for that. Neither I nor my ex filed new lawsuits, but family court continued our case every month. Eventually we were appearing "on the court's own motion." With their own court-appointed lawyer and social services involved in the case, they had the jurisdiction to do just about anything they wanted with my family.

By this time there was a Children's Protective Services worker who agreed with me, a mediator who agreed with him, an annoying therapist who insisted on "neutrality," a guardian ad litem—court-appointed attorney for the child—who seemed to agree with whomever he was talking to, and, finally, a court-appointed psychiatrist who reminded me alternately of Barbara Walters and Marianne Faithfull and administered the Minnesota Multi-Phasal Personality Inventory—a long and bizarre true-false quiz—to everyone involved. Far be it from me to guess why they needed to know whether statements like "I enjoy mechanics magazines," "I sometimes stare into fires," and "My father is (was) a good man" were true or false to determine my or anyone else's fitness as a parent.

Our case had taken on a life of its own and led us into a labyrinth of "help" services peopled by "experts" of all kinds. Although each of these professionals was supposed to help my family, his or her job, it turned out, was more to "evaluate" than to assist.

How would they evaluate my family? How would they evaluate me? I didn't give this much thought at first. I figured I was like most people: a human being made of shadows and light. I figured I was a confident, good-enough mother, a mother who gave child-rearing much thought. I figured anyone could see these things. But I figured wrong.

Sure, I am like most people. But these professionals were not there to empathize with my universal dilemmas. They were on duty to uphold and enforce all of our conflicting expectations of mothers.

I cannot tell you what the professionals said about my ex or about my daughter—that's their business. But I can tell you that all an alcoholic or drug addict has to do to get a second or third or even hundredth chance in family court is to ask for it. And I can tell you that by the time the professionals were done "evaluating" me, every decision I had ever made as a mom—including my decision to become one—had been scrutinized, put on trial, and, ultimately, found lacking. When the dust finally settled, I had been called too young, too serious, too quiet, too aggressive, overinvolved, neglectful, hypervigilant, oblivious, promiscuous, prudish, hysterical, and remote. Along the way I had been advised to "speak up," to "shut up," to "let go," and to "never let go." I was characterized by one professional as overly soft and giving, and by another as an ice queen with a vendetta. I was faulted as a mother for working too much and, at the same time, I was billed tens of thousands of dollars for the insults.

When I frightened these professionals with the truth, they called me angry. When this made me angry, they nodded and recommended therapy. When I went to therapy I was diagnosed as suffering from an "adjustment disorder with mixed disturbance of emotions." Translation: failure to adjust to a crazy system.

I bit my lip and asked the therapist, "But if I adjust, won't you say I'm totally dysfunctional?"

She nodded.

When I asked for an alternative remedy, she threw up her arms and laughed. "Revolution? Gardening?"

As far as these family-court professionals—and the greater culture their opinions reflect—are concerned, we mothers are all damned if we do, crazy if we don't. We are handed a tangle of conflicting expectations and faulted for having conflicting responses to those expectations.

God knows what would have become of me if I had been accused of any actual wrongdoing. As it was, my time with those professionals stripped me of most of my confidence, and some of my kindness, too.

IN THE END I "won." My original wishes became my reality. But the ultimate restraining order did not come from family court. I'd probably be sitting in a family courtroom right now waiting for my ten minutes but for a small miracle. It turns out that I wasn't the only one who thought my ex was dangerous. The local police department and the Immigration and Naturalization Department had had enough of him, too. He was deported as a criminal illegal alien the same week our court-appointed lawyer was threatening to have the court bust me on contempt charges for refusing to deliver my daughter to his doorstep. There is a ten-year ban on my ex now, and an all-borders lookout. The local cops and the federal government don't want him in the country terrorizing our nameless citizens. But with the same information in front of them, the folks at family court didn't seem to think there was anything wrong with him continuing to terrorize my family.

I "won." And although the news from the INS came as a tremendous relief, I couldn't bring myself to celebrate. I was, by that time, so exhausted by the whole process, I felt like I'd climbed Mount Everest only to discover that the elixir I'd come for was a bus ride away from my house. I breathed in the news and walked home slowly. I padded up the stairs into my apartment, read my daughter a strange bedtime story filled with fairies and ripening fruit, and I sang her to sleep. In the dark, I burned my court file and all those contradictory reports and told myself I wasn't too-anything. I wasn't crazy. I'd been stuck in a crazy system for all those years.

I slept soundly and rose with the sun to do some potted-plant gardening and some thinking. And while I rested on my blue patio chair, contemplating the fresh dirt under my nails, I decided that those family-court professionals—who never agreed with one another—were all right. I *am* too-everything. And I wouldn't have it any other way.

Now give me a catch-22 of motherhood and I will swallow it whole: I stay at home and I work for pay. I am modest and I flaunt it. I subscribe to *People* and to *Ms.* I am single and I am in love. I do dishes constantly and my sink is full. I am wildly ambitious and I loaf for hours on end. I am the best mother any child could hope to have and I am the worst. I am good at making money and even better at wasting it. I am clear-headed and I am completely insane. I am a Cancer, Scorpio rising, shy and fierce. I am angry, but I am right.

I get letters from young mothers periodically. They tell family-court stories that, like mine, taste of chaos and injustice. I am not usually at a loss for words. But what can I tell them?

I learned a good deal during my six-year odyssey in family court (although perhaps none of what the professionals meant to teach me). I learned that small miracles come after a lot of hard work and a good fight (revolutions are made of a hundred thousand small miracles). And that those miracles do not come out of family court. I learned that two professionals on a case are usually worse than none. That three can be dangerous. And I learned that to live well and mother soulfully amid all of these contradictions, storms, and dysfunctional court orders, we cannot have to adjust to any of it. The remedy is distilled from equal parts gardening and revolution.

Young, Black, and Too White

KAREN GRIGSBY BATES

IT IS SUNDAY AFTERNOON and I am dressed in high heels, pearls, and yellow silk in 80-degree weather, sitting on a hard chair talking with several women I do not know. We are gathered at the home of our hostess, a mother of three, to do what I couldn't imagine myself doing until recently: being prepped for initiation in Jack and Jill, a national organization for black children. More than thirty years after the crescendo of the civil rights movement, I am doing this to ensure that my six-year-old son has enough black friends.

It's a paradox that would have made Martin Luther King, Jr., laugh—or perhaps wince. After the decades the previous generations spent battering down the doors to segregated institutions, the first generation of those civil rights beneficiaries— us—has grown up, and we now have children of our own. Per the plan, we are living lives that are extremely integrated. Maybe (and here's where the wincing comes in) too integrated.

"She talks like a little white girl," one friend complained of her adolescent daughter. "She assumes that everyone lives the way we do. I've got to get her more grounded." The daughter in question attends an expensive private school, vacations abroad, and swims in the family's backyard pool in a suburban neighborhood heavy on the standard accoutrements of the upper middle class and light on minorities.

Another friend regaled us with a recent scene from her dinner table: "My husband and I were talking about corporate politics—he's the only black partner in his law firm—and concluding that race might have had something to do with what had gone on in the office that day. Our fourteen-year-old daughter just exploded. 'You people—you think everything is about race! You should just get a grip! People are not prejudiced like that anymore!' " My friend paused. "She was just *screaming* at us, and she was serious. She thinks racism is kaput. We didn't know whether to burst her bubble right then or let her find out later, on her own." (They decided to let her make this discovery on her own.)

The irony, of course, is this: A whole raft of us—black, gifted, ambitious—did what the architects of the civil rights movement would have wished. We stormed the bastions, convinced (or at least impressed) the skeptics, and performed competitively in educational venues that had not long before been forbidden to us. We went on to be the Lonely Onlies, many of us in workplaces that had heretofore been white—or that had never had a black manager, editor, head resident, faculty member. We married, usually to people who had had experiences much like our own, and had children. And thanks to the slow death of restrictive residential covenants, overall increased interest in multicultural living, and the expanded incomes that those good jobs afforded us, we sent our children to elite schools or moved to affluent, often suburban neighborhoods that were Safer, with More Advantages.

And then we began to notice that our kids weren't, well, as *black* as we had been. Whether we'd grown up in the 'hood or had integrated suburbs, we had been grounded, if not in black neighborhoods, then by the black churches to which most of us returned every Sunday. If the schools we were integrating didn't teach black history and culture, our Sunday school teachers made sure those critical gaps were filled—packed to bursting, in fact. So along with the proverbs and parables, we learned about how the DAR refused to let Miss Anderson sing in its old building, and how her friend Eleanor Roosevelt hooked her up for a milestone concert at the Lincoln Memorial on Easter Sunday. We learned about the contributions of Charles Drew and Paul Robeson and Paul Laurence Dunbar and Constance Baker Motley. If our hometown papers politely neglected to mention the war against segregation being waged in the South, our Sunday school teachers kept us current and passed the felt-bottomed plate so we could contribute to the struggle too. ("Those little children in Mississippi and Alabama are fighting for *your* freedom too," they would tell us. "Don't you think you could give up your candy money to help out?" Out would come the coins, bound for freedom schools.)

If Sunday school gave us a sense of community and history, Jack and Jill gave us a sense of place. There was a hidden agenda when we nice Negro children got together once a month for fun and fellowship. Even as we took our monthly excursions, the cultural message was hammered into us: Black is not just ghetto. Black is not socially or aesthetically inferior. Black is vital to American culture. In addition to picnics, movies, and parties, we visited museums to admire works by black artists and dutifully trooped to hear André Watts in concert—"one of ours," a supervising mother would gently but unfailingly point out.

Initially started almost sixty years ago by twenty black mothers in Philadelphia who were anxious that their privileged children have black playmates, the organization quickly blossomed. Today it embraces 216 chapters across the nation, in thirty-five states and the District of Columbia. There is even an international chapter in Germany. Then, as now, mothers gathered monthly to plan activities for their age-grouped children. The charter requires that these activities be educational, fun, and/or culturally uplifting—but they also had the unstated purpose of making sure that these children teetering on the edge of Total Integration would not fall and be lost, perhaps forever. "We are sending you out into Their World," was the message, "but we want you to remember where Home is too."

It worked. For children fighting their way through the pressure cooker of educational integration, Jack and Jill was a godsend. I spent my days playing field hockey, conjugating French verbs, reading Wordsworth and Tennyson (never Hurston and Ellison), the Only One in my class at a prim girls' day school. I had friendly relationships with many girls, but no truly good friends. My good friends came from the neighborhood, and from Jack and Jill. And because of that, I remembered where Home was.

I am not so sure my child will—or perhaps it's more accurate to say I don't want to chance that he won't. Given the state of Los Angeles public schools and the impossibility of decoding what needs to be done to gain entry into the fully subscribed magnet system, it's likely that he'll spend his entire precollege years in nominally integrated private schools, because the choice is that stark. I want him to have experiences that are self-affirming, and even the most liberal private schools cannot protect against the assumptions of superiority that are sometimes voiced by white students and their parents.

It was the stories told in muffled voices by parents saddened but not shocked to find that their children aren't being judged solely by the content of their character that made me decide. The one black boy in his circle who did not get invited to his "best friend's" birthday party. (And the friend's mother, when confronted about the exclusion, could only stammer, "I'm sure race didn't have anything to do with it." Uh-huh.) The eight-year-old who agonizes over her dark skin because it's different from that of "the pretty girls" in her class. The white child from a liberal, wealthy family who thought he was complimenting a black honor student when he asked, "Why is it black people never say anything intelligent? Except for you, of course; you're different."

It's because we know these slings and arrows are going to whiz at our children, no matter how we try to protect them, that Jack and Jill is becoming fashionable again. Once it was seen as an exclusionary bastion of the Negro elite, to the point that admitting to membership was considered certifiably counterrevolutionary in the late sixties and early seventies. (This even though some of the most avid revolutionaries on Ivy League campuses were Jack and Jill alumni—although they'd rather be shot than 'fess up.) Now it's viewed as just another tool, another safeguard, to keep black children with more and more options outside the black community culturally grounded.

"My child is fourteen," confided the woman sitting next to me. She was slim and elegant in a navy pantsuit and queenly cornrows. "His school is fairly integrated—I mean, he's not the only one—but I want him to have other children as friends too. Right now, his best friend is white, and I'm fine with that. But I worry about the future." She means when her son is dating age and, all of a sudden, the groupings get to be more homogenous and the kids who are "different" find themselves excluded, or included as cultural mascots, badges of white hipness.

A neighbor whose child is in a Hollywood-heavy school empathizes with the Jack and Jill initiate's worry: "Here I've been, Afrocentric all his life, pointing out the beauty of black women, the importance of black culture. We vacation in Africa and the Caribbean, in part so he can go somewhere and feel what it's like to be the majority culture. And after all that, who does he bring home as a steady girlfriend? Some little blond girl! I don't want to be prejudiced, and I'm trying to live with it, but it's hard."

Although Jack and Jill is the oldest and most established of the social organizations for children, it's not the only one. A rival, Hansel and Gretel, has several chapters nationwide. And across the country, black parents are struggling to establish informal, local groups that address the same need. Here in Los Angeles, a group of concerned parents got together to found Onyx Village. Many of the parent members are in the entertainment industry—LaTonya Richardson, actress and wife of Samuel L. Jackson, is one of the founders. They live incontestably affluent lives, often in neighborhoods where black children have to be ferried to visit one another. The group meets monthly to inculcate children with black culture and history, and to provide them with an additional circle of friends who just happen, in the words of poet Lorraine Hansberry, "to be young, gifted and black."

It's for those same reasons that many of my friends hasten back to Martha's Vineyard every summer. One lifelong summer resident confided as we sat on the beach several summers ago: "It's important for our kids to have some time where they can all run around together and see that black is many things—not just what they see in the movies or on TV. Black Ph.D.'s,

M.D.'s, artists, bankers—all those folk are just as real and just as black as rap stars and professional athletes. Is it convenient to come here? No. Is it essential? Yes."

Which brings me back to why I was dressed in stockings and silk on a beautiful day when I could have been doing something else. Was it convenient for me to join Jack and Jill, with its labor-intensive mothers' committees and onerous dues? No. Is it essential? That answer is still, I'm afraid, yes.

Expecting the Worst

I STILL REMEMBER the relief and gratitude I felt when I first opened *What to Expect When You're Expecting.* I was standing in a bookstore, having just learned I was pregnant, and it occurred to me I had been quite drunk on at least two occasions since this totally unplanned infant was conceived. When I read what the other pregnancy tomes had to say about this, I grew faint. Then I came upon *What to Expect.* The cover featured a pastel drawing of a pensive pregnant woman in a rocking chair against the backdrop of a floral quilt. Inside I read: "There's no evidence that a few drinks on a couple of occasions early in pregnancy will prove harmful to a developing embryo." I promptly bought this wonderful book.

With almost 6 million copies in print, *What to Expect* is one of the nation's top-selling pregnancy books. Women like it because, in a world of stern, scary pregnancy guides, it is easy to use, gentle, and reassuring. The authors are women, but they aren't grinding the feminist ax that makes *Our Bodies, Ourselves* both so interesting and so useless. Arlene Eisenberg, Heidi Murkoff, and Sandee Hathaway write for mainstream women who would not necessarily mind an epidural.

But they are not, I soon discovered, anywhere near as friendly as they initially appear.

Most women want to have big, robust babies and look willowy two seconds later. I was certainly no exception. *What to Expect* had the answer: the Best Odds Diet. I studied it with interest. It is called Best Odds because, the authors assert, it offers your infant the best odds for being born healthy. The authors refer to this diet on just about every page, and claim that it helps with morning sickness, fatigue, stress, insomnia, dental problems, premature labor, stretch marks, depression, and constipation. What a remarkable diet! Of course, it will also keep you from getting fat. And, as the book reminds us on many occasions, "delivery won't make thighs and hips thickened by overindulgence during pregnancy magically disappear."

If you ask me, that's an unnecessarily demeaning way to describe weight gain, but still, I had always prided myself on being slim and I wanted to stay that way. Early on, I thought I might actually follow the Best Odds Diet. Looking back on it, though, there was no chance. "Before you close your mouth on a forkful of food, consider, 'Is this the best bite I can give my baby?'" the authors write. "If it will benefit your baby, chew away. If it'll only benefit your sweet tooth or appease your appetite, put your fork down."

And they really meant it. I had no problem meeting their vegetable quota. It was the variety of foods the book strictly forbade that stumped me: white rice, white flour, refined sugars, anything fried. Once a week, you're allowed to "cheat" by eating a bagel or a honey-sweetened bran muffin. Once a month, you can indulge in "something terribly wicked—cake or ice cream or a candy bar." In what circles is a slice of pie considered "terribly wicked"? And why couldn't I be wicked a little more often?

I started to notice there was something icky about the prose. I also noticed these women had a lot of ideas about why I needed to exercise, what I should wear, and how I could "keep the love light burning" with my husband. "When you leave the practitioner's office after your next visit," they suggest, "surprise him with a pair of tickets for his favorite opera or sports event." Sure, that's a nice thing to do . . . I guess. Except it reminded me of the simpleminded marital tips that magazines of the 1950s used to dole out to happy homemakers, right next to the ads for cake mix. The more pregnant I became, the more plastic *What to Expect*'s advice seemed. And as I got bigger and bigger, that unpleasant diet began to make me feel really bad about myself. I was pregnant and exhausted and I was supposed to prepare a soup of tomato juice, tomato paste, and skim milk sprinkled with a dusting of wheat germ?

Well, yes. The book offers control-freak suggestions for just about every eating occasion. Trouble sleeping? Try a light snack: say, whole-grain cookies (fruit-juice sweetened, of course) or some cottage cheese or unsweetened applesauce. What if I wanted sweetened applesauce? What if I wanted baklava? Wasn't I smart enough—wasn't I old enough—to pick my own bedtime snacks?

Apparently not. And I could forget about trusting my instincts at a restaurant. Several pages were devoted to instructions for avoiding the cunning ways in which the bread basket might disguise its useless calories and reminding readers to keep a running mental tally of their fat allowance for the day. Then, pregnant women, as your companions dig into fried calamari, you turn to your salad, with the dressing on the side "so you can stay within the Best Odds Diet guidelines." Order the steamed fish (but skip the side of white rice). As you watch your husband enjoy some pecan pie, you remember that "Desserts should, except on special occasions, be limited to unsweetened and unliqueured fresh or cooked fruits and berries (with a dollop of whipped cream if you wish)."

There is something so niggardly about that dollop of whipped cream. There is something so prissy about nibbling fruit-juice-sweetened cookies and toting around "a small flask of toasted wheat germ (you CAN develop a taste for it . . .)." Even if you don't see the point of all this self-denial (I mean, pregnant women get big, it's what they do), your husband might. In the chapter for fathers, a man worries that his pregnant wife will become "fat and flabby." Instead of telling him where he can stuff it, the authors propose techniques for helping the little mommy-to-be stay on her diet: "If you must indulge in dietary indiscretion, do so out of your home and away from your wife," they counsel. "If she slips, nagging will only help her to fall faster and farther. Remind, don't remonstrate. Prod her conscience, don't try to become it. Signal her quietly when in public, rather than making a pointed announcement to all within earshot about her ordering her chicken breaded and fried."

I can't quite forgive the authors for this one. I've tried to picture my husband quietly signaling his disapproval of my fried chicken. I would have divorced him. By the time our daughter was born, I actively detested *What to Expect.* I had surpassed their recommended weight gain and I felt like a mountain. I guess by their calculations, I got what I deserved. But then again, the baby was big and healthy. After breast-feeding for a few months, I weighed less than I did when I got pregnant. So there.

It seems so obvious that you should eat well when you're pregnant. And we'd all be healthier if we never ate dessert. But pregnant women need less to feel bad about, not more. Does a piece of fried chicken really jeopardize your child's well-being? During one of the most alarming, astonishing, and creative times of your life, do you really need a book that makes you feel guilty for eating a Pudding Pop?

A Mother of a Year

STEPHANIE COONTZ

THROUGHOUT 1997, a series of sensational stories about individual mothers and their problems kindled passionate emotions among the general public. In my aerobics class, which serves as my personal focus group on these issues and many others, hardly a week went by when our warm-up stretches and post-exercise showers weren't enlivened by intense discussions or animated debates about something a mother did or failed to do, according to some press report.

The birth of septuplets in November, for example, divided my workout companions right down the middle: Half thought it was tremendously moving, a miracle; half found it an irresponsible contribution to overpopulation or a waste of medical resources and energy that could be better devoted to the thousands of kids stuck in the limbo of foster care.

The death of Princess Diana, on the other hand, united the entire class in mourning, from starstruck youngsters who had copied her hairstyles to earnest students who appreciated her work with AIDS victims to older married women who identified with Diana's very public mistakes and victories as she struggled to find happiness outside a loveless marriage.

The killing of baby Matty Eappen and the ensuing "nanny trial" were equally engrossing, as our changing room echoed with debates over how much responsibility for the tragedy should be borne by Matty's physician mom. Some of the women thought Deborah Eappen was selfish for working three days a week when she could "afford to stay home" (a standard they never applied to Diana's prolonged vacations from her children). Most just blamed Eappen for bad judgment in letting a "mere teenager" care for a baby and a toddler. The nanny teenager, though, got a lot more sympathy than the teen accused of killing her newborn at her prom dance several months earlier. That teen was widely condemned as a monster.

Even the women who most disapproved of Deborah Eappen's decision to continue working while her kids were young had been outraged by a May cover story in *U.S. News & World Report* that accused middle-class working parents of "lying" about their need to work. To a woman, my classmates felt that this criticism was aimed exclusively at mothers, and a few had statistics in hand to refute the charge of "selfishness," pointing out that college tuitions have risen by 90 percent over the past twenty years, while family incomes have risen by only 9 percent. But the decision of the vice president at Pepsico to quit her high-powered job in order to spend more time with her family drew almost universal approval, though a number of us wondered whether she might have just cut back if her husband paid equal attention to his own priorities.

The discussions in my aerobics class, like the media coverage from which they originate, are skewed in many ways. Often, for example, the intensity of anxiety stands in inverse proportion to the prevalence of the problem. The prom newborn death was featured in a *People* cover story asking whether America is seeing a scary new generation of kids "without a conscience," a question that most of my classmates answered in the affirmative. In fact, however, the killing of newborns by their moms is at its lowest level ever in American history. We find the case so shocking not because it is typical but because it is so rare. Far less attention and energy were devoted—in either our changing room or the nation's newsrooms—to the much more common tragedy of impoverished teenagers struggling to raise babies by themselves without adequate finances, support services, or even educational information.

Similarly, most comments about whether middle-class mothers should "trust their children to a stranger" did not address a much more serious question. No one brought up the looming child-care crisis in America posed by the new welfare law. The "success stories" of welfare reform typically involve single mothers who land minimum-wage jobs requiring up to a two-hour commute each way by public transportation. While the largest national study to date found that good child care plus good parenting confer a double advantage on children, former welfare recipients must often leave their children in substandard care for ten to twelve hours a day. The number of kids needing subsidized child care is expected to triple as a result of welfare reform, and already many states are dropping the children of the working poor from subsidized-child-care slots in order to make room for the children of former welfare recipients. Yet this unfair and self-defeating practice generated no debates comparable to those over whether Deborah Eappen should have been away from her children for the three days a week that she worked out of the home.

These strange silences in otherwise loud debates are partly connected to racial stereotypes that lead many people to wrongly assume that most poor people are on welfare and most welfare recipients are black, and that there is no "story" in the problems they face. Thus the Boston nanny trial made Louise Woodward's face and name instantly recognizable around the nation, stimulating impassioned arguments over how heavy or light her sentence should be, especially in view of her youth. Not one of the women in my class—all of whom had strong opinions on Woodward's sentence—had ever heard of Lacresha Murray, an eleven-year-old African American girl found guilty of causing the death of an African American infant in another unregulated home-child-care setting and sentenced to serve twenty-five years in a Texas jail.

But racial bias is not the only reason for the way these discussions are skewed. It's popular to blame distorted ideas about such issues on the gullibility and ignorance of the American public, but where does such ignorance come from? It's not my classmates' fault that Lacresha Murray never made the national news, except for a lone commentary on National Public Radio. Few of the women who rush off from our aerobics class to work or to other family responsibilities have the time and resources to look behind the newspaper cover stories or the evening news. There they are bombarded with the sensational, the surprising, the photogenic, and therefore almost by definition the exceptional cases where our emotional response cannot easily be connected to political or social analysis.

The unique, atypical stories that generate intense audience response are those that tap into real anxieties about the dilemmas of contemporary parenting, especially the double binds and contradictory messages faced by modern mothers. This is what gives these stories their emotional power, as well as creating the "conflict quotient" so necessary for talk shows. But it is also what prevents people from seeing the patterns behind the individual stories. And no constructive solutions are possible until we understand the social conditions under which women have to make their personal choices regarding work, marriage, and mothering. As long as the underlying issues are refracted and diffused through the lens of sensationalism, we will lurch from indignation to pity, praise to blame, with each new incident that pushes our buttons. Instead of debating what to do about child care, work policies, and changing gender roles, we will keep on discussing killer nannies, wicked stepmothers, and dead princesses.

In my view, this is a bigger tragedy than the death of Princess Diana, sorry as I felt for the whole dysfunctional family and the burdensome, all-too-public conditions under which Diana had to struggle to grow up. And it is an avoidable tragedy. Most of the women in my aerobics class, like the majority of the population, support investment in education, job creation, after-school programs, and paid parental leaves. Like most other Americans, they worry about divorce, but don't want to go back to the days when people had to prove or invent fault in order to get out of a rotten marriage. In my own experience discussing family issues with the public, I have found it's easy to get even broader agreement on such issues once people begin to understand the revolutionary and irreversible changes in the nature of marriage, motherhood, and family over the past half century.

Debates over whether it's better for a particular mother to quit work after childbirth, for instance, need to be put in historical perspective. The entry of mothers into the workforce is occurring in every country of the world, regardless of its laws, traditions, or family values. In America, the proportion of mothers who work has risen steadily ever since the abolition of child labor early this century. Today three fourths of all married mothers with children, and an even larger proportion of single mothers, work outside the home. Women with kids under six are the fastest-growing component of the female labor force. In 1997, a milestone was reached: A solid majority of new mothers now return to work before their child reaches his or her first birthday.

We are not going to jawbone or guilt-bait most mothers out of the workforce. Whether or not Deborah Eappen should have quit her job is irrelevant to the big picture. Married women earn, on average, 41 percent of their family's income. In 23 percent of working couples, the wife brings home more than the husband. Most of these women simply cannot afford to quit work. Yet America's haphazard, unregulated, and under-funded child-care system means that most of us agonize over whether our children will be safe and nurtured. Some couples work opposing shifts to make sure they've got child-care cover-age, but that puts terrible strains on even the most cooperative marriage, and of course this strategy is out of the question for single parents. Studies show that working mothers have only twenty-six minutes a day less direct interaction with their kids than at-home moms and that they usually make up for this on weekends. Meanwhile, though, they balance guilt about their parenting against pressures from employers to prove their loy-alty with more "face time," while sacrificing sleep and personal recreation. They hardly need sideline commentators pointing out their every flaw.

Women who quit work after childbirth have a different set of problems. Many appreciate the extra time and put it to good use. But full-time homemakers are more likely than other women to experience depression, and a woman who quits work after childbirth often suffers a sharp drop in marital satisfac-tion and self-esteem. She resents her loss of access to the pub-lic sphere and worries that her children are missing out on the benefits of having a hands-on father who is fully involved in child care from Day One. But her husband, often working extra work hours to compensate for the loss of a wife's income, can't understand why his wife isn't more grateful. Researchers find that such conflicts are a potent cause of marital distress. And the woman who stays home faces the frightening prospect that if she does get divorced, she and her children are far less likely to regain their former income than a mother who went back to work within the first year.

Like it or not, divorce is simply a fact of life that women must take into account. In some cases, it's a needed option; in others, an unwelcome surprise. But divorce has been rising steadily since the 1890s, well before the institution of no-fault divorce laws. If we disregard the short-lived dip in divorce rates during the 1950s, our present divorce rate is exactly where you would predict from its rate of increase in the first fifty years of the century. The increasing economic independence of women means that women do not have to stay in unsatisfactory marriages. But foregoing that independence to play the role of loyal helpmate, as the Lorna Wendt case showed, is no protection against divorce. And it's a rare homemaker who has the luxury, like Mrs. Wendt, of arguing over whether the settlement will be $20 million or $100 million.

Divorce, however, is only one of the reasons that marriage organizes a smaller and smaller proportion of people's lives and meets fewer people's needs. The age of first marriage for women is now at a world historic high, while the age of first marriage for men has tied its previous high of 1890. More youths are living outside the family than ever before, yet for 60 percent of them, incomes and medical benefits are still falling even after four years of economic recovery, making it ever harder for them to achieve self-sufficiency. At the other end of life, a person who reaches age sixty can expect, on average, to live another twenty-seven years. Together, these trends mean that we can no longer assume that all the needs of children or the elderly—or, for that matter, the physically or mentally ill—can be taken care of within the nuclear family. Failure in such care is not due entirely to individual flaws; it is often built into the circumstances of modern life.

The crisis of caregiving in America cannot possibly be solved by telling working mothers to quit work if they can afford to. Even most stay-at-home mothers must resume work at some point in their child's school years; few can afford not to work during the teen years, given soaring college tuition costs. But children can get sick at any age, while the parents of teens today may actually need more job flexibility than parents of toddlers, to provide occasional after-school supervision or deal with the ups and downs of adolescence in a world where the age of sexual maturity has never been lower.

Even when the children finally leave home, family obligations don't necessarily end. Almost one in four households today, triple the number of a decade ago, has extensive care-taking responsibilities for aging relatives.

At a personal level, we can debate how well individuals are dealing with their new challenges. But before we deal out too much blame for their failures, we need to remember that our political and economic institutions have made almost no accommodations for these massive rearrangements of family life. Our work- and family-leave policies are forty years out of date, constructed for a time when the majority of mothers did not work outside the home and the majority of fathers were happy to leave child rearing entirely in the hands of their wives. Our school vacations are one hundred years out of date, designed for a time when most families needed their children's labor on farms during the summer and only a minority of students finished high school anyway. Our school hours are out of sync both with new medical research and new economic realities: School begins way too early for teenagers' body clocks and gets out way too early for their parents' time clocks. Our medical insurance and hospital care have not caught up with the needs of aging Americans and their families. No family, whatever its form, is getting the investment in after-school programs, education, child care, or elder care that it needs.

Under these stressful conditions, we are all scrambling to do the right thing, making sacrifices to do so, resenting the lack of support for whatever choice we've made, and regretting the trade-offs we have to endure. As usual, women bear the largest share of the costs, whatever choices they make, and are assigned the largest share of the blame for any failures.

In the absence of explicit political discussion of these dilemmas, it becomes easy to project our fears and resentments onto someone else. Any historian can tell you this is the classic recipe for scapegoating.

It's also a classic recipe for unrealistic fantasies. If bestowing sainthood on Princess Diana was one symptom of this, so was the hope raised by the Promise Keepers, who were hailed by many in my aerobics class as God's gift to overstressed wives and mothers. Never mind that the Promise Keepers movement is financed by groups who oppose birth control, child care, abortion rights, and even public education, advocating that every political policy and school lesson be sifted "through the grid of Scripture." Never mind that its spokesmen have urged men to "take back" leadership in the house, telling them to "consult" with their wives but to remember that "every organization needs a Chief Executive Officer." At least, said my harried and worried fellow exercisers, the organization asks men to recommit to marriage and get more involved in fatherhood. Perhaps that will take some of the pressures off women.

But the Promise Keepers movement offers no more of a solution to the dilemmas of modern motherhood than the short-lived success of Princess Diana in rising above her unhappy marriage. Most of the Promise Keepers recruits did not start out as newfangled "secular cynics" who suddenly saw the error of their ways. They were old-fashioned fundamentalists behaving badly. Belatedly, many have realized that traditional chauvinism undermined their Christian vows of fidelity and kindness. Now they are trying to catch up with the changes that have occurred since the 1950s, but there's no way they're going to be up to 1990s speed by the time we enter the next century. The benevolent paternalism they offer their wives may be a step up from their former self-centered autocracy, but it's no substitute for the mutual accountability and equal sharing of both work and family roles that is the most sound basis for modern marriage and parenthood.

Women don't need men to go weep about their sins at football stadiums. Nor do we need to spend any of our already overloaded time second-guessing the choices that other women make. What we need is more help, at both the individual and the institutional level, in adjusting our work life and family life so that both men and women can share the rewards and responsibilities of each. To do that, we should relegate fairy tales about princesses and knights in shining armor, as well as scare stories about wicked witches, to a past that is largely mythical and at any rate completely unrecoverable. And instead of debating the guilt or innocence of each woman who falls off the tightrope we're all asked to walk, let's figure out how to broaden the path to success for every family.

Stop the World,
I Want to Get Off

SUSIE BRIGHT

WHEN THE good mommies of *Salon* approached me to write a personal opinion for their "Time for One Thing" column, they thought they had a sure bet. Other exhausted mothers might write the quintessential plea for a decent cup of coffee or wax poetic on the utter loveliness of an afternoon nap. But someone like me, someone who has written for decades about the importance of jilling off, could certainly be expected to write an impassioned editorial on "The Significance of Owning a Vibrator"—and what its daily use means to womankind.

I guess I can. I have two vibrators plugged in next to my bed, as close to me as my reading lamp. They are my favorites, after trying every model that ever came into the feminist vibrator boutique I worked at for six years.

One of them is the trusty Wahl One-Speed, made by a Catholic company in Chicago, which after all these years still advises in its manual to "avoid use on the genitals." *Ha!* The darn thing is virtually useless anywhere else. I like the Wahl because it is what we in the business call a "coil-operated" machine, meaning it's virtually silent, very intense, and perfect for sneaky little orgasms that you don't want to draw your entire household's attention to.

My other love is a Hitachi Magic Wand, and "Magic" is the key word here, for it was my very first vibrator, and it seemed like nothing less than a miracle to me that this purring ball of sensation could give me a screaming clitoral hard-on in less than a minute, then leave me gasping for air a few seconds later. Before I turned on a Magic Wand, I had been someone who needed a good half hour to meet my orgasm, and by then my poor hand was numb and aching. I didn't even want to ask lovers for oral sex—they'd have to be a martyr. (Later on I learned just how many people like to be hung up on that particular cross.)

Vibrators are liberating, no doubt about it. They bring women up to speed, literally. They erase the "time differential" between men's and women's sexual responses. Once I had gotten over the novelty of coming as quickly as a spastic teenage boy, I realized the divinity of arousing myself to sexual plateau and remaining there in bliss, as long as possible, before I fell off. I learned so much, so quickly about how my orgasms worked (now that I wasn't too exhausted and embarrassed to notice them) that I became a much more skilled lover, with or without my vibrator, alone or with others. It was like a ticket out of the world's worst small town.

Now, is that a testimonial or what? But here's the thing . . . I blushed when I read my *Salon* editor's suggestion. The horrible truth is that buzzing off *isn't* the one thing in my daily life I make time for. No fucking way.

I know you're shocked.

My lists of "must do this today" are much more indicative of a burn-out case than a sensual woman. I *should* masturbate every day; I'm sure it would do me a world of good, and clearly I would have a smile on my face for at least a few minutes of every morning—if I only made the time. But I don't—and truly, I can't tell you why. I'll tell you what I *do* make time for:

- I must have my graham-crackers-with-butter-and-jam snack.
- I must watch my *Law and Order* reruns.
- I must read my daughter chapter eight of *Heidi* because I'm reliving my *Heidi* infatuation all over again. I want a bowl of goat milk with my graham crackers.
- I must be alone with the door closed—alone, alone, alone. I'd give anything for more privacy.
- I must read travel books about places where I'm not and peruse mail-order catalogs for clothes that couldn't possibly fit me.
- I must log on to my computer and see what all the people who irritate me are saying in my favorite forums so I can make up all sorts of hilarious responses to them that I'd never actually post. I am so hooked on some of these on-line personalities' dramas that I can hardly go to sleep at night wondering if "UserID Betty" will disown her daughter or tattle on her supervisor or confide to her husband that she's cheating on him just like she has to everyone else on-line.

Just reading this pathetic little list makes me want to have a nice, clean orgasm and begin a new day with fresh habits. I wish that everyone would believe that I did indulge in imaginative sex every twenty-four hours with a variety of fascinating lovers and new sex toys direct from the manufacturer. Someone's got to be a role model, and at least I've made an attempt.

But here's the truth: There *are* certain days that I must buzz off (or pounce on my lover), no matter what, and they are obviously tied to my menstrual cycle. Much to my partner's disappointment, when I am not driven by a hormonal surge, or the occasional romantic inspiration, I often act like I don't have a body, let alone a sexual appetite. I am much more comfortable in my head than my "container," and I often wish I could leave this aching, tired thing by the roadside.

I do not approve of this condition. I feel betrayed by my body's cranks and pains. I can't believe that now, at age thirty-nine, when I know so much about sex and what I like and how to be the world's most intoxicating lover, all I want to do is have one more graham cracker and then go to sleep. For a very, very, very long time.

I have a feeling that when I woke up from such a sleep, unabated by an alarm, the coffee grinder, the door creaking, the kittens mewing, my daughter calling, any sort of call at all from any grasping voice—in that perfect moment, I would turn my electric blanket on low and bury my face in my pillow, where I can always find my very best fantasies. I'd reach out to that shelf that my fingers can find blind, I'd grab my little piece of magic, I'd let out a very big sigh and take a long, long ride, right out of my mind.

DRAMA QUEEN *for a* Day

Spaghetti Weevils

LESLIE GOODMAN-MALAMUTH

NO ONE in my family is naturally svelte, on either my mother's or my father's side. My mother battled the scale her entire life, a struggle complicated by the fact that she craved alcohol as much as food. I think the time in her life when she was happiest was during the late forties and early fifties, when she was a flight attendant—"hostesses," they were called—for TWA. What glamour! What prestige! The curling black-and-white photos with the deckle edges show my mother and her party-gal roommates, in halters and dark lipstick, perching decoratively on chaise longues outside their beach-front rental house near Los Angeles.

Among the hostesses who clustered south of LAX, the gals from TWA were considered the elite. "Teenie-weenies," they were called, and they had to live up to their billing. They were weighed in like jockeys before each flight, and if overweight, they would be warned, fined, grounded, or even fired. So my mother lived on three packs of cigarettes a day, black coffee, and skim milk. Once she was grounded for good after marrying my father (in those days flight attendants had to be single), her desire for either a good meal or a stiff drink played itself out at the family table throughout my childhood. The drinks usually won.

My mother defined herself as much by what she wouldn't

cook as what she did. She tantalized us with memories of occasional drop-dead-delicious meals—stuffed cabbage, sour-cream enchiladas, lasagna. "I'll make that when we all lose some weight," she'd say balefully, lighting up another Kool. Our dinners typically comprised naked, broiled lean meat or fish and a green salad, with brown rice or a baked potato on the side if Mother really felt like pushing the boat out. As often as possible, I gravitated to my paternal grandmother's kitchen, where the pantry overflowed with treats seldom, if ever, seen in my mother's house. At Nana's, two slices of Pepperidge Farm raisin bread cradled a thick slab of sweet butter; at home, Wonder Bread was spread meagerly with diet margarine, the kind with such a high water content that beads of moisture lolled on the surface. The wrapper warned against using it "for cooking or baking purposes."

But one day I came home from school to the intoxicating aroma of a meat sauce simmering on the back of the stove. All afternoon, it sent thick ribbons of scent through the air. And there was garlic bread! I couldn't wait. I don't know what the occasion was, but when dinner was announced, we all dashed to the table and waited expectantly. My father opened the sliding plastic top on the green, foil-wrapped cylinder of Kraft grated Parmesan cheese and shook a generous amount onto each plateful of spaghetti.

As I watched the steam rise, some of the crumbs of Parmesan began to walk dizzily around on the mounds of pasta. The cheese was infested with weevils, in a fairly appalling weevils-to-cheese ratio. We all wordlessly took our plates to the sink and dumped them down the garbage disposal. "I put the same cheese on the garlic bread," my mother murmured.

We had Wonder Bread and diet margarine for dinner. Green salad, too.

A Mother's Body

KATE MOSES

I'M IN THE BATHTUB with my nine-year-old son. His sister is a baby, a dedicated nurser, and proprietary of me. He'd asked me to join him in the tub, and yes, I hesitated, and yes, I reprove myself: He is still a little boy and he needs the contact of my skin just as his tiny sister does. When I slip into the water behind him, Zachary has finished arranging his bubble-bath hairdo, a mushroom cap of suds with a long curling flourish, like a Hershey's Kiss. He smiles sweetly, so happy to have me to himself for a few minutes, and leans into my body. Carefully, very consciously, gauging my reaction, he lowers his soapy head to my chest, leaning his chin on my breast and looking up into my face, then lifts his hand from the water and places it over my heart. A trigger of concern goes off in my brain—physical boundaries: when to impose—but when he sees my even expression (my poker face, hitched to genuine pleasure at the closeness of my child), I'm just his mommy gazing back at him, and all the tension goes out of his body. He knows he's my little boy, curled up with his mother in the bathtub for one of the last times; we both know it, and relax.

The erotic shimmer of motherhood, the light-on-water of physicality that underscores contact with our children, with everything after our children. Can the erotic and the sensual, the spiritual and the corporeal, ever be completely separated after you've become a mother? In the simplest terms perhaps, but parenthood renders the simplest terms impossibly complicated and conditional.

FOR YEARS after Zachary abruptly stopped nursing, shortly after his father left, I continued to produce milk. I didn't know what to think of my breasts any more—they had been part of the erotic being I'd become, they had kept a child alive. The transactions of my flesh had seemed clear-cut; now my milk dripped uselessly in the shower.

My body had gone missing. Eventually, someone brought it back. I would see his long silhouette on the cheap paper window shades after I'd put my son to bed. He rapped on the glass in a silly pattern to amuse me—but lightly, so as not to wake the baby—the nodding leafy shadows of trees framing him. He once brought me a fragrant lily; the dark saffron pollen drifted over my skin, over my bare feet.

I was leaking milk all over the sheets. My body felt foreign; I didn't know how to behave. But he ran his finger over the dark outer ring of my breast, traced its edge, in to the beading nipple. He rubbed the drops into my skin like a salve. *No one is like you*, he said. *You are more than a mother.*

Lovers make you a gift of your body; so do children. The body again becomes distinct, edged, a marvel you'd forgotten, retrieved by the unexpected: your belly slimy with gel, fingers and toes waving like sea anemones on a grainy sonogram screen. Or your newly shaved leg, buffed by the smooth ecstatic face of a sybaritic three-year-old.

My daughter, now two, has started licking me. The start of a hug, arms around my neck; or I'm bending down, picking up little plastic kitty cats off the floor, and her tongue laps my cheekbone, flicks the crater of my eye. Moist, warm—and immediately cooled and thus just the slightest bit aggressive and startling—her licks are inseparable from her voice and her velvety skin, the salty, nutmeg smell of her hair. Her licks have the power to completely alter my mood, capture my full attention, put me under her spell, which is no doubt part of the reason she loves to lick me.

As a young woman, I thought about my body all the time: how to disguise it, to shape it, to present it, to comfort it; what everyone else thought of it. Motherhood taught me to live in it. In the last weeks of my pregnancies, when each of my children tried to leave my body too early, eager party guests with someplace better to go, I sank back to the bed where they were made, defying gravity and the inevitable. My focus shifted to the babies inside me, sloshing in their safe balloons, lulled by the rhythm of my heartbeat.

The body is frontier territory to children—their own, with its discoverable landscapes, and their mother's, a fortress at the edge of the known, where they gather what they need before their journeys. I can see that my children are cataloging everything about me—my voice from another room tumbling down the tunnel of sleep; my hair, which sweeps their faces when I say good night; the feel of my hand shielding their eyes, the warm soapy water pouring over their shoulders—just like I memorized my mother. I thought she was beautiful and so did everyone else, but I judged her beauty from a child's perspective: What fascinated me were her long, fine bony feet with their red-polished toes. I think of this on a recent afternoon when I walk down the hallway, the rare lipstick applied in preparation for some meeting, and my two-year-old greets me. "Candy mouth," she says.

The same bold boy who touched my breast in the bathtub won't kiss me anymore—at least, not on the lips. Celeste, his sister, mashes our mouths together, gripping my hair, with all the passion in her forceful small body. But Zachary will only brush his face past my ear. At first I was hurt: You must kiss me, I thought. I'm your mother!

I couldn't understand why; then I realized that I know exactly why. It's time for my son, a decade out of my womb, to test his own boundaries, take possession of his body. Zachary's body isn't mine any more, not like it once was. We've been moving this direction since the day he was born, when I held him swaddled in flannel and watched every possible emotion roll and brighten and twitch over his face, like a symphony warming up, like clouds passing in front of the moon.

TEN YEARS OLD, my son holds my hand on the walk to school—no kisses. In a year, his body has changed: tall and lanky still, yet his thighs have grown muscular, almost manlike, his fine towhead hair darker and musky, so thick that when I pour water over his head in the bath it runs off in sheets, like rain off a duck. Some days he strips unself-consciously in front of me, burbling a list of toys he wants for Christmas; other days, his door is shut and locked.

Celeste scampers ahead of us down the sidewalk, ducking under signposts, looking back mischievously. Finally ready to begin to let go of her fading infancy, the sweet milk breath, damp cloth against my skin, I weaned her. Mostly, she's cooperated. But sometimes at night she reaches between the buttons of my nightgown, croons to me flirtatiously, feeling for my breasts, talking me into it—and I want to give in. For her, yes, but for myself also. I miss her hands on my breastbone, her little massages, her little bites.

They both still want to sleep in my bed, captured under my arms like baby birds, tucked under my wings, tucked beneath the heavy comforter. I *am* the heavy comforter, the hand over their hearts. I'm the one who remembers their slick hot entrance, their folded bones. I carried them in my body; now I carry them on my body. Their touch marks me. "Stay close by," I call to her as she runs. "Stay by Mama." Each day, she runs a little farther away, turns her head and laughs.

WE ARE AT the ocean, a beach bordered by a hillside of tall evergreens and boggy horse pasture. It's clear but cold, too cold for the snowy egrets we've sometimes seen here standing like lonely, hunch-shouldered angels in the cattails. My daughter is playing, making a comfortable seat from a chunk of driftwood, running from the surf, crouching in the sand, which is not quite normal sand: At close range, it's composed of infinitessimally small rounded pebbles the color of Italy—oxblood, smoke, lapis lazuli, mustard, stone.

I'm watching her, holding her shoes, my back to the November sun, when I notice she's playing in my shadow. My hair is blowing, my long shape darkening the colorful sand—and there she is, my little girl, inside me again. "Celeste!" I say, waving my arms. "Look! You're in my shadow."

She does look up, looks around, but she doesn't understand or doesn't see, or maybe she's just so intent on the mossy stick in her hand that it doesn't matter. I follow her closer than I need to before I finally give up, keeping pace as she wanders, trying to get her attention, trying to get her to see my shadow and herself in it.

A few days later, I've moved her toy table into the kitchen while I make dinner. She sits in a yellow chair with her watercolor set, some wide sheets of paper, and a cup of water. Kiddie songs natter in the background. She loves to paint—the muddy pools of color, the swampy paper bleeding pink and orange and blue.

When I turn back to her a little later, a pasta mist on the darkening windows, she is so still, her hand poised, holding a slim plastic brush over the spilled water cup, that I think maybe she's fallen asleep. But no—it's her shadow she's discovered, her fingers duplicated on her painting, moving as she moves. She's so focused I wouldn't dare disturb her, and watch instead as she wags her thumb, tips the brush, moves her hand entirely away and back again. She's blocking the light, and letting it in. Learning that her body is ripe with miracles. Seeded with powers beyond her imagining. I know my place. I stand back, ready with another cup of water, out of her light.

My Other Mother

LORI LEIBOVICH

WE TAKE our mothers where we can get them—and they are not always the women who gave us life. When my mother checked out of my life for six years, I looked for mothering wherever I could get it—from teachers, babysitters, and friends. I found it in the form of a didactic eighty-year-old woman.

When I was fourteen, my parents were divorced and my father moved to another town. Six months later, my seventeen-year-old brother, Phil, disappeared from my life when a car accident left him with severe brain damage and in a coma, unable to speak or move. Suddenly, the world that should have been opening up to me felt like it was closing in. I was depressed and scared, desperate for a firm place to stand. But then the person I wanted to turn to, my mother, left me too—moved into my brother's world, funneling her energies into the child that she felt needed her most. For years, she spent her days at the hospital at his bedside—attending physical, speech, and occupational therapy with him; changing him, reading to him, mopping his brow—and returned home at night, exhausted.

It was my mother's mother, Florence, who stepped in to fill her shoes. Florence lived a few hours away, but she seemed ever-present, visiting often and phoning all the time. "So, what are you having for dinner?" she'd ask, calling right around six. "Pasta? How are you fixing it?" "Be careful tonight," she'd warn every Halloween. "People do crazy things." She drove from New York to Boston with my grandfather every month, always arriving in time to cook dinner. She was the pair of eyes my mother no longer was. Though my mother came home every night, it seemed that she never saw me; I existed somewhere beyond her peripheral vision. Her thoughts were at the hospital even when she wasn't, with the child she was trying to keep alive. So it was Florence who picked off tiny bits of lint from my sweaters, noticed when a button was loose or if a color was less than flattering. It was Florence who made sure I was fed well and clothed, who paid attention when I talked about the latest styles.

My grandmother divided the world into two categories: things she was for and things she was against. Ready-made cake mixes? Against. Hair spray? For. Demi Moore naked and pregnant on the cover of *Vanity Fair*? Very, very against. By contrast, my mother, a 1960s-trained therapist, was all about gray areas and allowing me "space to grow." When I was ten years old and asked her permission to stay up past my bedtime to watch the two-hour *Love Boat* special, for example, she said, "You'll have to use your own judgment." Had I posed the same question to Florence, she would have replied, with her hands firmly on her hips, "If you stay up late to watch that junk, you'll be exhausted tomorrow and your eyes will be puffy."

Looking back on it now, it is ironic that I was suddenly being raised by the woman my mother had tried to push out of her life. Growing up, my mother had felt suffocated by Florence's black-and-white worldviews; when she left home for college, she vowed never to live near her mother again. Under other circumstances, I might have resented Florence's style of mothering too. What fourteen-year-old wants anyone, let alone some-one generations older, telling them what to do? But as my world unraveled, I wanted *less* space to grow, and Florence's binary views and autocratic manner gave my life the boundaries I needed.

With her blunt, unyielding words, Florence educated me about the rights and wrongs of womanhood. Walking out the door without lipstick was akin to leaving the house undressed. Dressing in black before age twenty was "morose." Going bra-less in public was out of the question. (My grandmother insisted she was "modern"; she was all for a woman showing her "shape," as she called it, as long as she didn't "spill.")

The summer before ninth grade, Florence took me to purchase my first bras. She notified the store beforehand of our mission. The shop sold bras exclusively; no panties, bathing suits, peignoirs, or other "intimate apparel." Such frivolous diversions might distract customers from the serious task at hand: finding the right bra for every breast on Long Island. I would need one standard white bra, one beige bra to wear underneath white summer shirts, one navy-blue bra for winter (black was too racy), and one pink bra—"just because."

I stood in the dressing room in nothing but my shorts, arms folded across my chest. The saleswomen buzzed around me, leaving the door wide open while they tugged and futzed, cupped my breasts with their hands, wrapped tape measures around me. It might have been my body, but it was their canvas. Florence directed the sales team from her perch outside the dressing room and provided her own instruction: Always bend at the waist and shake your breasts into the cup; if the material bunches or gapes, get rid of it. When you find a bra that fits well, get a few. "A well-fitting bra is a gift," Florence said. "And like lipsticks, bras can be discontinued." I left that day with four new bras that my grandmother said were perfect for my new, womanly shape.

Florence had standards for underpants and bathing suits too, and was adamant that they completely cover a girl's "tushy." "Too small and they might slip into the crack," she whispered. Once I convinced her to let me try some high-cut briefs, rather than the hip huggers she was partial to. When I modeled them, she just stared at my pubic line in disgust. "I can see every hair on your crotch," she said.

Did my mother miss mother-daughter moments like these? I'd like to think so, but I'm not sure. Although we've talked about that period in our lives a lot—as I said, my mother is a therapist—we have always tiptoed around that part. The topic is just too excruciating for both of us. I do think that for once she was grateful for her mother's intervention. With Florence watching over me, my mother didn't have to balance my "normal" teenage traumas—boys and bras and prom dresses—with my brother's daily needs—pain medications, wheelchairs, health insurance.

I LOVED LEAVING the stillness of my house and visiting Florence's gleaming home, where the television always hummed and china candy dishes were always full. In the late mornings after breakfast, when my grandfather disappeared into his study, she turned on one of the half-dozen soap operas she watched religiously and got to work kneading dough, skinning chicken, or lovingly chopping liver. She eschewed modern conveniences like electric mixers and Cuisinarts, preferring to dominate her batter by hand. Each buttery chocolate-chip cookie was tinged golden brown, each matzo ball shaped like a perfect globe. Visits to Florence's meant a release from the ten-minute chicken dishes my mother and I ate in silence when she returned home from the hospital. At Florence's, I devoured thick slabs of London broil, mashed potatoes, and slices of homemade pie, letting her serve me seconds—and sometimes even thirds—trying to fill myself until the next visit.

Although Florence never did teach me how to cook, she liked me to keep her company while she cooked. She'd sit me on a stool and go about her work, chatting on and on about how none of the other ladies on the block could make a decent pie crust, or she would ask me questions about things she'd read about in her women's magazines. I was a fresh audience, unlike my grandfather, who had heard about her various quibbles with neighbors and friends dozens of times before. I can still picture her darting about the kitchen in her "comfort clothes"—stretchy polyester pants with a matching cotton blouse and an apron—her bleached blond hair relentlessly in place through long hours in the steamy kitchen, petrified as it was with layers of Alberto VO5 hair spray.

As far as I know, there was only one problem that my grandmother couldn't vanquish with a time-tested rule or dictum: my parents' divorce. Florence never got over it. Sure, she knew the statistics about divorce—she watched *Oprah*. But in her family?

Since the day she met my grandfather, Sam, at a temple dance when they were both twenty-three, they had remained giddy and inseparable. Once, while sitting in her kitchen, I asked Florence straight out: What kept them happily and eagerly bound, made them want to sit down together every day for breakfast, lunch, and dinner? My grandmother put down her paring knife and smiled mischievously, her blue eyes dancing. What kept them from losing interest, getting bored, straying, or giving up, she explained, was that they both relished small freedoms and let each other indulge in those freedoms apart from, but not in violation of, their relationship. In short, they were both shameless, unapologetic, and very gifted flirts.

We joked that Florence had her "boyfriends" and Sam his "lady friends," most of whom lived in their neighborhood. Ladies on the block called Sam in "emergencies." "Sam," Regina would say breathlessly into the phone, "I forgot to grease my pan before I put it in the oven. Can you come over and help me get the cake out?" And Florence let him go, never asking why Regina's husband, Stanley, couldn't do the job. Florence's daily shopping rounds were opportunities for steal-ing glances. She had a thing for the man at the fruit stand. He liked her gumption, he told her, because she insisted he weigh her fruit with the stems off. I also suspected she had an eye for the butcher. While he wielded his cleaver, shirtsleeves rolled up just enough to reveal his muscles, she would pose questions about cuts of meat, the business—anything in order to linger. Sometimes he would wink and add an extra slab of beef to her order.

Well into their eighties, my grandparents were sitting on a plane holding hands when a flight attendant asked how long they had been married. "We're on our honeymoon," Florence replied.

When I went off to college, Florence continued to mother me from two thousand miles away. She reasoned, correctly, that I wouldn't be able to find a decent bagel in the Midwest, so she sent me three dozen every month, individually wrapped and labeled, along with homemade cookies, brownies, and noodle pudding (with directions for heating). She stuffed boxes with chocolate, pasta, cinnamon-flavored gum, and cans of tuna fish (as if I couldn't get such items in the Midwest, either), along with rolls of quarters for laundry and a couple of new pairs of underpants. On a piece of notebook paper, she'd write in her neat, condensed script, "Lori, dear—This package was made with love by Grandma and it was sent with love by Grandpa who took it to the post office."

My mother was only able to come back into my life nearly six years after she left it, when my brother died from a respiratory infection. But by then, I couldn't let her back in completely. Florence was the mother who had been there when I needed her, and it was still Florence whom I looked to for direction and approval.

My relationship with my mother had changed irrevocably. It was awkward, as if she were an old childhood friend who had dropped into my life and couldn't possibly know the person I had become. I don't begrudge my mother the choice she made; I don't know what I would do in her situation. But in choosing to be there for Phil, she had let go of me. I know that she still feels guilty about it. She overcompensates now, wants to be close to me, wants to *know* me again. But the daughter she knew is gone; the adult me was born during the years she wasn't around, shaped into a woman by another woman's hands.

When I was twenty, Florence died in her sleep on Valentine's Day, with Sam by her side. My mother and uncle had been invited to my grandparents' home for breakfast that morning, but when they arrived, they learned that Florence was dead and called the family. She lay peacefully in bed, her peach-colored nightgown modestly buttoned up to her chin. The smell of coffee wafted from the kitchen—she had set the timer on the pot the night before. Rows of bagels stood at attention in the oven, waiting for her to turn the knob to "bake." A kaleidoscope of fruit—melon wedges, oranges, berries, and nectarines—was meticulously arranged on a platter in the fridge.

And the small china pitcher she used for special occasions was filled with milk and covered with Saran Wrap.

I have to think she planned it this way, that she somehow felt comfortable dying only because she knew that my grandfather would not be alone and there was plenty of food in the refrigerator. (In fact, Sam lived for a year on the frozen meats and baked goods stored in the freezer.) Florence's death paralyzed me—even more than the death of my brother, whom I had really lost years before he died. She was my one strand of stability during those desperate, lonely years, and when she left me, I felt unmoored, unclaimed.

Dressing for temple two days later, I remembered one of Florence's more counterintuitive decrees: Never wear black to a Jewish funeral. She couldn't remember the origin of that rule, but as a girl she was told that wearing black was somehow disrespectful to the deceased. So I went to her closet, chose a fuzzy blue Angora sweater from the shelf, pulled it over my supportive bra, and left to say good-bye.

Can This Child Be Saved?

KIM VAN METER

WHEN I THINK back to that long weekend when I decided to turn my back on a child, I think not of the difficult parts, the tantrums, the constant emotional distress, the intense pressure to decide the fate of a little girl I hardly knew. Instead I remember one of the few moments of peace that we were able to create.

After dinner one evening, my partner, Margi, and I walked along the sidewalks with Julie.* It was getting dark, and on the corner an enormous stone ball rested inside a granite stand, a thin sheen of water gliding along its polished surface. A group of boys surrounded the ball, pushing it in its stand, as it began to slowly rotate.

Julie watched for a moment, then pulled away from me. She rushed to the other side of the granite globe and began to push. The boys laughed as they pushed harder, and the orb continued to rotate. I placed my hand on the smooth rock, let the water wash across it, and began to push too. With Margi and me on either side of Julie, we all pushed and suddenly our strength took hold. Together, it felt like we were moving the weight of the world.

Margi and I had been trying to have a baby for more than a

*Some of the names in this piece have been changed.

year, and in addition to our many failed attempts at donor insemination, we had done extensive research on adoption. Although we had been preparing ourselves for a baby, when we heard about Julie, a five-year-old in trouble, it didn't take long for us to imagine that this could be the child we had been waiting for.

My mother had called us late one night, breathlessly saying that my cousin Anne had somehow gotten temporary custody of an abandoned girl in Tennessee. Julie had been abused and neglected for years, and her mom finally gave her up on a street corner, signing away parental rights just before catching a bus out of town with her boyfriend. Anne was keeping Julie at her house, but she couldn't continue to take care of her and was desperately looking for someone to adopt. Were we interested?

I knew nothing of this cousin except that she was a born-again Christian who had become something of a family outcast after marrying an out-of-work, right-wing Southern Baptist twenty years her senior. And she knew nothing of me until my mother called and told her I might be interested in adopting Julie. Anne hesitated at first because she thought Julie needed a "mommy and a daddy." She would think about it, she said.

Finally, she came around. "All Julie really needs is someone to love her," she told me on the phone, then launched into the story of the child's troubled past. Julie didn't know how to use silverware, Anne said. She had been eating out of Dumpsters. When Anne bought her some chicken to eat, she stripped away the meat and began gnawing on the bones. After her mom left her on the street, Julie told Anne that she had been hoping for a new mommy. She used her hands to show how one of her mother's boyfriends had raped her.

Julie also talked about her younger brother. He was just a baby, she said, but then he had a heart attack and died. "Mommy buried him in the backyard," she explained. There were so many of these stories and they came up so casually, Anne didn't know what to believe. "I just don't know what to do with her," she said finally, betraying her earlier hopeful optimism.

Anne had made one strong stand—she convinced Julie's mother to sign over legal custody rather than just abandon her daughter on the street. Since that moment of calm reason, however, she had become terrified that someone—in particular, the state foster care system—would take the child away. She asked how soon I could get there.

I told myself that maybe by going to Tennessee, talking to Anne, talking to Julie, and getting some legal advice, Margi and I could make a difference. We could help to make some sense of the situation. But part of me could think of nothing except that this one trip, one long drive across five states, might miraculously turn us into parents. Surely we could make this okay. I thought vaguely about therapy, private school. We could help Julie talk it all through. Maybe together we could make a new life.

During the slow, 750-mile drive to the foothills of the Great Smokies, Margi and I could think of almost nothing but meeting Julie. This part of Tennessee is tourist country, thick with souvenir shops, carnival rides, and outlet malls, and it took us more than an hour to drive the last ten miles from the interstate through a drenching downpour. The morning before, the boyfriend of Julie's mother had called Anne, demanding money and threatening to steal Julie back if they didn't get some. So Anne and her husband, Richard, were hiding out in a motel, trying to stay out of sight until Julie passed safely out of their hands.

Anne met us on the street with a large envelope stuffed with custody papers, Julie's Social Security card, a birth certificate, her parents' divorce decree—the paper trail of her life thus far. Then she led us to a musty basement room in the motel. I could hear a television playing inside as Anne unlocked the door. There was Richard, a man in his sixties with white billowing hair, perched on the edge of the bed, watching a TV evangelist while Julie sat at a desk, coloring a picture.

It had been almost impossible for me to imagine the reality of having this child in our lives without seeing her. But here she was—small, dark-eyed, with freckles across her cheeks and a little turned-up nose. Her hair had been long and thin, snarled and damaged beyond repair, but Richard had taken her to have it cut short and blunt at her chin.

"She's been coloring that picture for you," Anne whispered. As we talked, Julie ripped a page from her coloring book and handed it to me. Then, without prompting, she began packing her bags. "Do you want her to stay with you tonight?" Anne asked, but the question was rhetorical; it was clear that this had been decided before we arrived.

"Well, if she wants to," I stammered, not sure what to do. Somehow I couldn't say no, but I knew things were moving much too fast. Was this girl, whose papers we had just been given as if we were buying a dog, really going to become our daughter?

As Julie stuffed a Barbie into her backpack, Richard confessed in a hushed tone that he had told her a nice lady was coming who might want to be her new mother. "I'm ready," Julie said in a sweet, slow drawl, and she took my hand. Anne gave a few nods of encouragement and said that they would be going home now that Julie was safe with Margi and me. Then we were out the door and on the street.

We took Julie back to our hotel room, let her deposit her suitcase and backpack, and then set off to find something to eat. At a restaurant, we watched her devour as many pieces of pizza as the two of us put together. Although she had been eating regularly for at least the last week, with my cousin feeding her as often as five or six times a day, she still was obviously captivated by food. Her hunger, her incessant demands for food, became a regular refrain for us throughout that weekend. She seemed hungry always—for food, for attention, for comfort.

When we left the restaurant, we walked aimlessly along the sidewalks among the crowds of tourists shoving their way from one souvenir shop to the next. At a crosswalk, Julie grabbed my hand. "Hold my hand, Mommy," she said. *Mommy.* She had known me for little more than an hour and already I was Mommy. I said nothing. I wasn't her mommy, and I wasn't sure if I ever would or even could be. I glanced at her surreptitiously and saw that she had quickly cut her eyes at me as well.

We soon found that every public outing that weekend would be charged with the possibility that without warning Julie could reel wildly out of control. I remember our one aborted shopping expedition. We wanted to buy her some new clothes to replace the few ragged shorts and stained T-shirts that she had brought with her in her small, flowered suitcase. Before arriving at my cousin's house, Julie had spent the last few weeks sleeping outside on the ground. Her legs were covered with inflamed bug bites, and we stopped at a drugstore to buy her some medicine for her skin.

We were inside the store for less than a minute. Julie was bouncing from shelf to shelf, grabbing things, running. I tried to calm her, to hold her, talk to her, but she began to yell and struggle. Within an instant, she was like a two-year-old having her first tantrum. I picked her up and carried her to the car as she screamed. We sat there for what seemed like hours as Julie continued to scream and cry inconsolably. Finally she was quiet, her arms wrapped around her chest, curled in a fetal ball. She closed her eyes as if asleep, but I had already learned in our short time together that her sleep was not always real. It was a state she could enter seemingly at will, in a moment—a pretend sleep that took her to a place where she could escape, a place where she was safe.

Margi and I decided that stores were out of the question. Too much stimulation, too much in her face, and certainly too much for us to handle. In the hotel room, things seemed more manageable. We shampooed Julie's hair, got her to eat Cheerios and bananas, said no to television and put her to sleep with stories and songs. At night we would fold out her bed and read from the books we had bought for her. She could pick out some letters and numbers, and she giggled with delight over the cartoonish figures tumbling over letter blocks. I had the eerie feeling, however, that somehow this wasn't real, that she was consciously "playing" the role of child for our benefit. We tried out the alphabet song, not sure if she would know it. The second time around, she quietly joined in, singing as if she were reciting a creed. She seemed to be trying desperately to engage with something normal, to grab hold of the childhood that had been torn away from her until now.

On Sunday, Margi and I took her to Anne's house, with the hope of talking over some legal details before we saw an attorney on Monday. Although we had just eaten breakfast, Anne made Julie a plate of fried eggs and toast and sat her in front of the television with her food and a can of Coke. Margi and I talked to Anne about the necessity of seeing a local adoption attorney, someone who was an expert on Tennessee custody laws. Anne became increasingly nervous. Although she appeared to have every legal right to retain at least temporary custody of Julie, she was terrified that Julie would be taken away by the state. "You can't see an attorney," she said, holding back tears. "Just take her, there's no reason you can't just take her."

Julie had eaten half of her eggs and begun to wander through the house. She asked Anne for a piece of candy. "You'll have to ask your mommy," Anne said. I cringed. Anne was clearly ignoring reality. In her mind, I was already Julie's mom and we were free to take her "home."

Julie sat down at an old electric organ in the corner of Anne's living room. I sat next to her, realizing that we weren't going to get anywhere with Anne. I began picking out a one-fingered tune on the organ. "Sing!" Julie commanded. I launched into a lackluster, off-key version of "Chattanooga Choo-Choo" and Julie rocked back and forth on the bench, trying to sing along. I put one arm around her as I plunked through the melody of the song with my other hand. Suddenly, she screamed, pushed me away, and wrapped her arms tight around her ribs, sobbing. It was as if the touch, the unexpected intimacy, had overwhelmed her. The boundaries between Julie and the rest of the world seemed to be constantly in flux, and in one abrupt moment my casual touch appeared to intrude unbearably.

Anne had begun to cry as well. "You have to take her," she pleaded. "Just take her in the car and go." But we didn't go. We waited for Monday morning, when we hoped to find someone who could bring some expertise to the situation.

By Monday it was clear that Julie's problems were bigger than anything we might have imagined. When we looked for a place to eat, she would become hysterical, desperately warning us away from fast food places on the strip. "That one has worms," she would insist. Julie would randomly pick out men on the street and run to them, hug them. In our hotel, she rushed up to a man in an elevator, grabbed his leg, nestled up against him. He laughed, slightly uneasy. "Where are you from?" he asked.

"Here," she said.

"From Tennessee?"

"Just from here." And I realized she was right. She was from wherever she happened to be at the moment. She had no real place, no real connections. She was just *here*.

Her explosions became more frequent. One moment she would be snuggling against one of us, reveling in the physical closeness, the next she would be crying, screaming, struggling to get away. And then there were repeated offhand references to sex as she would point at her crotch, recalling some unknown "him" putting his "thing" in.

When I finally got through to an attorney on Monday, I explained Julie's situation as best I could and said we had been considering adoption. She agreed that our legal position was sound but questioned whether we knew what we were doing. "Do you know what these kids can be like?" she asked.

I did not. At that time, I had never heard of attachment disorder, the condition marked by severe emotional detachment and often violent fits of rage that can occur in children who have not had a consistent caregiver in their lives. Since that weekend, I've read the horror stories—the couple who lost control on the plane ride home with the girls they had adopted from a Russian orphanage, the Colorado woman who beat her adopted toddler to death. These were children who had been isolated and possibly abused, who might never develop the resources to control their impulses or form intimate relationships. But at the time I kept thinking of Anne's words: *All Julie needs is someone to love her.* I wanted to believe that.

"Some of these kids just can't connect, can't attach," the attorney continued. "They can end up robbing you, hurting you. They can ruin your life." I became terrified as I listened. I knew I wanted to have children, but was I ready for *this* child? Were we ready for the years of therapy, the sadness, the anger? And if we weren't, who would be? I wanted to run for my car and head north without looking back. Instead, I arranged an appointment for a psychiatric evaluation of Julie.

Margi and I had reached a state of barely restrained panic by the time we sat in the psychiatrist's waiting room. As usual, Julie did not hesitate to walk away with a total stranger. She willingly took the doctor's hand and followed him to the playroom where they would talk while we endured a tense forty minutes of waiting. Finally, the doctor waved me over to his office. He began with the good news: Julie was bright, possibly even above grade level. The bad news was that she seemed to have definite "attachment" issues. He gave me a frightening timeline: For every year of abuse—which as far as we knew had been since birth—he projected maybe two years of recovery before she could become what he called an "attractive" child. He reminded me that puberty was hard, and she would be getting there in just about six years. "And this is a child who shouldn't be in a house with other children," he added.

"Because she'll need a lot of attention?" I asked.

"Because she could be dangerous," he said.

I asked him about foster care. "It's bad here in Tennessee," he said, echoing Anne's fears. "You've probably got a fifty percent chance of additional abuse if you go that route."

My stomach tightened. I felt trapped. We could take her home and commit ourselves to raising a child who was in trouble and who might never be out of trouble—or we could commit her to a system that might be worse for her than the mother who had been unable or unwilling to protect her in the first place.

"These kids can have a lot of anger and resentment," he continued, "and it's usually aimed at the person they spend the most time with, the person who makes the rules. I'm not sure this is a child who would grow up to love you. I'm not sure if you could ever have a positive adult relationship with her."

Back in our hotel room, we looked out the large windows, watching the traffic go by. I had been furious at the doctor when we left his office—I realized now that I was really angry because he and the attorney had confirmed what I already knew inside.

When I called my cousin and told her the news, she refused to believe it. "You can't tell me that she can't attach," she cried. "She's the friendliest little thing I've ever seen." And it was true. Julie would be friendly with the nearest mass murderer if he would talk to her and buy her next meal. She couldn't discriminate; she could attach to anyone and no one.

I started to list my reasons for not adopting Julie, emphasizing the technical problems. It would be months before we could complete all the necessary paperwork to get us approved as adoptive parents, months before we could even take her out of the state, and Julie needed a place to go immediately. As I rationally ticked off the reasons, however, I realized that they were really just rationalizations. Partly I was afraid—not that I wouldn't be able to handle it, but that I didn't *want* to handle it. This wasn't the kind of parent I wanted to be, the kind of family we wanted to have. In reality, the best reason not to adopt Julie was that neither Margi nor I was sure we wanted to. We finally decided against it.

When we asked Julie if she wanted to go back to live with Anne and Richard for a while, she yelled, "Yeah," I think without truly understanding. Within minutes she was packing her suitcase. We added to her backpack the books we had bought, the tapes, the crayons and markers. On the way back, she chewed stick after stick of gum while we listened to an endless tape loop of Wee Ones music.

We said good-bye to Julie in the parking lot of an evangelical church. I handed the envelope of papers back to Anne, and we embraced on the asphalt with this child between us, a child whose future we could only guess at.

"Can I have another piece of gum?" Julie asked. Margi fished around in her bag, trying to retrieve the pack we had plundered on the drive down.

"Sugarless gum!" Anne exclaimed. "She wouldn't chew that when I gave it to her."

"That's because she wouldn't let me have any candy or pop," Julie said, pointing at me with, I felt, a touch of pride. By the time we were ready to leave, however, she would no longer look at me. She turned away as first Margi and then I hugged her. She ran to the open doors of the church as Anne called her back. It was a hot night in August, and the congregation was in revival. There would be kids' church every night for the rest of the week, for the rest of the summer.

Then Julie was gone, through the doors and inside, and we were gone too, speeding out of Tennessee as fast as we could drive. For a moment I felt nothing but relief. We were free. We could go home and reclaim our lives. It was only when we were two states away that the relief slowly became stained with regret.

At home, with the help of the Internet, I began to search for families who had planned for and were ready to take on a high-need child like Julie. By Sunday I had found a couple in Florida who had already completed all the necessary adoption paperwork. Within days they could drive to Tennessee and legally take her home with them.

My last news of Julie came a few days before her new family came to get her. At breakfast, she calmly told Anne about her mother and her mother's boyfriend killing somebody with a kitchen knife. She described how the man had been cut, how they had pulled him from the house, where they had put his body. She didn't know who he was. I have since learned that one of the characteristics of children with attachment problems is that they will often make up stories—frightening, ghoulish stories—and tell them as truth. Anne called the police, who said they would investigate, but we don't really know if the story is true. I wondered what other stories Julie will have to tell in the years to come.

I would like to think of this as a happy ending, but I know that the likelihood of there being a happy ending for Julie is small. Now she has a family who will make sure she is fed and loved, but who knows what kind of lasting neurological damage may have been caused by the abuse and neglect of her first years of life—or even before birth? Will love be enough to conquer the demons her childhood filled her with? Yet the regret I began to feel on our drive home from Tennessee is with me still—regret for a life that I could have made but didn't, for a child that was not mine but could have been. Mostly, however, I feel regret for a girl's life that was twisted and nearly stamped out before it had a chance to begin.

Common Scents

CHITRA DIVAKARUNI

IT'S A COOL December morning halfway across the world in Gurap, a little village outside Calcutta where we've come to visit my mother. I sit on the veranda and watch my little boys, Anand and Abhay, as they play on the dirt road. They have a new cricket bat and ball, a gift from their grandma, but soon they abandon these to feed mango leaves to the neighbor's goat, which has wandered over. Abhay, who is two, wants to climb onto the goat's back. Anand, who is five and very much the big brother, tells him it's not a good idea, but Abhay doesn't listen.

Behind me the door opens. Even before I hear the *flap-flap* of her leather *chappals*, I know who it is. My mother, fresh from her bath, heralded by the scent of the sandalwood soap she has been using ever since I can remember. Its clean, familiar smell pulls me back effortlessly into my childhood.

When I was young, my mother and I had a ritual every evening. She would comb my hair, rub in hibiscus oil, and braid it into thick double plaits. It took a long time—there were a lot of knots to work through. But I was rarely impatient. I loved the sleepy fragrance of the oil (the same oil she used, which she sometimes let me rub into her hair). I loved, too, the rhythm of her hands, and the stories (each with its not-so-subtle moral) that she told me as she combed. The tale of

Sukhu and Dukhu, the two sisters. The kind one gets the prince, the greedy one is eaten up by a serpent. Or the tale of the little cowherd boy who outwits the evil witch. Size and strength, after all, are no match for intelligence.

What is it about smells that lingers in our subconscious, comforting and giving joy, making real what would otherwise be wooden and wordy? I'm not sure. But I do know this: Every lesson that I remember from my childhood, from my mother, has a smell at its center.

The smell of turmeric, which she made into a paste with milk and rubbed into my skin to take away blemishes, reminds me to take pride in my appearance, to make the best of what nature has given me.

The smell of the rosewater-scented rice pudding she always made for New Year is the smell of hope. It reminds me to never give up. Who knows—something marvelous may be waiting just around the bend.

Even the smell of the iodine she dabbed on my scraped knees and elbows, which I so hated then, is one I now recall with wry gratitude. Its stinging, bitter-brown odor is that of love, love that sometimes hurts while it's doing its job.

Let me not mislead you. I wasn't always so positively inclined toward my mother's lessons—or the smells that accompanied them. When I first moved to the United States, I wanted to change myself, completely. I washed every last drop of hibiscus oil from my hair with Vidal Sassoon shampoo. I traded in my saris for Levi's and tank tops. I danced the night away in discos and returned home in the bleary-eyed morning smelling of vodka and sweat and cigarettes, the perfume of young America.

But when Anand was born, something changed. They say you begin to understand your mother only when you become a mother yourself. Only then do you appreciate all the little things about her that you took for granted. Maybe that's true. Otherwise, that morning in the hospital, looking down at Anand's fuzzy head, why did I ask my husband to make a trip to the Indian store and bring me back a bar of sandalwood soap?

I have my own rituals now, with my boys, my own special smells that are quite different. (I learned early that we can't be our mothers. Most times, it's better not even to try.)

On weekends I make a big chicken curry with turmeric and cloves. Anand helps me cut up the tomatoes into uneven wedges; Abhay finger-shreds the cilantro. As the smell of spices fills the house, we sing. Sometimes it's a song from India: *"Ay, ay, Chanda mama"*—"Come to Me, Uncle Moon." Sometimes it's "Old MacDonald Had a Farm."

When the children are sick, I sprinkle lavender water on a handkerchief and lay it on their foreheads to fend off that other smell, hot and metallic: the smell of fever and fear.

If I have a special event coming up, I open the suitcase my mother gave me at my wedding and let them pick out an outfit for me, maybe a gold-embroidered kurta or a silk shawl. The suitcase smells of rose potpourri. The boys burrow into it and take deep, noisy breaths.

Am I creating memories for them? Things that will comfort them in the dark, sour moments that must come to us all at some time? Who knows—there is so much out of my own childhood I've forgotten that I can only hope so.

"Watch out!" says my mother now, but it's too late. The goat, having eaten enough mango leaves, has decided to move on. He gives a great shrug, and Abhay comes tumbling off his back. He lies on the dirt for a moment, his mouth a perfect O of surprise, then runs crying to me. A twinge goes through me even as I hide my smile. A new lesson, this, since motherhood: how you can feel someone else's pain so sharply, like needles, in your own bones.

When I pick him up, Abhay buries his face in my neck and stays there a long time, even after the tears have stopped. Is he taking in the smell of my body? Is he going to remember the fragrance of the Jabakusum oil that I asked my mother to rub into my hair last night, for old time's sake? I'm not sure. But I do know this—I've just gained something new, something to add to my scent shop of memories: the dusty, hot smell of his hair, his hands pungent with the odor of freshly torn mango leaves.

Boys Without Men

CELESTE FREMON

JUST AROUND THIS TIME three years ago, Academy Awards Monday to be exact, a tiny vascular balloon exploded in the brain of my son's father, inundating his left frontal lobe with blood. The cerebral aneurysm didn't kill Will's dad, who is also my ex-husband, as at first we were terrified it might. Instead, it unhinged the mechanism with which he encodes and decodes speech. When he talks to us, it's as if he's reaching from the bottom of a Lewis Carroll rabbit hole, trapped in a realm where the only language spoken is a jumbled blend of real words and jabberwocky. Will still sees his father for dinners and occasional outings, yet his role is more caretaker than it is child.

Now that I'm raising my son as a single parent in the truest sense, I attempt to be the best mother time allows, while also trying to do those things I imagine a father might. Will and I river raft, fish, and ski together regularly (he snowboards). I've taken him parasailing, rock climbing, tracking wolves in the wild. I've even promised to take him sharpshooting at a firing range because, although I abhor firearms, I want to ensure that guns aren't an attractive mystery.

But I'm not a father. And the older he gets, the more I see the effects of that lack. I try my damnedest to model for Will the way to be a good person. However, I cannot, by definition, tell him how to be a good man. I can't, for example, tell him how a guy should deal with a bully.

My limitations came particularly into focus a year after Will's dad got sick. Will, who was by then in the fourth grade, began coming home from elementary school in a state of high distress. He wouldn't say what was wrong but left a visible trail of emotional bread crumbs: bursting into tears at the smallest homework-related frustration; staring absently into an interior distance, his ten-year-old shoulders tensed as if against a defeating blow. Finally, after days of prodding, I got him to confess that he was being pushed around on the playground by a fifth grader. The bullying was mostly verbal: threats, name-calling, and some personal form of insult that Will considered so egregious, he refused to reveal it.

My son is a bright and, in most ways, fearless child. He jumps his bike and skateboard with an abandon that gives me the vapors. During the weeks spent at our summer cabin in West Glacier, Montana, he always manages to become friends with any new neighbor faster than I do. However, when faced with this typical schoolboy badgering, Will seemed to have no defenses.

Concerned, I rummaged around in my own experience for what I hoped was helpful advice. "Don't pay any attention to that kid. He only picks on you because he doesn't feel very good about himself," etc. The Psych 101 approach fell woefully short of the mark. "You don't get it, Mom," Will said quietly, then laid himself down on his bed and turned his head away from me. Over the next week, the bullying continued, with my son still unable to ignore or confront his juvenile harasser. Instead, he developed stomachaches and pleaded to stay home from school.

I asked Will if he wanted me to speak to the bully. He said, "No," with extreme prejudice. I tried reporting the kid to the school principal, an unnaturally cheery woman who informed me she could do nothing unless my son would come to her office and repeat to her exactly what the other kid was saying. Then she could bring both boys in for "conflict resolution."

"Yeah, right," Will said with a horrified roll of his eyes.

"I wish I could talk to my dad," he said. Yes. Of course.

Groping for a substitute male perspective, I called my brother, a good and caring man, hoping he could help. He offered Will a string of snappy retorts he might toss back at the offending child. While the quips were great in theory, and made Will laugh, in practice he wasn't destined to be the Noël Coward of the playground. The bullying, the stomachaches, the distress continued. Then, just when it seemed he must somehow hang tough until the fifth grader left for middle school, aid materialized in the most unexpected manner: Crazy Ace called from prison. Deus ex gang member.

I had been working as a journalist specializing in East Los Angeles street gangs for seven years. It's an admittedly peculiar specialty for a middle-aged white woman, and there were times during those years when I found myself shuttling schizophrenically between yuppie Cub Scout meetings and urban shoot-outs, a fact that did not, I'm sure, add to my son's sense of security. However, there were payoffs too, in the form of relationships. I got to know scores of gang members well—some of whom call me from correctional institutions when they get locked up. A homeboy with the street name of Crazy Ace was then among my most regular callers.

In order to rise high in the ranks of street gangs, one must possess intelligence, a bad-ass, ultra-cool persona, and the ability not to blink in the face of danger. Ace had all those qualities in lavish abundance. So the next time he called, on a whim I decided to apprise him of my son's dilemma and ask if he had any advice. He suggested I put Will on the phone. Will had met Ace only once in the past, but remembered him vividly. Wide-eyed, he took the receiver and listened.

Afterward I asked Ace what he'd told my kid. "Just mainly to try not to let it get to him," he said. Exactly what both my brother and I had already advised. But coming from the infamous Crazy Ace, it had weight. Within days, Will seemed calmer.

A week later, I dragged another gang member into the role of counselor. This time it was a homeboy named Grumpy, who imparted essentially the same tips Ace had given. "But," he added, jotting something down on a piece of paper, "give your son my pager number. And tell him, if that kid keeps giving him trouble, to just page me. I'll come up and have a word with that little fool."

This last was said as an affectionate joke, and I passed it all on to Will as such. Joke or no, the bodyguard idea cheered him up immensely. Grumpy, as his name suggests, looks like a huge, tattooed version of the bad-tempered Disney dwarf. The idea, however fanciful, of this enormous gangster suddenly showing up on the Topanga Elementary School playground to growl menacingly at my son's attacker, "You got a problem with my friend Will?" . . . well, it was delicious beyond expression!

The bully problem wasn't solved overnight. But somehow Will ceased to be tormented and, under the unlikely tutelage of Grumpy and Ace, a new confidence bloomed in his demeanor. The bullying incident also precipitated a sea change in me as a single parent—albeit a discomforting one.

When I first began investigating gang life, I recognized right away that, although there are many causal threads leading to the tragedy of gang warfare, one thread is most consistently present: The majority of gang members are boys raised without fathers. Without male role models, they turn to one another and the street in order to fabricate their manhood. The results are chronicled each night on the evening news.

In the beginning of my research, I failed to connect the homeboys' problems with the kind of issues my own son was likely to encounter. After all, they were born into grinding poverty, raised by overwhelmed mothers who found themselves trapped in a permanent underclass. Will, on the other hand, was being brought up in an enlightened, affluent neighborhood, with a caring extended family and a mother who attempted daily to open to him a myriad of possibilities. Looking back, I think my inability to see obvious points of similarity was partly denial. It was also partly a result of the fact that Will was still young, and the no-father crisis had yet to reach gale force.

Following the bully incident I began to see a different picture. Surely, my son was in no danger of becoming a gang member. But what of more subtle threats to his soul and psyche that were looming outside the periphery of my gender-specific vision? After all, most of these homeboys had caring mothers too. Yet each spoke of the loss of the primary male in their life as an unhealable wound that caused pain beyond reckoning. How could I be so naïve as to believe that the pain—although acted out differently—was any less for my kid?

Will's dad and I divorced when Will was four. Even then, my ex was alcoholic, undependable, not the kind of guy who was ever going to coach the neighborhood softball team. I hoped, after the divorce, I'd remarry in a few years. Then Will would have a new male role model in the terrific husband/stepfather I'd no doubt soon meet. In the meantime, I made sure he had plenty of contact with his grandpa, my own dad, and my brother. But then the years came and went. My dad died. My ex had the aneurysm. And I didn't remarry.

After the bullying, it began to occur to me that remarriage might be an ever-receding mirage that would come after Will's most crucial need for a father had already passed, if it came at all. Suddenly each interview I conducted with a gang member felt unnervingly instructive. "By the time I was twelve," one homeboy told me, "I thought I was the man a' the house, an' ain't nobody gonna tell me what to do. If you the only *vato* in the house, you grow up thinkin' you the man. An' you don't know a damn thing about being a man."

I cried as I drove home from that particular conversation, frightened because I already saw inklings of the pattern in Will—a dislike of teamwork, the hardheaded desire to do things only as he saw fit, a visible well of loneliness that I often couldn't penetrate—and I dreaded what such signs might imply. In the early years of childhood, a male child can cling to his mother. During the prepubescent years, he must push away and look to his father. But what about the boys who have no dads to turn to? Some become mama's boys. Others spend a lifetime proving that they are not. When a boy is at that age when he should be identifying with the father, and there is no one, who does he understand himself to be? If he isn't mama's boy, he must be nobody's boy.

Of course, I knew that plenty of guys grow up without fathers and turn out perfectly fine and happy. When I ran across their profiles or biographies, I'd try to squirrel away each new example as a hedge against my worry. But, in truth, the successes of faraway men seemed too abstract. I needed to see some happy endings at closer range before I could believe they had any real significance for me or for Will.

During the first few years of my gang research, the situation in East L.A. was at its most calamitous. Nearly every night, teenagers whom I knew and liked were shooting at other teenagers whom I knew and liked. But time passed, truces were made, and boys I'd met at fifteen entered their twenties. Some went to prison, others morphed into their absent fathers and disappeared into crack, alcohol, or equivalent chasms of despair. But there were still others who attempted against impossible odds to build decent lives for themselves. Take, for example, Crazy Ace.

One of seven children, Ace's main male role model was a father who repeatedly knocked his mother to the floor and beat the kids on a regular basis. When Ace was six, his dad and his uncle strode into the house and pulled a gun, announcing that "this time" they were going to kill his mother. "All of us kids jumped on both of them," Ace told me. "That's the only thing that made 'em stop."

Awful home life notwithstanding, during his elementary school years, Ace showed promise in athletics. Then, at age twelve, as he was walking home from school, he was waylaid by local gang members who hurt him so badly, he spent the next two months in a coma. When he came back to consciousness, he formed a gang of his own.

Crazy Ace got out of prison in the spring of 1996. For the first half-year following his release, his future looked dicey at best. Although he successfully completed a job training program, he couldn't seem to leave gang life behind him, wavering for months between genuine adulthood and the magnetic pull of his past.

Then one day, optimism reached critical mass inside him and he made the leap for real. Now, he's working on staff for a Warner Studios–produced ABC TV series, and his bosses just love him. A few months ago, he told me that he'd recently gone to court to fight for joint custody of his daughter. Giddy with amazement, Ace described how he'd stood in the courtroom and presented his parenting strategies to a judge who ruled firmly in his favor. He credits his newfound victories to the fact that a couple of people believed he could be a different kind of man than the one he grew up imagining. One of those supporters is a priest whom he views as a surrogate father. Another is a woman: me.

Ace's transformation isn't the only miracle I've been blessed enough to witness. There's Ramon—aka Speedy—who came so close to suicide that the priest and I had to keep him on the phone while calling the cops on a second line to forcibly intervene. Now he's working for a company in San Francisco and is planning a big church wedding in June. And there's Alex, known as Flea, who went crazy three years ago after his non–gang member brother was mistakenly murdered in his place. Today he's helping other young guys like himself move away from the gangs toward a hopeful future. And Timothy—Tiny—who, when I met him, told me he was "dead already," but now is married and working for Sony Studios while shooting his own documentary on weekends.

I could name at least a dozen other young men, all originally considerably more at risk than my son, all of whom, at least for the present, have roused themselves out of the emotional quicksand that fatherlessness predicts. While I realize that today's good achievements are no guarantee of tomorrow's well-being, either for the homeboys or for Will, I'm gradually coming to regard these stories as countersigns.

My son is now in sixth grade and attends a public school for highly gifted children. He's a wonderful kid in whom I see new sprigs of maturity sprouting so fast it takes my breath away. I'm still parenting him alone, a process that's a constant roller coaster of challenges. Some weeks I feel brilliantly up to the task. Other weeks, I'm convinced any fool in the world could do a better job than I seem to be able to manage.

Just the other day, the subject of bullying came up anew. "At our school," Will told me, "the eighth graders try to beat up the seventh graders, and the seventh graders try to beat up on us." Oh, God! I thought. Here we go again.

"But I know how to keep people from messing with me," Will continued.

"You do?" I asked.

"I've learned how to have this look. It's like, 'I'm really crazy so don't try anything or I'll mess you up.'"

We were in the car at the time—a frequent venue for our mother-son conversations—so he was able to demonstrate the technique by narrowing his eyes slightly and staring hard at the motorist next to us (who remained oblivious). Will's mad-dog glare was a junior version of the challenging gaze I'd seen a hundred different homeboys use. On his young face, it looked somewhat silly and ill-fitting. And yet, there were also glimmers of calm and focus behind the look that suggested a self-possession I'd never seen before—still unformed, latent, but present nonetheless.

"Oh," I said, carefully. "That sounds like a . . . smart strategy. I think laser stares are good tools to have." The self-possession vanished and Will glanced at me sharply to check my face for irony. Finding none, he looked away, his pleased expression ducking quickly behind his recently acquired veneer of sixth-grade cool.

We didn't talk about it again. But that evening he gave me an extra hug out of nowhere, and solicited my company more than usual as he finished his homework, pausing every few minutes to tell yet another dumb joke to keep us both amused.

Okay, here's what I know: My son will never be able to sit down with the male whose face his own most resembles and talk about first dates, first fights, first cars, first any and everything. And he may never get to observe, under his own roof, what grown-up, day-to-day intimacy between a man and a woman really looks like, with both its raggedy edges and its joy. Yet, no life is without stupendous holes. We grieve for those we can't fill, and fill in those we can.

So, if there is no father to bequeath to my son the cloak of manhood, maybe the needed influence can be quilted together piece by piece. One quilt square from his uncle, who talks computers with him; another square from Sean, the neighbor who takes him surfing; another square from his dad, whose way with animals he has inherited; another from his late grandpa; his friends' fathers . . . and so on. Plus a square or two from Grumpy and Crazy Ace.

And maybe some of the quilt pieces are fashioned, not just by males, but by women—mothers even—in whose eyes our boys can see reflected glimpses of the men we know they can become.

Toy Story

JOYCE MILLMAN

I'LL NEVER FORGET the first time I saw Daniel. Actually, it was the second time—the first time I saw him, he barely registered: I just stuffed him in a desk drawer and went back to work. But four years later, as I was packing up to leave my job, I found him again, under a pile of press releases, magazines, and snacks. And I immediately fell for his somber little face. Luckily, I was a mother by then, so I had a use for him. I took him home, never imagining that a small stuffed tiger would someday reduce a rational, even cynical, woman to a delusional, paranoid, sentimental fool. But, then, I was woefully naïve about motherhood, too.

Let me tell you about Daniel. He's rusty brown with black stripes. He has a streak of what used to be white beginning just under his tiny peach nose and running down his belly, where a tag reads "Yomiko," whatever that means. He was some sort of special edition Russ plush animal and he was sent to me by a local TV station as an enticement to review its show about Marine World/Africa USA. (This is the type of graft TV critics get—toys and the occasional chunk of chocolate.) Sitting on his haunches, Daniel is seven inches tall—the perfect size for snuggling at bedtime, carrying along on trips (he's flown cross-country twice), and sitting not too obtrusively on the table in restaurants.

My five-year-old son, Mark, sleeps with Daniel, watches videos with him, makes little hats and rocket ships and race cars for him, and tells me that he talks to him in his head when he's at school. Daniel's clear plastic whiskers are bent at weird angles. He has a smudge of black (marking pen, maybe) near his mouth, which itself is just three little stitches of thread in an inverted Y. He's threadbare in spots; more than once, I've had to sew up the hole in the back of his neck. And he's downright dirty, because I don't know if his tail will hold up through the spin cycle. Daniel is every inch a child's favorite toy, and he is damn cute.

I guess what gets me the most about him, though, is the expression on his face—he looks very, very serious. He's wide-eyed and his head is slightly cocked, as if he's permanently waiting for something to be explained. He reminds me and Mark of Daniel Striped Tiger from *Mister Rogers' Neighborhood*—hence the name. And the voice. Which is my voice.

Not long after Daniel came home, Mark asked me to make him talk and I launched into the Daniel Striped Tiger voice, soft and scratchy and worried. Gradually, Daniel developed a personality of his own; younger than Mark (because that's the way Mark wanted it), he'd ask questions that Mark already knew the answer to, or mix up words and meanings so that Mark could get all superior and correct him. You know how it turned out, don't you?

I'm being asked to make Daniel talk *all the time* now, and the truly insane part is that, mostly, I do. He is, after all, my son. Mark, I mean. Well, Daniel, too—somewhere in there, Mark decided that he was Daniel's father and I was Daniel's mother and Mark's father was Daniel's grandfather. I know this all sounds very *Chinatown*, but part of being a kid is having imaginary friends, we figured, so who's it gonna hurt?

Well, *me*, apparently. I realized that I had become deeply and ridiculously attached to Daniel in the winter of ninety-six, when a wild storm knocked out power to Mark's preschool for four days. The school was closed and the terrible thing was, Daniel was inside—I had forgotten to check Mark's backpack for his stuff. Mark was a mess at bedtime, marginally consoled by our reassurances that we could go to school early the next morning and find Daniel. But there was no school the next morning, or the next. On the third day of Daniel's absence, Mark sniffed, "I know he's not hungry because I packed him a good lunch," and I felt my throat close up, just close right up.

I had my own worries, too. I worried that Daniel *wasn't* at school, that maybe some kid took him home—we'd had a narrowly thwarted Daniel abduction before. What if some inattentive parents didn't have a clue that Daniel wasn't their kid's toy but *mine*? I wrote a plaintive yet stern note ("Lost: Small stuffed tiger. Needed for bedtime! Please check your child's cubby and return ASAP!") that I planned to tack up on the bulletin board, but I didn't need to—when school finally opened again, there he was, on the floor of the playroom where Mark had left him. My son didn't shed tears of joy, but I did. How could I have become so dependent on a dusty little *thing*, I wondered. But deep down, I knew: The thing wasn't just a thing.

A few weeks ago, I was looking at some photos from a trip we took last summer. And there, in nearly every photo—like that enigmatic black statue all over the cover of Led Zeppelin's *Presence*—was Daniel. Mark and Daniel on the Cape Cod railroad. Mark and Daniel at Grandma's. Mark holding Daniel aloft in extended family portraits. Daniel is even in the picture when Mark's *behind* the camera—he's sitting on my lap or perching on the shoulder of an aunt. And that's how it is in our family: Daniel is almost always where Mark is.

Sometimes, when Mark is at school or out playing with his dad, I'll come across Daniel lying forgotten on the living room floor, or squished into a crack between the sofa cushions or sitting at the kitchen table, and I'm always startled by his silence. I never make him talk without Mark around—it just wouldn't be fun and, besides, it might even be considered the teensiest bit psycho. But I often hear Mark making Daniel talk when he's playing alone in his room. He can make Daniel come alive all by himself. I can't. When I stumble over Daniel during the school day, the little tiger just stares at me—neither one of us, I think, is quite all there without our little animator. Those are the times when I see Daniel for the shabby baby toy he is and I know his days are numbered. And it hits me hard, the dread of how awful Daniel's silence is going to feel when my child no longer needs him.

DRAMA QUEEN *for a* Day

Dogsitter/Mother/Nurse Puncher

ARLENE GREEN

THE WORST DAY of my life was the day my second child was born. Operation Desert Storm had happened and my husband was stuck in Germany for the duration. I woke up that morning, took one look out the window, and groaned. Pouring down rain. Great. I had to feed my friend's dogs. She had been called away on a family emergency and I was the best dogsitter she could come up with on short notice. I waddled out to the car and squeezed my two-weeks-overdue bulk under the steering wheel.

When I arrived at Linda's, there was a body of water comparable to Lake Michigan all over her hardwood floors. Her sulky Doberman had chewed through the king-size waterbed. As I was surveying the damage, I felt my first contraction. It hit hard. Catching my breath, I decided that the baby would wait long enough for me to at least sop up the water and drain the bed. Then the second contraction hit.

I couldn't find the draining attachment for the bed. Maybe it was possible to drain it with a hose, which happened to be outside in a ridiculously overcrowded storage shed. After much pulling and tugging and four contractions later, sopping wet, I got the hose loose and dragged it inside. The bed would not drain. Searching my brain, I recalled that you could siphon gas by sucking on the hose to get it started. So I began to suck, still in labor. Finally I got a mouthful of disgusting fluid. I then decided it was time to go to the hospital and called a cab.

I got to the hospital and they checked me in. I lay there strapped to the monitors when suddenly my contractions slowed down. I was eight centimeters dilated and the nurses had wandered off. I had to pee but I was strapped into everything and couldn't very well drag it all into the bathroom. I stood up and grabbed a bedpan with every intention of unhooking myself when another contraction hit. Bedpan clamped between my knees, I peed through the worst contraction I had ever experienced. The nurse returned. I less than politely inquired if she shouldn't, in fact, check to see how far along I was. She did this and then exclaimed, "Oh my gosh, you are all the way dilated and your water has broken."

Suddenly the room was a flurry of activity. I was too far along for them to move me to the delivery table, so they just wheeled my bed into the delivery room. At this point a nurse stationed on my left grabbed my leg and pulled it up so far that my knee was touching my ear. I looked at her with all the calm I could muster and instructed her to let go of my leg. She looked at me and said, "Push, push!" I more forcefully requested that she let go of my leg. She told me to push again. A third time I told her to let go of my leg and a third time she told me to push.

Finally I doubled up my fist and punched her as hard as I could. She let go of my leg. I gave birth to an eight-pound baby boy. They wheeled me into recovery and I promptly fell asleep. When I awoke, I made a couple of promises to myself—that I would never again dogsit for anyone with a water bed or give birth in a military hospital if I could help it.

Sex and the
Seven-Year-Old Boy

MONA GABLE

MY SON IS in love with me. This is no surprise. After all, I have nice green eyes and Jennifer Aniston–type hair, though regrettably not her long-stemmed legs. More important, I can tick off the names of the Los Angeles Lakers, play a tough game of Junior Monopoly, and have a high tolerance for jokes that revolve around the letter *p*. What seven-year-old boy wouldn't adore me?

I grew up in a house of rowdy boys, boys with no-nonsense masculine names like Jack and Tom and Jim. In some ways this made it easy for me when my son came along, red-faced and furious and eager to devour the world. I knew what to expect. Loud grunting noises and flying objects. Toilet seats never put down. Clothes left in a heap on the floor as if the Wicked Witch had just waved her broom and made the person in them disappear. A preference for toys with an excess of body parts and names like "venom."

What I was not prepared for, what caught me totally off-guard, was my son's romantic feelings for me. A few mornings ago I was standing in the bathroom, looking like a mean raccoon. My hair was piled loosely on my head, mascara ringed my eyes from the night before. "You look like hell," I said to the mirror. Suddenly, there was this little voice. It was so quiet and small, so unlike my son's normal, full-throttle roar, I almost didn't hear it. "No, you don't, Mom." I looked down. My son was staring up at me, his huge sea-blue eyes full of longing, his heart banging furiously in his little bony chest. "You're the most beautiful woman in the world." The scary thing was he meant it. What guy ever said that to me with such purity of motive and heart?

This intent pining for me began, normally enough, when he was four. I'd go to sit down on the couch or a chair and he'd slide his hand under me, grinning madly. I'd go to hug him and he'd burrow his little head into my breasts, lingering there a minute too long. I'd be taking a shower and suddenly the curtain would be flung aside by a pint-sized blond in Ninja Turtle briefs. "Mommy's in the shower," I'd say. "Oh," he'd say, holding his ground.

That my son was intense didn't help matters. He was, as the books charitably call it, a "spirited child"—which is to say volatile and active and completely unlike my friends' babies. Fervor extended to everything he did.

For a time when he was two and three, he was obsessed with his father. My husband would do something fairly nonthreatening—leave the room, say—and our child would go insane, flinging his skinny toddler self on the floor, or worse, hurling himself after my husband out the door.

I remember in particular one long, miserable weekend in Solana Beach. We'd driven down from Los Angeles to relax, have a good time, which only goes to show you how delusional as parents we still were. Every time my husband wanted to head out to go bodysurfing or for a swim in the pool he'd have to sneak out of our hotel room or frantic screaming would ensue. It mattered not that I, the mother, the one who had spent thirty hours in mind-altering labor, was readily available for fun and games, a romp in the pool. No, my son wanted his father. And how dare I presume to be a worthy substitute? Nothing like the rejection of a three-year-old to make you feel really small. But by then I had another baby and I didn't have much time to brood about it.

So when my son latched on to me again, it came as somewhat of a shock. He wanted me, but now he wanted me like Lyle Lovett crooning about unrequited love. He pouted if I didn't hug him tightly enough or cuddle with him on the couch. He cried if I wouldn't lie down next to him after I read him a story at night. "All right, leave!" he'd say angrily, turning his back to me in bed, as though we'd just had a lover's quarrel. Then, of course, he'd protest loudly when I did.

I tried not to let all this bother me. I knew that little boys did this, developed erotic feelings for their mothers around the time they turned four—it said so right there in the updated edition of Dr. Spock—and that eventually these feelings would abate. Some of my friends' sons were also behaving this way, acting like drunken high school boys on a date trying to cop a feel. I was damned if I was going to be uptight about it, do something that would make my son feel bad about himself, or, God forbid, cause him to grow up sexually repressed. A child of the liberated seventies, I was going to handle this right.

We had talks. Frank, straightforward talks. About how mommies and daddies touch each other. About how mommies and children touch each other. Whenever his hand would stray into the no-touching zone again, I'd remove it and gently remind him to keep his little mitts to himself. I bought a children's book that discussed boys' bodies and girls' bodies, with cartoonlike illustrations of vital parts. We said the words *penis* and *vagina* with devil-may-care abandon.

Every so often, my husband would happen in on one of these conversations, roll his eyes, and accuse me of hopelessly confusing our son, perhaps even warping him for life. "He's too young. He doesn't understand," he'd say. "Of course he does," I'd snap back. I had no idea whether he did understand everything I was telling him, of course. It's not like you can give a five-year-old a sexual comprehension test. But I was doing what I felt was right. I answered questions when he asked them. I kept the explanations simple. We rented *Look Who's Talking*, and in the opening scene when the talking sperm are frantically trying to penetrate the egg and my son turned to me and asked, "What are those little wiggly things?" I didn't flinch, didn't turn off the set. I said they were sperm and that they came from the daddy's penis and that they went into the mommy's body. "That's how babies are made," I said. "Eeeeuuu!" my son squealed with a mixture of wonder and disgust. I knew then I'd done my job.

Then gradually, mercifully, the sex problem went away. My son grew older, got distracted from his passion for me, lost interest. There was another girl in his life, Sarah—Sarah with the long blond braid and slate-gray eyes, who raced him every morning on the school blacktop. I was relieved.

Then a few months ago, something happened that jolted me back awake. It began with my son and his best friend, James, who lives next door. I adore James. He's as round, mellow, and dark as my son is wiry, incendiary, and pale. If there were a movie made about the two of them it would be called *Buddha and the Little Beast*. Another reason I adore James is because he finds it impossible not to tell the truth. This is bad for my son, but good for me.

On this occasion James was over at our house playing basketball on the patio. He and my son were talking about James's teenage brother. I was in the kitchen when I heard them giggling wildly and in the next split second the uncommon phrase, "He sexed her."

I came out to the patio. I stood on the steps. I looked at them. They looked at me. More giggling. I smiled. As Joan Didion once wrote of a scene involving Nancy Reagan plucking a rose for a cameraman, the moment was evolving its own choreography. James held his hand over his mouth and giggled again. I could see I was going to have to deal with this.

"What do you think that means, 'he sexed her'?" I asked in my most neutral voice.

"He put his tongue in her mouth," James giggled.

"He rubbed on her with his shirt off," my son added, even more hysterical.

I was tempted to say, "Boy, are you guys misinformed," but held my sarcasm in check. I'm not exactly sure what I said. I think I told James he might want to have a talk with his parents. I think I also said something to the effect that sex is not a verb but a noun, turning this potential sex education moment into a grammar lesson. But it was clear I was not off the hook.

After James went home, I got my son a Popsicle and sat with him on the porch steps while he ate it. I thought about what to say. On the one hand, I didn't want to make a big deal out of it, insist that James's brother had absolutely not been having sex and how could you think that? and launch into a detailed explanation of sexual intercourse. That seemed a bit neurotic. On the other hand, I wanted to be sure he had a handle on the basics, that he understood sex was not just an act, but caught up in all sorts of complicated and lovely emotions.

"Do you remember what I told you about sex?" I said.

"You mean about the penis going into the vagina?" my son said with a silly grin.

"Yes," I said. "But sex is not just how people make babies. It's the way mommies and daddies show how much they love each other."

This piqued my son's interest, so I went on. I babbled on about how sex was the most beautiful thing in the world that two people who loved each other could share. I talked about the magic feelings surrounding being in love. Then suddenly I noticed my son looking at me in a strange, sort of horrified way, as if I'd just blithely informed him his pet goldfish had died.

"What's the matter?" I said.

"You love Daddy more than me because you two have sex!" he said, beginning to cry. "I don't ever want to ever hear about sex again!"

Well, I just about fell over, I was so stunned. Here I'd given my seven-year-old what I thought was an inspiring lecture on sex and love, and he'd managed to twist it into some bizarre Freudian conspiracy pitting parents against their children.

I tried to repair the damage. I told him that's not what I meant at all, but that mommies and daddies feel a different love for each other than they do for their children, which only made him howl more. I told him I loved him more than anything and that he was being silly, which only made him madder. I tried hugging him, and he pushed me bitterly away. No matter what I said, he refused to calm down. Unfortunately, sometime in here my husband showed up, demanding to know what the hysteria was all about. I don't think I explained the situation very well because his immediate response was, "What did you tell him that for?"

Over the next few weeks, my son showed distinct signs of regressing. He trailed me wherever I went, refusing to let me out of his sight. He was like cat hair on a wool skirt; I couldn't get him off me. Whenever his father tried to hug me, he threw himself between us in a preemptive jealous fit. But he wasn't mad at my husband, it was me he was furious with. No matter how much affection I gave him, he accused me of giving his sister and his father more. I felt terrible, guilty. After all, wasn't I the one who'd screwed him up, made him hopelessly insecure?

"What should I do?" I asked my friend Maura on the phone one day. "He won't leave me alone."

"I don't know," she said. "Have you tried seeing if anything's been written about it?"

The next day, I went to a bookstore near my office in Westwood. I sat down on the floor in front of the parenting section and scanned the titles until my eyes felt bloody. There were books on infancy, books on potty training, books on "growing girls," books celebrating motherhood, books exposing motherhood. There was also, to my great relief, an entire shelf of books on adolescence and, to my general annoyance, a slew of books on the "new father." But nothing vaguely titled *How to Deal with Your Seven-Year-Old Son's Sexual Interest in You.* Sitting there, I suddenly felt this lump in my throat, which I recognized as a perverse nostalgia for the days when I could flip open Penelope Leach or T. Berry Brazelton and find exactly the advice I needed on tantrums or separation anxiety or when to introduce solid foods. I looked so hard that when I finally stood up I felt disoriented, like I do when I've been at the Glendale Galleria too long with the kids and if I don't get out of there in the next ten seconds, I'm going to start screaming in Hindi.

Time passed. I was quiet. I did not open my big mouth about sex. When my son was overly demanding of my attention, I tried to give it to him without being indulgent. I told him I loved him often, as I had done from the moment he was born. "You have no idea how much I love you," he said to me at night when I tucked him in bed. "Oh, yes, I do," I sighed.

Then one Saturday afternoon, he was playing out on the patio and he said, "I'm not going to worry about sex anymore." Just like that. I wanted desperately to ask him what had brought him to this newfound state of inner peace, but I controlled myself. I smiled. He smiled back. I was happy he felt okay again.

Things have calmed down considerably since then. I wish I could tell you why. I wish I could say it's because of some incredibly wise thing I did or said. Or some marvelous chapter in a book I'd read. But the truth is, I think my son's attraction to me was like every phase of childhood, only a matter of his growing out of it, of the vagaries of character. Of a little boy who will always be passionate about everything in his life. Especially me.

The other morning we were sitting on the living room couch together. My son had his head in my lap and was looking up at me in a certain bemused way—a way that means he's either going to tickle me or do something wonderfully silly. Then he began speaking, like he sometimes does, in mock French.

"Oh, my cherie, you are ze most buuteeful voman in ze world," he said.

"Oh, no," I said, laughing.

"Oh, *oui oui!*"

The Baby Girl I Gave Away

AT A POETRY READING, I sit next to a woman I have known since our daughters, who are now finishing high school, were small. Between poems, my friend says, "I read your article about Florence Crittenton."

I'm taken back. She's referring to an article I wrote ten years ago for a local parenting magazine.

After the reading, she says, "We should have lunch sometime. I was there too." We're in our early fifties, but talking about where we were thirty years earlier makes us both look around to see who might overhear.

"You were there?" I say. She seems so well adjusted that she's the last person I would have expected to have relinquished a child after a stay in a maternity home.

"I was there in 1965," she says. "I was eighteen, just starting college. I went to rush week at Colorado University and then I found out that I was pregnant, so I had to leave before my first semester even started."

"I know."

"I hated the lies. We told everybody I was in California working as a nanny for a rich family."

"It was the same kind of thing for me. Did you think about abortion?"

"It wasn't legal. Was it?"

"No, it wasn't."

"I just went along with it. All of it. What else was there to do? My mom took care of all the details. My family told people I couldn't handle school. I would rather have told them I was pregnant."

The crowd has thinned by now. Her husband is looking at books.

"What was it like for you at Crittenton?" I ask.

"Full of shame and fear."

"I no longer remember that so fully. Meeting my daughter a few years ago softened my memories. Have you met your child?"

"No, I don't think boys are as interested in searching as girls are." She adds, "I'm RH negative, and that first delivery was the only normal one I had. After I got married, I lost my first child. We tried again. I had a very anxious pregnancy with lots of amniocentesis. There were complications, and I had to have a C-section. Then it was hard for me to connect with my daughter. My husband had to tell me to go down to the nursery and see her."

"I went the other way. I was overprotective, afraid of separations. My daughter had complications at birth too, and I had to leave the hospital without her. It was harder than it should have been." I feel my friend's assent. She must understand this better than anyone.

"I've worked on my grief. I've worked in therapy, I've written, I've done body work."

"I have too. But the grief doesn't go away entirely. I didn't grieve then. Did you?"

"Oh no," she says. "I just put it all away and went on with my life."

Before the 1970s, most unmarried teenage mothers put

their babies up for adoption. A 1993 *New York Times* article recalled that pregnant teenagers were treated as "pariahs, banished from schools, ostracized by their peers or scurried out of town to give birth in secret." Their secrecy was protected in unwed mothers' homes; the most familiar of these, Florence Crittenton Homes, offered sanctuary to unmarried mothers in most major cities for decades.

Twenty-five years after I gave birth to a daughter at Denver's Florence Crittenton home, my out-of-wedlock pregnancy was redeemed by meeting my daughter—an intelligent, intense, warm, amazingly verbal young woman, obviously cherished by an adoptive family well equipped to care for her. Yet I still think about that pregnancy. A woman I know asked me recently, "Why not just focus on the good that came out of your pregnancy? The birth was good, after all." She's right, of course. The birth was good, the child I gave birth to a blessing for her family and for me. Why not leave it at that? I don't seem to be able to; somehow, I resist telling myself or anyone else the easy story—the story of my child's birth and my reunion with her, the story that ends simply and happily.

At nineteen, I couldn't face the enormity of what was happening or understand what relinquishing my child would mean for me or for her. For a long time, I was afraid to acknowledge how complex my feelings were about the decision I made. But I've come to realize that giving up a child for adoption was the first act of my adult life. That means I need to get the story straight for myself, to tell the whole truth about the experience. I need to tell the whole story to honor the young woman I was.

THE STUDENTS I teach now in college-level composition classes, even my own adolescent children, think the sixties were a time of free sex, abundant drugs, and bra-burning women's libbers. But I was there, and I know that this picture isn't adequate to describe the whole decade. When I started college in 1964 at age seventeen, I didn't even feel tremors of the widespread social and political changes to come. The early and mid-sixties were simply an extension of the fifties, when race, ethnic background, religion, class, breeding, grammar, and table manners all mattered. Concern for keeping up appearances was pervasive, the sexual double standard taken for granted.

If free sex means guilt-free, open sexuality, it was a foreign concept in my college experience. All the sex I was aware of was explored and pursued stealthily, secretly. But evidence that other students were having sex came to light: unplanned marriages, children given up for adoption, and abortions sought even though they were illegal.

I was just finishing my sophomore year. Disappointed in college, disappointed in my performance in college, I was on shaky ground. It had always been school that stabilized me. But those first two years—with their large classes and the impersonality of lecture and test, lecture and test—left me feeling alienated and disconnected. I'd collected a transcript full of B's and C's and was wondering how I'd find a place for myself in the world.

Looking for something my college experience didn't offer me, I explored my sexuality timidly. I slept with David twice. He was a premed student at CU Boulder, someone I had wanted to be in a relationship with for many months. The relationship was tenuous, based more on mutual attraction than a deeper sense of connection that might have anchored a lasting relationship. And David's ties to his upper-middle-class family were very strong. My middle-middle-class family didn't really measure up, and his mother, who kept a close eye on her sons, must have hoped that I was just a passing fancy.

I don't remember how I told David that I was pregnant. But his response was clear: My pregnancy marked the end of our relationship. I didn't see him or hear from him after that. He retreated into his family. I learned later that he did tell them about my pregnancy, but at the time I wondered whether he had the courage to do even that.

I do remember telling my mother that I was pregnant. She was sitting on the couch in the living room; my older sister was hovering in the doorway, listening. Mom cried; it was the first time I'd ever seen her cry. I remember that she said, "I'm so sorry your first child has to be born under these circumstances." I didn't have to be told that I had to get out of my parents' house and out of their community. I suggested that I go to Denver. She knew how to arrange it. And she said she'd tell my father.

I was in turmoil. I knew something even worse than what I was telling people. I'd slept with someone else. It was a one-night stand with Harry, whose last name I didn't even know. I'd gone to a bar and a party with my roommate. Drunk, I'd slept with Harry. I couldn't justify that act to myself, much less tell anyone about it. It was unacceptable to be nineteen and pregnant, but to be nineteen and pregnant and not even know the father's last name was unspeakable.

I felt I had to maintain my story that David was the father of my child with my parents, my friends, David, of course, and my social worker at Florence Crittenton. Because the social worker would see to my child's adoptive placement, I had to protect myself and my child from what I thought would be certain rejection and absolute shame by claiming that I'd at least had something of a relationship with the child's father. At least

I knew his name and the particulars for an adoption study. At least I had cared for him, had been cared for. And on paper, he and I made good birth parents: Our child was considered a high-background baby, one slated for an especially good home.

I went over and over my story in my head, clarifying the details I would tell, making sure I was consistent. My story was believable, and I would start to believe it myself. But then I'd rub up against the true story: that night with Harry and the fact that I really didn't know who the father of my child was.

THE DENVER FLORENCE CRITTENTON HOME was a three-story red-brick building. It looked ordinary enough from the street, but once inside there was no mistaking the purpose of the building: dorm rooms, kitchen, school, even a hospital where girls gave birth, and a nursery where the babies were housed until they were taken off to foster homes and adoptive homes. There were forty girls, high school and college students primarily, most of us within a month or two of term, all of whom had somehow managed to get by in the outside world until we had to come to the institution for cover.

Cover. That's a good word for what the home did; it covered us until we gave birth and could return to school, to our families, to our friends. Until then, we used no last names; I was simply C.C., even on the labor and delivery record. In the adoption study, I was reduced to: nineteen-year-old, green eyes, light brown hair, five-nine, fair skin, allergic to sulfa. I even relinquished rights to my child in court under an assumed name, Constance Anne Brown. To keep our secrets, our families concealed our whereabouts from extended family, even brothers and sisters, and friends who might ask questions. Mine said I was working as a nanny for a wealthy family, that I had dropped out of college after my sophomore year, needing a break.

What was it like at Crittenton? On the one hand, it was a safe place designed to protect us from censure. And it was comforting to me to discover that the other residents were very ordinary girls, including the daughter of a minister, the daughter of two teachers, the daughter of a Wyoming rancher. On the other hand, we knew we had done something so terrible that it required that we be segregated. We were hiding away, putting our real lives on hold.

We followed a strict, institutional schedule. Far from finding it limiting, I welcomed the structure. We woke early, had breakfast. The younger girls went to school while the older girls did their assigned jobs. Mine was to help the cooks fix lunch by cutting up fresh vegetables; preparing large bowls of Jell-O, a different color for each day of the week; and serving bowls of cooked, limp, butter-soaked vegetables. This was one of the sought-after jobs, much better than swabbing floors or cleaning up after lunch. After our work was done, we could go out to walk or shop. Curfew was at four-thirty and lights out at 9:00 P.M.

I don't remember how I passed the rest of the time. I don't remember what I read. Or thought. Or felt. Did my friends send letters? I think so, but I don't know how often. My mother sent letters. I remember a package with her handwriting on the label. I don't remember its contents. I can see myself in the downstairs lounge, where the library cart was placed and where I took knitting lessons. I don't think I watched TV—it was on all the time, quiz shows, as I remember, during the day.

My dad came to see me once, unannounced. I'd taken up occasional smoking and was embarrassed to be carrying a pack of cigarettes, which I couldn't hide because my maternity smock had no pockets. My father didn't mention the cigarettes sitting in my lap or my prominent belly, although he must have noticed both.

No one took photos. There were no autograph books, no addresses were exchanged, no one kept mementos. We would leave our maternity clothes in a community closet so the new girls could use them, just as the girls before us had left clothes behind for us. Maybe there was wisdom in the conventions. Does an experience go away if it's not mentioned? In some ways, it does. Without the anchoring of words, without the repetition of a story, experiences do drift, get less distinct.

Over the years I've told and retold the story of my child's birth to myself, protecting the most profound experience I'd had in my life. I was afraid that it was in danger of getting lost. In fact, for years I thought I had written the birth story over and over again. But when I looked through the boxes of journals I keep in my basement, the account wasn't there. I realized that it was an oral history, one I recited internally.

My parents took me out to lunch on Easter, the only time they had taken me out since I had gotten pregnant. By that time I was about two weeks past my due date. I can't imagine what we talked about. Maybe their taking me out into public was enough. Maybe they had told themselves people might think my husband was in the army, my hands too swollen for my wedding ring. Or perhaps people would think my husband had died and that I deserved great sympathy. Whatever they told themselves, they braved being seen with me in public, but didn't linger after lunch.

At about nine that evening, I started to have contractions. I walked up and down the hall as I'd been told to do in a birth preparation class to test whether these pains were the real thing or false labor. The contractions began to come closer and closer. When I was convinced that this was the time I'd been waiting for all those months, I walked upstairs to the third-floor Mary Donaldson Hospital, where a single nurse was on duty. I was scared and excited, but for the nurse, I was just another unwed mother who'd come to term. She hurried me into a nightgown and brusquely showed me to a bed. She prepped me for delivery without speaking and then left me alone.

Later, the nurse gave me Demerol, which she must have assumed would slow down labor, so I wouldn't deliver until morning. But the next time she checked me, at midnight, I was fully dilated and ready to give birth. Horrified that I'd dilated so quickly and without a doctor for the delivery, she ordered me to slow down, not to push while she summoned someone. An intern from Colorado General came just as the baby arrived. The nurse said perfunctorily, "It's a girl," and whisked the baby away as if my seeing her or touching her would harm her. I looked over my shoulder at the nurse, bundling the baby in a blanket. Captive on the delivery table, I had no choice but to lie still and quiet while the intern stitched me up.

I wasn't surprised by this cold treatment in the delivery room; the people who worked in this institution simply shared the attitude of the larger culture. But I was unprepared for the incredible elation I felt, the exhilaration of having carried a child to term. Even the dreary hospital, the cold nurse, the impersonal intern couldn't dim this realization. I knew I would never be the same. It was, in fact, the very impersonality of giving birth that impressed me. I was Everywoman. It hadn't mattered what my name was, what color my hair was, what my age was, what my marital status was; I had delivered a child, a real child.

Not only Everywoman—I was for a few hours Everyparent, stepping back to consider another, putting self aside, not so much as an act of heroism or altruism or compassion, but bowing to procreation, the beat of life expressed in a new person, separate, marvelous.

The exhilaration was short-lived. In the midst of enormous hormonal shifts and all too aware of my raw emotions, I found the days after my daughter's birth difficult. I took pills to stem the flow of milk in my breasts and more pills, green ones, to stop the tears that flowed after I saw my child. We were allowed to see our children and hold them, even nurse them if we chose. They were, after all, legally our babies. I opted not to hold or nurse my child on the advice of other mothers, who said it only made relinquishment more difficult. I did pin my hospital gown together with a clothespin and shuffle down the hall to see my daughter in the nursery. Outside the glass, I looked closely at her, tracing her head, her ears, her nose, her mouth with my eyes. I must have visited three or four times. When it came to the nurses' attention that I was crying after each visit, they told me I must stop because I was upsetting the other girls.

Several days after I gave birth, my social worker drove me to the Denver City and County Building, where I gave up my child and promised never to attempt to contact her or learn her whereabouts.

WHEN I returned home, of course, nobody in my family mentioned the fact that I'd had a child. Twenty-five times a day, I wanted to mention it casually: "By the way, I gave up my child for adoption last week," or "By the way, my child's ears were shaped just like mine." But I said nothing. My parents and older sister said nothing. My younger brother, who didn't even know I'd had a child, of course said nothing. I sunbathed, dieted, and exercised, erasing the visible traces of my pregnancy. By summer, I was tan, fit, and thin, ready to return to college.

I didn't know then that the feelings that lay dormant in me, the ones I hadn't made a space for, would develop a life of their own to emerge later around the births of my other two children, my divorce, my children's gaining a stepmother, and single parenting. The grief, the loss—all the themes opened by relinquishing a child for adoption—would demand their due. Sometimes they arose as questions: Am I a fit mother? Would I be fit with the addition of a husband, money, education, maturity? Can I be loving to a child? Is this pattern of walking away when parenting is inconvenient something I'll do again? Will I be chosen for marriage? Is something wrong with me? However, it wasn't only the doubts that remained; the exhilaration and pleasure also remained as a benchmark against which I would measure later experiences.

Time passed. A new, more forgiving era emerged. I had long since finished college, earning close to a 4.0 grade point average those last two years. I even acquired a master's degree. I married and divorced. I had told my husband about my first child, and when my children were old enough, I told them. I hoped someday I'd meet her. It was stronger than a hope, really. I longed to know what had happened to her. I needed to know how the decision I had made on her behalf had turned out. I even joined a birth-parent group in which several mothers were actively searching for children they had surrendered for adoption. I stopped going to the group when I learned some of the mothers had illegally located their children's adoptive families.

I signed up with a birth-parent registry called Soundex, which matches birth parents and children only when both are searching. They didn't even make matches until the child reached eighteen. I knew I wouldn't be imposing myself in her life, but I would be available to her if she was searching.

Eleven years after I registered with Soundex, I got a call from the daughter I had given up for adoption. That was six years ago, when I was forty-five and she was twenty-five. She told me her name, Kristina Marie Zarlengo—after all those years of waiting, her name, this prize, was handed over so simply. We talked and talked: She had good parents. Her father had died when she was fifteen, she had an adoptive sister, her mother had remarried recently. She was in graduate school in comparative literature at Columbia University; she'd been raised in Arvada, Colorado, and then south Denver. All of a sudden, the facts of her life were right there, *she* was right there.

My memories of the reunion are not as clear to me as my memories of Kris's birth. There is no reason for me to protect them so fiercely. This could be talked about openly. I wrote about it, Kris and I wrote each other letters, I could tell my friends, and, of course, my children; they told their friends. This was a more public story. And I realized it was a changing, evolving story. The first phone call was superseded by others; the original letters from Kris—reflective, intense, intelligent— were superseded by new letters—equally reflective, intense, intelligent.

Kristina and I agreed to meet for lunch at a tearoom in Castle Rock. Walking toward the restaurant, I saw a young woman on the sidewalk. She was about my height, dark-haired. It had to be Kris. Seeing me approaching, she said, "Ceil? Do I call you Mother?"

"Call me Ceil," I said. We hugged, somewhat awkwardly. It was hard to know how to respond when so many emotions were surfacing.

I don't think either of us ate much lunch. Mostly we stared at each other. I didn't want to turn my head away. I wanted to take her in, savor every angle, every expression. I wanted to hear her voice, impossibly a little familiar even though she had learned to speak in a household unknown to me. I'd last seen her when she was a few days old. Now a full, complex human being sat across from me—mother, father, sister, grandparents, cousins, aunts, uncles, friends, teachers, lovers all unknown to me.

After that first meeting, I saw Kris from time to time when she came to Colorado for school breaks. We wrote, both curious and respectful. And then the story became more complex. After a couple of years, she wanted to find her birth father. I told her, had to tell her, my dilemma: The father I'd named might not be her real father. Actually, I'd gone farther than that in my mind. I'd convinced myself that Harry, the Harry with no last name, was Kris's father. And I'd built a whole scenario—one I'd never tested, of course—that he would have been more loving and accepting of me had I told him about my pregnancy than David was. It was an imaginary cushion I'd built into my private story, easier to live with than the truth.

Respecting Kris's wishes, I located Harry, rousing him from family and life to tell him I thought he was my child's father. He didn't even remember our encounter. Poor Harry. We met. I appreciated the disguise of middle age, my intrusion into this man's life somehow easier for me because I was almost fifty.

Harry had blood tests done: They were negative. The story I'd brandished when I was pregnant was no fiction. David really was Kris's father.

Nearly thirty years after I'd last phoned him from Florence Crittenton, I reluctantly wrote David, sending him a photo of Kris. I knew it was essential to Kris to know her birth father. In fact, locating him might be the only thing she would ever ask of me.

I was relieved to find that David was open to his child and to me. He had thought of her through the years. He even explained why he had withdrawn when I was pregnant: He didn't have the strength to see the situation through. He'd had to withdraw to protect himself. It was an honest response, and although my feelings about David were far from resolved, I could tolerate that.

About the time that Kris met David, she told her adoptive mother about having met me. Shortly after that, Kris invited her adoptive mother, her stepfather, her adoptive sister, me, my son, her birth father, his wife, and their nineteen-year-old daughter and her longtime friend to a picnic in Boulder, where we ate chicken and salad and chips and watermelon and talked. I got to meet the woman who was my daughter's mother. I sat across the picnic table from her, asking her question after question and learning what it was like to be Kris's mother—to be the one who brought her home after she was born, who was there when she cut her first tooth, who took her to ballet, who saw her through her father's death, who sent her to Europe and then to college and graduate school as a single parent. I met the woman who had been Kris's sister her whole life. Meeting Kris's family, I realized I was not full author of this young woman's tale. Genetic influence stretches only so far; I could see that my part in her life had been early and relatively minor. My private story—the one thing I'd held fast to all those years after Kris's birth—was outdated and limited.

Ironically, it was in finally meeting my daughter that I realized I really gave her up—and how great my loss was. The opportunities for me to know her in the way I know my other children are gone: I gave them to her parents and her sister. And in that way, I have had to give her up a second time. But now I know how the story I nurtured in isolation all those years connects to Kris's life and her family. Now, because it is a story my daughter shares, it is whole.

Coyote Dreams

CYNTHIA ROMANOV

IN THE MONTHS immediately after I filed for divorce from my husband of twenty-seven years, I was possessed of the strange conviction that I was going to have an affair with Peter Coyote. We'd never met, but there was enough of a tangential connection to prevent dismissing this notion as completely deranged: Peter Coyote is the friend of a man I'll call Patrick, who was briefly friends with my closest friend, whom I'll call Alexandra.

I vaguely remembered seeing Coyote in *E.T.* and *Jagged Edge:* tall and dark, terrific voice. Then one night, searching the Internet for information about Allen Ginsberg, I stumbled upon some prepublication chapters posted from Coyote's (as I learned he was called) loopy, psychedelic-soaked memoir of his days as a capital-H Hippie, a high-profile member of the legendary Diggers, and a performer in the original San Francisco Mime Troupe. These chapters did not break any new ground in the gray-haired-ponytail memoir genre. But they were, for me, incredibly evocative of the era, and delving into them was akin to experiencing an acid flashback.

I read them straight through, amazed at the power of the memories they commanded. Revisiting the era's heady dangers and pleasures—the giddy sense of infinite possibility, the seeming surety of social and political revolution, the electric charge of ingested psychotropic substances—I also revisited my own youth, remembering where I had come from, what conscious and unconscious compromises I had made as I grew up and bore children, what I had gained and lost. And recalling the artless lasciviousness of the times also brought into high relief my own muted sexuality, shaped by a long marriage to a man whose enthusiastic middle-aged plunge into the gay community surprised no one.

The timing was exactly right. Coyote's unbuttoned romp through the fields of our common youth made me remember who I was before I was the wrung-out wife of a man whose midlife crisis left a bankrupt family in its wake, and in doing so made me aware of who I might be after I was a wife no longer. Emerging from the trip stunned and a little disoriented, I bonded, gratefully, to my guide. I felt I knew him. Then I realized, hey, I could know him.

This improbable sense of connection was oddly reinforced by the fact that the literary Coyote frequently came across as a jerk. The fearlessness with which he revealed himself through his writing—his reckless honesty, even about some pretty callow behavior on his part—seemed brave and worthy of respect. It spoke of integrity to the truth, a quality with enormous appeal to someone living with the damage wrought by evasion and denial. I respected this man who was not afraid to expose the soft, pale parts of his past to judgment that was sure to be harsh; it elicited the same random, swift tenderness and sympathy I feel when listening to solo vocal music or recited poetry.

The harsh exigencies of my own private life—an out-of-control, soon-to-be-ex-spouse with a pro bono lawyer; a pending bankruptcy; a car literally about to blow up; the cache of unopened letters from the IRS that my husband left behind; a thirty-day deadline to find housing with no credit, no transportation, and no money in a community with nearly no rentals; a crashed hard drive; one daughter away from home for the first time, another daughter frantic over leaving the neighborhood; having to sort through and pack up the house while working full-time—left little time for earnest fantasy cultivation. But at odd times (a warm, fragrant, full-moon midnight in my soon-to-be-abandoned garden, the "Casta Diva" audible through the open door), my Coyote conviction provided a focus for the fleeting moments of fierce longing for someone to whisper my name, invite me to set aside my burdens and lie down with him in the dark. My palms ached with a dim tactile memory of the way a man's head felt, cradled between my hands as it moved slowly downward: Now that head had a face.

Sort of. In real life, I wasn't sure exactly what Coyote looked like. He was wearing some kind of space suit in *E.T.,* and the character he played in *Jagged Edge,* creepier even than the serial killer, wore an expression that strongly suggested he was smelling something unpleasant.

I suppose I could have gone to the video store and looked up other movies in which he appeared, but I did not have the time—and besides, I saw him in my dreams, literally. Coyote had an ongoing, mostly platonic role in a series of dreams that loosely knit the slender threads upon which my fantasy hung. I had heard that he bought Patrick's art; in one dream, he was in my house to look at my friend Alexandra's paintings and was suddenly dancing—a dream-shill for Mark Morris, whom I really do know, and know would love the paintings. Another sequence of dreams placed him in my kitchen doing the dishes—I had heard that he really did this at Patrick's birthday party. In most of these kitchen dreams, I could hear him dutifully rattling dishes without actually seeing him. But once he was standing in front of the sink, inexplicably dressed in full scuba gear—flippers, tank, and mask—and I awoke in a minor snit over his imaginary dripping on the little Oriental carpet in the kitchen. And once only, I floated into the kitchen to find him completely naked and clearly ready to do more than the dishes.

I was aware that the very circumstance that precipitated my bizarre fantasy—extreme stress—also contained its scope. I was so busy and exhausted handling survival that it was impossible to give escape much attention. So I made a conscious decision not to worry much over what such a fantasy said about my state of mind (and my grip on reality), while allowing that there was at least an outside chance that it might actually come true (some enchanted evening, big party, mutual friends). Scuba tanks were never a part of such wistful ruminations.

It didn't happen. The hairline thread of remote possibility was broken when Alexandra decided that a relationship with Patrick required more effort than it was worth. She broke off contact with him; there would be no irresistible pull across a crowded room conveniently provided by mutual friends.

Meanwhile, during one five-week period, I underwent a surreal bankruptcy hearing, found a house for lease, jumped through a series of flaming hoops to override my lousy credit so I could rent it, researched and bought a used car with a loan from my mother, negotiated a payment plan with the IRS, finished packing, rented a truck, moved my family, reformatted my hard drive, and hooked up the washer, dryer, refrigerator, and sound system.

Last week I surfaced for air. I put on Maria Callas singing the "Casta Diva," poured a glass of the infused vodka my son had given me as a housewarming gift, and went out into the backyard: another full moon, different garden, cooler weather, earlier moonrise. I noted, with a pang, that the kitchen dreams had not ported over to the new house and the new season. I missed my demon lover, and I realized just how useful my cuckoo construct had been.

My summer's fantasy provided desperately needed diversion from the extraordinary pressures of my waking life. It had the fail-safe advantage of being so far-fetched that there was no question of having to act upon it, which would only have been an added stressor. I certainly did not have energy to devote to any sort of real dalliance, and needed time and privacy to heal from the multiple blows I had been dealt. And it was fun falling asleep with amused anticipation of what might be unfolding in my dreams that night. It balanced waking up with sober dread of what might be unfolding in my life that day. In this light, my fantasy can be charitably seen as a life-affirming, as opposed to psychosis-supporting, response to challenges that might otherwise have sent me screaming into the street—or up a bell tower. It's still a little embarrassing, though.

Summer's over, thank God. My divorce is final, and my ex-husband's lawyer has tired of freebie saber-rattling. My younger daughter, happily enrolled in school with her friends, has calmed down, and my older daughter is home. We're almost unpacked. My life is on more solid ground.

Now, in an elegiac mood, I review the arc of my brief but significant time "with" Coyote and think of him with exactly the same indulgent affection I feel for some of my real, long-ago lovers. Who wouldn't? He was there for me when I needed him, did the dishes without being asked, and never made eyes at other men. The tender gratitude I feel for this exemplary behavior is quite real, and it would be simply petty to keep carping that the affair was not.

Double Dare

SALLIE TISDALE

FROM THE TINY BALCONY of my dreary hotel in Marina Del Rey, California, I can see a sprawling shopping center, a busy freeway, and a small kidney-shaped pool glittering in the dirty light. A half-dozen people drowse or read in the plastic chaises by the water.

I'm alone, out of town on business, and I have two hours free—two hours to pretend I'm alone in the world, with no place to go and no one to please. I go out to the pool with a soda and a book and find an empty lounge, its vinyl strips still sagging in the shape of a departed bottom.

Three chubby girls with identical black hair and ill-fitting swimsuits are playing Double Dare in the shallow end.

"Dare, or Double Dare?" the biggest girl says to the smallest.

The smallest girl flips her heavy, wet hair. "Double dare," she says, without hesitation.

"I dare you to stand on your head under water."

"Eeeaaasssy," drawls the girl, jumping in and flipping over.

A heavy, self-conscious woman bobs in the deep end, watching the dark-haired girls.

Nearby, a pair of prepubescent sisters compete for the attention of an older boy. Their swimsuits bag on their attenuated bodies as they shriek and call; the boy, his bony chest puffed out like a mating frog's, takes turns flinging them away from him so they can splash and scream.

A slim Japanese woman in a black tank suit silently leads her timid little boy down the steps.

And weaving through, as fluid and oblivious as the water, slide two teens.

The girl is blooming, about fifteen years old, unblemished. Her shoulder-length brown hair is pulled back and clings to her small head like a cap. The boy is a bit older, perhaps, gawky and thin, and his shoulder-length brown hair is disheveled and loose around his long neck. In the tiny pool, in the noisy L.A. haze, they fold themselves together like gliding swans. He holds her for a moment like a man carrying a child, or a bride; then she turns slowly and wraps her arms around his neck. He comes in close to her ear and whispers; she turns her back to his chest and leans her glistening head on his shoulder. He pushes off the bottom and they float backward to the pool's edge and pause against the deck, beside each other. He turns and she lays herself on his back and he slides forward; she ducks out of his reach for a second and he stretches after her; she laughs and rolls back to him; they bounce gently face-to-face, murmuring.

This goes on for a long time.

I read my book, drink my soda. And all the time, I watch. People slowly, sleepily come and go. The dark-haired girls are called away. The boy demonstrates his skateboard to the sisters. A young man arrives with fresh towels. Trucks rumble by. The boy and girl slither through the water together without a thought, seamlessly drifting between the changing swimmers. I watch from behind my sunglasses, and suddenly she catches me watching and returns my stare, stony, self-contained. The difference between us is simple. I am just another voyeur, dismayed by the distant object of desire. She is not dismayed. She is a universe of Two.

I've left behind my thirteen-year-old daughter, my youngest child. She is young at thirteen, younger than her own body, interested in books and soccer and her pet turtle. She is still very interested in me, in my position of safety and control between her and the world. She likes to sit behind me when we watch television and mess up my hair and tell me stories that invariably begin, "Guess what?" and eat big, sloppy bowls of cereal right before going to bed. She misses me terribly when I'm gone, and this time I wrote a note for the kitchen bulletin board to remind her when I'd be back: "Mom, Sunday, 12:30." If she were here, she'd be winning Double Dare; she'd lie beside me, drinking soda and dripping on her mystery novel in the sun.

But that will end like everything else.

I remember how it feels, their dizzy height of obsession, the centering of the universe around Two. I remember how all else fades like a weakening signal, to a blur, how when you are together, all the world is the world made by Two, and when you are apart, there is only waiting to be together. I remember when love and sex were one thing, as unbroken as this moist ease in the sunlit water. I remember how one falls in love and longs for the body of the other and, longing, believes in love.

And I remember, oh I do remember, that the ghostly adults around you have no idea, because they have never felt like this, and so there is no reason to try to explain.

Many years ago, when my daughter was still toddling around with a ragged bear in her arms, I tried to explain to an old friend how it felt to be her mother. She was my third child and I was still trying to find the words.

My friend had no children, had no interest in children, tolerated mine with poorly disguised impatience. I wanted her to know why they mattered to me.

I pointed to my daughter on the floor beside us and said, "I'm the giver and taker of the world to her." I was trying to explain this enormous responsibility, the weight that sometimes feels intolerably large. "I bring good and evil whether I mean to or not. I might as well be God."

My friend sneered at me. "Well," she said, "aren't you special?"

The boy and girl slide through the water. I watch, furtively, and think: her mother. Somewhere her mother watches them make their smooth way through the water. He pulls her close to him, a large hand claiming her smooth belly. She strokes his cheek. I actually lean forward off my lounge, almost speaking, wanting only to beckon her to the poolside for a moment and whisper, "Be nice to your mother." But I say nothing at all, and pretend to read.

I see the accelerating future approach. I've done this already, after all, with two boys—grieved for the silly three-year-olds, the gap-toothed six-year-olds, the willowy nine-year-olds. They've died and will never return, and I grieve. She ruffles my hair when we watch television and my back actually arches, like a cat, pushing into her hand, asking for more. She brings goodness to me and makes me fear evil; she gives and takes away the world. There are so many mysteries ahead.

I remember the world fading into the universe made by Two, and I remember how it shatters when that ends—and then, how it begins again, brand new. So much to do, so many mistakes to make for the first time. And what is there to regret? This is how the world goes, this is how it must be. I don't grieve for her—I grieve for me, sitting by some poolside in a few years, pretending to read so my sunglasses hide my hungry, tearful eyes as she glides by, oblivious.

I haven't seen my childless friend in many years, but I've replayed that conversation again and again in my mind. I hadn't thought I needed to say to her that it's terrifying to be God. I thought such a thing goes without saying. The risks are so enormous—the losses so sharp. For years, I've wanted to tell her how powerless that power feels. How it is to be a voyeur, subject to the most pleading of desires. I wish my friend were here, and I could say: I dare you to try this. I double dare you.

Dancing with Death

CAMILLE PERI

ROSE OPENS her eyes and he is there—his breath soft on her face, hollow little chest, eyes lit like half-moons in the night. When he was four, nightmares of fire would send him bursting into their bed to wedge his body between hers and his father's. Now he is whispering to her to come and see the midnight stars. They stand outside, two tiny human figures under an enormous sky. Rose is shivering in her robe and slippers. Toby's feet are on the ground but his head is floating somewhere above, her eight-year-old guide through the galaxy.

Rose opens her eyes again. He is not there. Toby, the eldest of her three sons, died eight years ago, but he comes back to her often in her dreams. *A parent's worst nightmare.* Now she wonders, Is that watching your child die or outliving him? For a while, it seemed that she was sentenced to live out the nightmare literally. Sleep would plunge her back into his early dreams of burning buildings and dizzying cliffs, and she would be helpless to save him. After a while, his dream-self got older. Now sometimes he is a young man, robust and healthy, as he was before cancer killed him at the age of thirty. When she has these dreams, she knows it will probably be a good day.

. . .

I MET ROSE when I was twenty-four in what now seems like another life. Nancy, a law student and dancer, had become my best friend and Toby my boyfriend when they each came out to San Francisco to start their adult lives. All of us were shedding childhood and convention, trying to figure out our places in the world; within the triangle of our friendship, I felt safe to be anything, to try out everything.

Nancy and I were friends until her death from cancer four years ago, just after her fortieth birthday. I thought Toby had left my life years before, when we split up and went on to marry others. Yet as he and Nancy were linked in my life, so were their deaths—they died four years apart to the day. Each died within weeks of my sons' births—no sooner was I flooded with the overwhelming instinct to protect my children than I was up against the jarring impossibility of doing that. Since then, I have been unable to separate them from my children—I often see Toby in the eyes of my older son, Joey, and hear Nancy in the laughter of my younger son, Nat.

For a long time, the lingering connection to my dead friends both fueled my love for my children and made me fearful. When my children were babies, I could avoid probing those feelings, but as they grew older and I started saving baby teeth or wisps of hair, trying to hang on to the parts of them that were slipping away, I could no longer ignore the promixity of loss. I began to think of Toby and Nancy not only as my friends, but as other mothers' children. And so this year, on the anniversary of their deaths, I found myself drawn to their mothers, and through them, back to my friends.

TOBY WAS my first real love. We met in the clouds, on the twenty-fourth floor of a posh Nob Hill hotel where we both waited tables. We were both creative and ambitious and romantic—and that drew us together for five years. When we got off work at two in the morning, we would sneak into the supper club where performers like Tony Bennett and Ella Fitzgerald headlined, and Toby would do a private show for me, playing Gershwin or Bach on the piano until the security guards kicked us out.

At that time, Toby was studying photography. I remember he would wind my legs around each other like taffy or sit me naked near a window to catch the light falling in halos on the curves of my body, shooting photos while a pot of spaghetti sauce bubbling on his tiny gas stove provided the apartment's only heat. He was the perfect first love—artistic and sensitive and playful. When he was hell-bent on moving in with me, he showed up at my door to woo me with a bowl of freshly made chocolate-chip-cookie dough; when I was angry and he didn't know what to do with me, he'd turn me upside down by my heels and shake me. He gave me beautiful and quirky gifts—a finely embroidered antique blouse, a bolt found while hiking under the Golden Gate Bridge. He pried open the French doors that had been carelessly painted shut in my tiny apartment so that I could hear the bells from Grace Cathedral on Sunday afternoons.

Toby quit school after a year; five years later, he was assistant cameraman at George Lucas's special effects studio, Industrial Light and Magic. When I think of Toby, I think of light and stars: I picture him on the roof of our building, sitting in a director's chair under an indigo sky, guiding me through the constellations before the fog wrapped around us and swept the view away.

The other person who opened up my young adult world was Nancy. We met in VISTA, the domestic Peace Corps, working at a San Francisco law office that represented children. In my eyes she was worldly—she had worked for the defense in the San Quentin Six trial and became friends with celebrated defendant Johnny Spain; and she was chic—she wore high heels with shorts and let her bra straps show long before it was stylish, a perfect role model for the shy woman I was then. She had a blessed sense of how to pamper herself and others— together, we drank freshly ground coffee, with cream, in bed; took saunas; ate oysters when either of us had any money; browsed at tacky lingerie shops.

Nancy was steely determination and generosity entangled with a wry, sarcastic sense of humor. When she became a partner in a criminal defense practice, she provided her clients with more than legal help—she gave them jobs, sometimes money and much of herself, in friendship and faith. But her first love was dancing. Even in a business suit she looked like a dancer—I used to imagine her gliding through court, her rib cage high, hands flowing in graceful arcs as she argued her cases.

Nancy held my hand through my breakup with Toby, at my wedding to David, and through my first childbirth. A few months later, when I learned of Toby's death, she was the first person I called.

IT WAS at Toby's wedding that Rose first noticed something wrong. Toby and Ellen, an animator and producer, had met at ILM and moved to Los Angeles, where they were married in 1989. "I remember looking at him at the ceremony and his back was shaking," says Rose. "He was pale and his eyes were kind of bulging. I wondered if he was high and for a minute I was irritated. Then I thought, Well, it's his wedding."

We are sitting in the den of their 350-year-old farmhouse in Connecticut. When I first came to this house almost twenty years ago, I thought she and Bob were the coolest parents I had ever met: Rose was a vivacious, thirty-nine-year-old mother of three sons—Toby, Todd, and Troy—and still looked like a model in a bikini; Bob was an illustrator who was just breaking into fine art with a series of highly sensuous paintings of dancers. I got much of my encouragement to make sense of the world through words here, from this family; it's difficult to be returning to write about them without Toby. This house is so familiar—the only thing new to me is the story of how he died.

The autumn after the wedding, Toby thought he had an ulcer; his doctors examined his upper body and found and removed a tumor in his lung. But by his first wedding anniversary, he still didn't feel well. The following month, they discovered cancer "everywhere," according to Rose—under his navel; in his rectum, the stomach walls, the portal veins to his liver. Rose remembers flying out to California to see him as if in a dream. "He just laid his head in my lap and said he was frightened. He looked so thin. I said, 'You'll be all right. We're going to get you well.' "

Toby's doctors had told Bob and Ellen that the cancer was terminal, but Rose couldn't believe it. "I felt like my stomach had dropped out," she says. "You hear things like they'll have one percent chance of surviving if it gets to the organs and you think, Well, my child is going to be in that one percent."

At Ellen's invitation, Rose and Bob moved in with them and began to take care of Toby during the day while Ellen worked. Rose remembers a night soon after, when Toby was in excruciating pain. "I wished it was my pain. I remember rocking him, saying, 'We're going to get through this.' And I believed we would—I had to." But by the time they got him to a hospital, he was almost unconscious. The oncologist told them he had three months to live. "He said, 'I don't want to see you back here again. Let him die in peace.' "

They did not talk directly about his death again. Instead, they lived with a kind of wordless understanding, taking their cues from Toby. Miraculously, he continued working as a cameraman on a television pilot. After he grew too weak to walk, Rose and Bob would help him to a director's chair on a crane. He finished filming three weeks before his death.

Bob had transferred his studio to Toby and Ellen's house. He was in the middle of a series for the Scottish Ballet production *What to Do Until the Messiah Comes*. His paintings suddenly became charged with anguish, the dance an allegory of Toby and Ellen's life. Toby would sit near his father, strumming his guitar while he watched Bob paint. One day he lifted an eyebrow and said, "Dad, if I die, I know you're going to paint me."

Ultimately, Rose and Bob believe, Toby died of starvation. His six-foot-two frame had shrunk to ninety-eight pounds, the skin stretched so tight on his face he could no longer close his mouth. "Two nights before his death, he came into our room and said, 'Mom, can I lie down there with you and Dad?' " Rose recalls. "He never left. Maybe he just wanted to crawl back into the womb. We'd just hold each other and reminisce. He said, 'Mom, if I kick the bucket, these are the things I remember.' He talked about how much he loved Ellen and Bob and me, about ILM; he talked about you. Then he said, 'If I live, these are the things I want to do,' and he talked about directing a movie, having children."

Rose says she can still see Toby's face in the moments before he died. "He looked at me with those big brown eyes—I remember they seemed bigger than ever because that was almost all that was left of him. He opened his mouth as if he was about to say something to me and then he closed his eyes and died. Maybe he was just taking a breath, maybe he didn't have anything to say. But that will haunt me until I die."

The family had all been there; she and Ellen were hugging him when he died. "We were talking with him until the last breath, telling him we loved him and not to be afraid," Rose recalls. "The only thing we didn't do was go with him. And I would have gladly taken his place."

PARENTS NEVER completely stop feeling responsible for their children; when a child dies, they still feel somehow to blame, no matter how old the child or what caused his death. For five years, Rose tells me, she reviewed Toby's life and found guilt in even the smallest details—from whether she let him eat too much candy as a child to a family fight that was a turning point in his life. Toby had been out drinking with high school friends when he flipped his parents' jeep. "Fortunately, no one was hurt, but Bob blew up," Rose recalls. "He said, 'After graduation you're out of here.' I think it was too soon—he had just turned eighteen and he wasn't ready. Intellectually, I know it didn't cause the cancer, but maybe it had some impact, weakened his immune system. Maybe I should have stood up to Bob more."

Alone in San Francisco, Toby got a room in a transient hotel. "He'd call and say, 'I'm thinking of coming home.' I'd say, 'Come back,' but Bob would say, 'Stick it out a little longer. I'm sure you'll find work.' He was talking from his own experience: When he was eighteen, he went to New York with his portfolio, stayed for a week, and came home. He didn't want Toby to have that regret." If Toby had lived, I realize, this would be part of his success story, what made him, but now it is forever tinged with sadness.

IN THE LAST century, when up to half of the babies born in the United States died in childhood and parents could lose all of their children in a single epidemic, it was a common practice to photograph the dead or dying. Most of the postmortem photos disappeared with the people who treasured them; some that remain, including many of children, are gathered in a collection called *Sleeping Beauty: Memorial Photography in America*. They are strangely beautiful, reminders of an age when people looked more steadily at death because they had no choice. In some, the grieving mother cradles a dead child in her lap like a stiff little doll. In one sequence, a ball lies on a bed near the limp, open hand of a dying boy; in the next picture, the child is dead. Postmortem photographs were often the only images existing of these children, and they were cherished—hung in homes, worn in lockets, sent to relatives and friends.

Bob did paint Toby. His work now hangs in their home: huge, grief-wreathed portraits of a young man whose gaze stays clear and serene while disease destroys his body. They are both beautiful and raw, filled with a palpable rage and tender, bereaved love. And for a year after Toby's death, they were almost all Bob could do.

"When a woman loses a child, she loses her past, present, and future," he says. "A man loses his future. Toby was an extension of me." The only way for Bob to reclaim him was through painting. "As long as I have pictures of somebody, I have them. I don't know that I could ever go back and do them now. I don't think I could do a realistic picture of his face any-more. But he's still there, in some way, in every painting I do."

DEATH HOVERED over the birth of my second son, Nathaniel. I had placenta previa—a condition that meant the blood flow to his body could be cut off at any time during gestation—and he was born five weeks too soon, weighing less than five pounds, his lungs not ready to breathe on their own. After he was whisked from my body to a respirator, the doctor told my hus-band he might not live through the night.

Nat was in the intensive care nursery for two weeks. When he was still too weak to nurse, I would go to the hospital twice a day with a cooler of pumped milk to bottle-feed him, then go home and empty my breasts again. I probably should have wor-ried that we weren't bonding enough, but I just felt lucky. Nat and I were on the edge of a world of children who were existing between life and death—some born weighing only a couple of pounds. I would see their mothers in the nursery day after day, standing sometimes for hours, their hands lying on their chil-dren's tiny bodies through portholes in the incubators. Some of those babies would make it and some would live for maybe six months and die. Then they would take the still child out of the incubator and disconnect the tubes and the mother would get to hold her baby for the first time.

Nancy was not at the hospital for Nat's birth. She joked that going through labor with me once was enough. But she was too sick, had been in too many hospitals herself by then. Or maybe the irony was too much. The same machines that were literally breathing life into my son were being used more and more fre-quently to keep her alive—and for how long?

I drove under an empty blue sky through the Massachusetts Berkshires to the home of Nancy's mother, Suzanne. "I've been planning to make a Nancy album," Suzanne says, carrying in a box of photos and notebooks as we sit down on the sofa. "But it was two years before I could look at these, and then I just put them in a box and couldn't touch it until today. And that's doing well for me."

On the mantel is a kind of shrine to Nancy—photos, candles, poetry, and an old Christmas ornament, a pair of ballet slippers dangling on a pink ribbon. Each year on the anniversary of Nancy's death, Suzanne goes to a peace pagoda near her home in Amherst and sits by herself with a book of poetry. "But I try to focus on her birth more than her death. I know Nancy would prefer that."

Then, as if it was on her mind, she recalls the day Nancy was born. "When they brought her to me in the hospital and I saw her huge violet eyes and blond hair, I couldn't believe she was mine," Suzanne says, ruffling her cropped dark hair, which is currently tinted the color of wine. "I always had a terrible fear that I would lose her—she seemed too good to be true."

On the wall is a photo of Nancy at her first tap recital, rosy rouge circles smudged on her cheeks. "She was always moving, always dancing," Suzanne says. "When she was a child, you could hardly catch her. You would reach out to hug her and she would slip through your fingers, she was gone."

AFTER RAISING four children with Nancy's father, Les, Suzanne reversed course midlife—she divorced, went back to college to study psychology, and fell in love with her current mate, Susan. Listening to her talk, it seems that sometimes during that period, she and her eldest daughter reversed roles.

"Nancy drove me to my first class and I was shaking like a leaf. She said, 'You're going to be fine. What time is class over? I'll be here to pick you up.' Like a mother taking her kid to kindergarten."

In 1984 Nancy married Howard, a psychiatric nurse and aspiring musician. Like Rose, Suzanne first became alarmed while her child was home for her wedding, when she noticed a mole on Nancy's leg. Nancy avoided having it checked out; when she finally did, it was melanoma, the most deadly form of skin cancer. Nancy's doctors immediately removed the mole and a large amount of tissue on her leg. They thought they had gotten all the cancer, and a few years later, she and Howard were able to adopt a baby boy, Aaron. But then a new tumor appeared on her lungs.

I ask Suzanne when she knew that Nancy was going to die. "August 26, 1991," she answers. "It was a beautiful sunny day, a few weeks after Nancy's thirty-seventh birthday. I answered the phone in the kitchen. As soon as I heard her voice, I knew. The cancer had reached her liver. Nancy was crying, but I felt like I had to hold it together for her. The mother has to be strong. If you're not, how will your child be?"

But when she hung up, Suzanne fell apart. "Shards of glass pierced my being," she wrote in her journal that night. She began having "dreams of dragons, mountains, and roads to travel—roads that are too long and I'm lost and I waken shaking. . . . I am melting in a pool of helplessness."

Nancy began commuting between her home in Oakland and City of Hope, a cancer treatment center in Southern California, where she underwent an agonizing regimen of chemotherapy, interleukin and interferon treatments. And Suzanne began commuting between Amherst, City of Hope, and Nancy's home. "I lived tentatively," she says. "I felt like my feet were never touching the ground, I was never firmly ensconced; any minute I might need to get on a plane."

Over the next three years, she watched as, one by one, parts of her daughter seemed to fall away—her work, her strength, her possessions, her beauty. "She had long hair when she went into City of Hope," Suzanne recalls. "The nurse gave her a pep talk. She said, 'You're going to lose your hair, but it might fix you.' I'll never forget the day she was combing her hair and chunks—not strands—chunks of her long blond hair were falling around her. She cried. I went back to my room and cried." Another night Suzanne broke into tears watching the Olympics, seeing the parents of the medalists bursting with pride. Yet she and her daughter rarely talked about death. They danced around the subject, talking instead about recipes or the weather or people they knew. Nancy would talk to friends about her treatments and feelings in front of Suzanne, but not to her.

Suzanne began to feel a free-floating anger. "I didn't even see it. I was really angry at God, but I didn't know how to have a conversation about it with God, so I started picking on other people. You think you've gotten your children through everything, that they're safe. And that's when the anger comes in."

The only person she couldn't get angry with was Nancy. She did once, six weeks before Nancy's death, and she still regrets it. Suzanne had scolded Aaron for something minor and Nancy yelled at her. "I went to my room and stayed in there like a little kid. The next morning, we were alone in the house and she said, 'Mom, why are you mad at me?' She patted the seat next to her and said, 'Sit down and talk to me.' I said, 'I'm not mad at you, I couldn't be mad at you.' And she said, 'Yes, you could.' I regretted it terribly. It was okay for Nancy to get mad at me, but not for me to get mad at her."

Suzanne's biggest regret is that when she could do less and less to protect her daughter from her growing pain, she found herself finally wishing Nancy would die. "If anyone had ever told me I would think for one second, Please, God, take her now, I would have told them they were crazy. But I couldn't bear to see her unable to get out of the bath or bed, unable to keep food down, unable to breathe."

At home on the Friday before she died, Nancy began gasping for air. "We turned the oxygen up all the way, got the bag that she kept packed for the hospital, and rushed her into the backseat of the car," Suzanne remembers. "Aaron started screaming, 'Mommy, don't go!' He ran after the car and I ran after him. We stood on the street, my hands on his shoulders, tears streaming down both of our faces. Nancy turned and looked back at us. I'll never forget the look of terrible pain and torture on her face—it's a look no mother would ever want to see."

The next day Nancy was well enough for Aaron to visit for the last time; that evening, she and Suzanne watched game shows on TV before she slipped into a coma during the night. I saw Nancy for the last time the next morning. She was as pallid as the hospital room, her limp body propped up in the bed. All that was left of her was her breath. I held her hand to my heart, as she had held mine in labor. She had not only been my friend—she had helped shape my life and I could not imagine the shape of a future without her. I couldn't speak the words I should have said; I said them silently and willed them into her.

At around midnight, Nancy's breathing became very labored and her doctor suggested increasing the morphine to ease her discomfort. Suzanne knew this could ultimately cause her to stop breathing. "What would you do if it were your child?" she asked him. "She won't live more than a few hours," he said. "I would turn it up and let her go quietly." So Suzanne and Howard agreed, and an hour later, Nancy's breath left her.

A SMALL CHILD who is separated from his mother cannot comprehend the loss—he still expects that she will respond to his cries. The child will look eagerly toward any sight or sound that may be his mother, using all his resources to recapture her any way he can. Psychologists call this behavior "searching." The mother is the center of the child's universe, and when the mother is gone, the child feels not only her loss, but lost himself.

A mother who loses a child often does the same. No matter how expected a child's death is, the mother's hope for a miracle can become a physical prayer, so strong that it continues even after death. A child's absence is simply too unnatural; if the parent is alive, her mind insists that the child must be alive somewhere too. If the longing is strong enough, she may see the child or hear him moving about or calling to her.

"For the first few years, I thought, Toby's just gone for a while. He'll be back," says Rose. The first time she saw him was on a stage in London, shortly after his death, when she was shooting photos of dancers in rehearsal. "The light was falling on his face and hair, but his body was partly hidden in the curtains," she recalls. "He was wearing his glasses, like he used to. My heart was pounding. I grabbed the telephoto lens to get a better look, but he was gone." Later, she found out it was the ballet's young composer. "But that used to happen a lot—I'd see a young man and think it was him."

Suzanne still remembers a phone call on the first anniversary of Nancy's death. "I picked up the phone and I heard Nancy's voice on the other end." The caller was her daughter

Julie, but the feeling was so strong, Suzanne kept waiting for Nancy to return. "I thought maybe she couldn't be here for a while, maybe she was with Aaron," Suzanne says. "Then one day I was thinking about her and the wind chimes outside started ringing, although there was no breeze. And I knew it was Nancy. Now I feel her close to me from time to time. When I'm really in a bad place and I ask for her to come, she does."

Suzanne talks to Nancy and also writes to her, filling up the pages in the journal that Nancy left incomplete. Her notes to her daughter are touchingly conversational—about summer storms, Aaron's growth—like the things they used to talk about, or a mother's letters to a daughter who is simply away for a while.

Aaron is now nine years old, and his curiosity about his mother brings her back to him. When he visits Suzanne, he likes to sleep in Nancy's childhood bed. This year he told Suzanne he would like to have the robe that Nancy always wore. "Sometimes I look up in the clouds and she's up there, she sees me," he said. "Sometimes I wish I'd die so I could be with my mommy."

NANCY'S JOURNALS, which begin before she was married, are like a window into our shared past: filled with poems, postcards, autumn leaves, quotes, and lengthy ramblings about torturous love affairs. Then the melanoma sneaks in, like a rude interruption. Nancy fantasizes about having George Winston music piped into the operating room and writes about a dance she will choreograph, "Hospital Dance," set to Winston's "Thanksgiving." There are program notes: "In mid-December, I was diagnosed with melanoma, a potentially fatal form of skin cancer. My life went through a series of abrupt, unexpected, emotional upheavals. I was not ready to die." Later she writes, "I'm too young and healthy and besides that it wouldn't be fair." Turning the page, I find a list of questions for her doctor about treatments and life expectancy and then her handwriting stops.

For a long time, I thought Nancy and I needed to talk about her death. When I was away from her, I would think of new ways to broach the subject, but she would always wave me off. I thought she was not following the necessary steps to dying in peace—she was "in denial," refusing to "bring closure," not taking her "journey of acceptance." Now I understand that she was dancing with death—making deals, buying time, agreeing to put up with whatever physical torture her treatments required to gain time with her son. Aaron was the one thing she could never let go of. She told me once, "Sometimes I think if I'm good enough, maybe God will let me live."

I remember the last time I saw her at home. Her burning blue eyes had almost lost their light, her body was shrunken, as she told her sister Julie, "to the dancer's body I always wanted." Just as she did not want to talk about her death, I had found it increasingly difficult to talk about my life. We were folding clothes in silence when she said, "I'm not afraid of the pain—I know the morphine will take care of that. I just wish I could figure out how to leave behind five years of clothes for Aaron and five years of frozen dinners."

Even as her wish to live drowned out everything else, she was preparing to die in a quintessentially motherly way: attending to tedious domestic tasks, cleaning up the messes she anticipated after she was gone. When she was strong enough, she tidied dresser drawers, labeled shelves in Aaron's closet, sorted through his clothes. She made a photo album for him called "Mommy and Me." She may have even started scouting for her replacement: After she died, Howard found the business card of a woman he had not seen in years. Nancy left a note saying that she had run into her and ended it: "P.S. She's single."

WHEN MOTHERS talk of a child's death, they say that the emotional pain becomes physical—overwhelming and unendurable, like the pain of childbirth. But women seem wired to forget the pain of childbirth, while the pain of a child's death appears to be limitless. Researchers trying to ascertain the endpoints of grief have yet to determine if there is a limit to parents' mourning. Rose and Suzanne would say there is not. "It softens after about seven years," says Rose. "It never goes away."

A woman carries a baby in her body and when that child dies, no matter how old he or she is, the mother feels that something has been cut out from inside her—the loss is as profound and permanent as becoming a parent. I asked Rose and Suzanne how childbirth and child death changed their lives.

"A woman named Elizabeth Stone wrote that having a child is 'to decide forever to have your heart go walking around outside your body,'" Suzanne says. "That's what becoming a parent is like. And now I've lost that piece of myself."

Rose thinks back to Toby's birth. "I remember holding him when he was a newborn, being scared to death. Here was this tiny human being that I was responsible for, and the love and commitment is for life, even after he's married and has children. And when you lose that child, it takes a part of you out that never returns—a part of your heart. A light goes out forever. You just learn to live with the loss."

. . .

I LOOKED AT photos of my children a lot on that trip. I memorized Joey's skinny knees and the deep brown pools of his eyes; the kissable curve of Nat's chin and the sprinkling of cinnamon freckles across his nose. I devised my own waltz with mortality. *I will become the perfect mother,* I thought, *I will write down every deed and phrase.* At home, Joey hugged me with his ever-ready love and said, "I felt empty when you were gone." Nat held back, needing to know that I was not going to disappear again. The next day, when I was untangling a hopelessly knotted shirt that he was trying to get over his head, he burst out, "I love you, Mom," and threw his arms around me.

But the problem with trying to live every day as if your children could die is that life gets in the way: Dishes pile up, homework needs to get done, bills must be paid. Work pressures rise, children misbehave. A few weeks later, Joey and I were at the grocery store. We were on our way to Disneyland and had a cart bulging with chips and SnackPack cereals, and he was whining for a twenty-five-cent toy in the gum machines. Suddenly, that toy became a point of honor, all that stood between me and spoiling him rotten.

Oblivious to my tough-love stance, the checker reached into her pocket and gave him a quarter. "How can you resist those big brown eyes?" she cooed. I shot Joey a look and he made the weakest possible effort to refuse her money, then ran off to the machine before she could finish insisting that he take it. The checker looked at me softly. "I know, it's not good to spoil them," she said. "But I lost my son when he was eleven, so let me spoil him just a little."

NOTES ON THE CONTRIBUTORS

ERIN AUBRY is a Los Angeles native and staff writer for the *L.A. Weekly*. She has written extensively for the *Los Angeles Times* and national magazines, chiefly on news, arts, and the cultures of L.A.'s black communities.

KAREN GRIGSBY BATES lives in Los Angeles, where she writes about race and popular culture. Her column appears regularly on the op-ed page of the *Los Angeles Times,* and she is a frequent essayist for National Public Radio's *All Things Considered.* Bates is the coauthor, with Karen E. Hudson, of *Basic Black: Home Training for Modern Times.* She is married and the mother of a young son.

SUSIE BRIGHT (www.susiebright.com) is a *Salon* columnist and was named "the best sex columnist in America" by the *New York Press.* She is the author or editor of fourteen books, including her latest, *The Sexual State of the Union,* and *The Best American Erotica* series. She lives in the San Francisco Bay Area with her partner and daughter.

STEPHANIE COONTZ teaches history and family studies at The Evergreen State College in Olympia, Washington. Her books include *The Way We Never Were: American Families and the Nostalgia Trap, The Way We Really Are: Coming to Terms with America's Changing Families,* and, with Maya Parson and Gabrielle Raley, *America's Families: A Multicultural Reader.* She is married and the mother of a college-age son.

CHITRA DIVAKARUNI, a longtime resident of the San Francisco Bay Area, now teaches at the University of Houston. She is the author of four books of poetry, the latest being *Leaving Yuba City*; the story collection *Arranged Marriage*; and two novels, *The Mistress of Spices* and *Sister of My Heart*. She is the recipient of an American Book Award and a Pushcart Prize. She is the mother of two sons, Anand and Abhay.

CELESTE FREMON is an award-winning journalist and the author of *Father Greg & the Homeboys*. She lives in Topanga, California, and occasionally in West Glacier, Montana, with her son, Will Hunter Mason.

MONA GABLE is a writer whose essays and articles have appeared in *The Wall Street Journal*, the *Los Angeles Times*, and numerous magazines. She lives in Los Angeles with her husband, Joel Sappell, and their two children, Jesse and Kate.

LESLIE GOODMAN-MALAMUTH, a former newspaper and magazine editor, is a coauthor of *Between Two Worlds: Choices for Grown Children of Jewish-Christian Parents*. She lives in Washington, D.C., with her husband and their three sons.

ARIEL GORE is the editor of the parenting zine *Hip Mama* (www.hipmama.com), a veteran family court litigant, the author of *The Hip Mama Survival Guide*, and Maia's mom.

ARLENE GREEN is a part-time freelance computer programmer and a full-time mother. She lives in Northern California with her husband and numerous children.

NORA OKJA KELLER is the author of the novel *Comfort Woman*. She lives in Hawaii with her family.

BETH KEPHART is the author of *A Slant of Sun: One Child's Courage*, a 1998 National Book Award finalist that reflects on the lessons she has learned from her only child, Jeremy. She is a winner of the 1998 Leeway Grant in Nonfiction and a 1997 Pennsylvania Council on the Arts grant in fiction, and was a 1998 Pew Fellowship Finalist. She lives in Pennsylvania with her family.

ANNE LAMOTT is the author of eight books and a columnist for *Salon*'s "Mothers Who Think." Her most recent nonfiction work is *Traveling Mercies: Some Thoughts on Faith*.

JANE LAZARRE is a writer of novels and memoirs, including her most recent book, *Wet Earth and Dreams: A Narrative of Grief and Recovery*. Her other books include the memoirs *Beyond the Whiteness of Whiteness: Memoir of a White Mother of Black Sons* and *The Mother Knot*; the novels *Some Kind of Innocence, The Powers of Charlotte*, and *Worlds Beyond My Control*; and *On Loving Men*, a collection of essays. Lazarre teaches writing and literature at the Eugene Lange College at the New School University in New York City.

LORI LEIBOVICH is an associate editor at *Salon*.

CEIL MALEK, a writer and editor for twenty years, is currently senior instructor in the Writing Program at the University of Colorado at Colorado Springs. She is also the single parent of two adolescent children as well as the birth mother of a thirty-one-year-old daughter.

JOYCE MILLMAN is a senior editor of *Salon* and a founding editor of "Mothers Who Think." She is also *Salon*'s television critic. She was a finalist for the Pulitzer Prize in criticism in 1987 and 1991 for TV columns she wrote while on the staff of the *San Francisco Examiner*. A Massachusetts native, she now lives in the San Francisco Bay Area with her husband and their son.

KATE MOSES is a senior editor at *Salon* and a founding editor of "Mothers Who Think." She was an editor at Berkeley's North Point Press and literary director at San Francisco's Intersection for the Arts. Her book criticism and essays have appeared in various magazines, newspapers, and literary journals. She is married, the mother of two children, and lives with her family in San Francisco.

BETH MYLER lives in Austin with her husband, Erik; her children, Julia and William; and Maggie, the dog with half a tongue.

DEBRA S. OLLIVIER is a frequent contributor to *Salon* and the French daily *Le Monde*. Her work has also appeared in *Harper's, Les Inrockuptibles, Native Magazine*, and numerous literary chapbooks. Originally from Los Angeles, she currently lives in Paris with her husband and son.

CAMILLE PERI is a senior editor at *Salon* and the editor of "Mothers Who Think." Her work has appeared in the *Los Angeles Times Magazine, Mother Jones, Parenting, Lear's*, and *Savvy*, and she was a contributing editor to *Hippocrates* magazine. She lives with her husband and their two sons in San Francisco.

JAYNE ANNE PHILLIPS is the author of two novels, *Shelter* and *Machine Dreams*, and two widely anthologized collections of stories, *Fast Lanes* and *Black Tickets*. She is the recipient of a Guggenheim fellowship, two National Endowment for the Arts fellowships, a Bunting Institute fellowship, and a National Book Critics Circle Award nomination. She was awarded the Sue Kaufman Prize and a 1997 Academy Award in Literature by the American Academy of Arts and Letters. Her new novel, *MotherCare*, is forthcoming from Knopf. She is the mother of two sons.

ELIZABETH RAPOPORT is an executive editor at Times Books/ Random House and the proud owner of a third-grade boy and a kindergarten girl. Her future bestselling books will include *Thin Thighs in Thirty Years: The Exercise Program for Mothers Who "Just Want to Lie Down for a Sec"* and *Take These Shrinky Dinks and Shove Them: A Manifesto for Shirking the Girl Scouts*.

JENNIFER REESE is a writer and mother who lives, works, and eats whatever she feels like in her native San Francisco.

RAHNA REIKO RIZZUTO is the author and editor of numerous articles and publications, including four young-adult mysteries under a pseudonym. She is associate editor, with Bino A. Realuyo, of *The NuyorAsian Anthology: Asian American Writings on New York City*. Her first novel, *Why She Left Us,* is forthcoming from HarperFlamingo. Born and raised in Hawaii, Rizzuto lives in Brooklyn, where she is raising two sons who are, thankfully, too young to read.

CYNTHIA ROMANOV grew up in Chicago and raised her three children in San Francisco. Her writing has appeared in the *San Francisco Chronicle,* a defunct Chicago newspaper, and various obscure professional journals. She is working on her first book.

CATHERINE A. SALTON is a writer and attorney in Northern California.

SANDI KAHN SHELTON is the author of *Sleeping Through the Night and Other Lies* and *You Might As Well Laugh: Surviving the Joys of Parenthood,* a collection of humor columns, many of which appeared in *Working Mother* magazine. She's married and the mother of three reasonably well-adjusted children in Guilford, Connecticut, where she works as a feature reporter for the *New Haven Register.*

ROSE STOLL is the pseudonym of a writer living in San Francisco.

SUSAN STRAIGHT was born in 1960 in Riverside, California, where she lives with her three children. She is the author of the novels *Aquaboogie, I Been in Sorrow's Kitchen and Licked Out All the Pots, Blacker Than a Thousand Midnights, The Gettin Place,* and a children's book, *Bear E. Bear.*

SALLIE TISDALE is a "Mothers Who Think" columnist in *Salon* and a contributing editor to *Harper's* and *Tricycle.* Her sixth book, *Pigs in Blankets,* is forthcoming from Riverhead Books. Her work appears frequently in magazines, including *Traveler, Saveur, Vogue,* and *The New Republic.*

KIM VAN METER is a writer and editor living in Iowa City, Iowa. She and her partner have recently become parents to a son and a daughter, Theo and Sophie, both of whom were adopted internationally.

CATHY WILKINSON lives near Prescott, Arizona, and has four children, ages fifteen, fourteen, thirteen, and eleven. She spends most of her time trying not to lose her mind. For now, her writing projects entail signing permission slips for field trips, but someday she hopes to sit around all day in a ratty bathrobe, sipping gin and writing novels.

ALEX WITCHEL is a reporter in the "Style" department of *The New York Times* and the author of *Girls Only: Sleepovers, Squabbles, Tuna Fish and Other Facts of Family Life*. She is married to the writer Frank Rich and has two stepsons. She lives in New York City.

ESSAY CREDITS